POVERTY AND PREJUDICE

Religious Inequality and the Struggle for
Sustainable Development

Edited by
Mariz Tadros, Philip Mader and
Kathryn Cheeseman

T0319628

BRISTOL
UNIVERSITY
PRESS

First published in Great Britain in 2023 by

Bristol University Press
University of Bristol
19 Old Park Hill
Bristol
BS2 8BB
UK
t: +44 (0)117 374 6645
e: bup-info@bristol.ac.uk

Details of international sales and distribution partners are available at bristoluniversitypress.co.uk

The research in this book was supported by UK Aid Direct, funded by the Foreign,
Commonwealth & Development Office (FCDO).

British Library Cataloguing in Publication Data
A catalogue record for this book is available from the British Library

ISBN 978-1-5292-2904-2 paperback
ISBN 978-1-5292-2905-9 ePub
ISBN 978-1-5292-2906-6 ePdf

Cover design: Hayes Design and Advertising
Front cover image: Artwork by Kathryn Cheeseman
Bristol University Press use environmentally responsible print partners.
Printed and bound in Great Britain by CPI Group (UK) Ltd, Croydon, CR0 4YY

FSC
www.fsc.org
MIX
Paper | Supporting
responsible forestry
FSC® C013604

Contents

List of Figures and Tables

Figures

Tables

List of Abbreviations

CLJ	Center for Law and Justice
CREID	Coalition for Religious Equality and Inclusive Development
FCDO	Foreign, Commonwealth and Development Office (UK)
FoRB	freedom of religion or belief
ICT	information and communication technology
IDP	internally displaced persons
NGO	non-governmental organization
OBC	other backward class
OSCE	Organization for Security and Cooperation in Europe
SC	scheduled caste
SDG	Sustainable Development Goal
ST	scheduled tribe
UN	United Nations

Notes on Contributors

Rosa Abraham is Assistant Professor at the Centre for Sustainable Employment, Azim Premji University, Bengaluru, India. She is interested in issues relating to India's labour market. Rosa's research focuses on informal work and women's employment, particularly issues at the intersection of labour statistics and women's work. Her most recent work looks at the impact of major life events – marriage and childbirth – on women's employment.

Haitham Abul-Eis graduated from Al-Mustansiriya University in Baghdad, Iraq in 1993 with an MBChB degree, practised in both south and north Iraq for 18 months and then for two years in Yemen. He has been a doctor in the UK since 2000, and obtained membership of the Royal College of Paediatrics and Child Health in 2003. He has been working as a consultant paediatrician at the Royal Alexandra Children's Hospital in Brighton, UK, since 2015. He has a special interest in gastro-enterology and nutrition in children.

Asif Aqeel is a renowned Pakistani Christian journalist, researcher and academic. Asif's area of expertise is the socio-economic exclusion of religious minorities in Pakistan. He is Deputy Director of the Center for Law and Justice and teaches sociology at the Lahore School of Law, Pakistan.

Vinitha Bachina is Research Officer at the Institute of Development Studies, Brighton, UK. A researcher with interdisciplinary training in development studies, Vinitha is currently working on a British Academy project that explores anticipation and decision making during extreme weather events in India.

Mike Battcock is Policy Advisor in the Education, Gender and Equality Directorate of the Foreign, Commonwealth and Development Office, UK. Mike has worked in international development for more than 30 years on a wide range of areas, from spice processing in Sri Lanka and training in Bangladesh to bee keeping in Zimbabwe and small business development in Peru. Mike joined the UK Department for International Development in 2000 and has worked on aid effectiveness, governance and accountability, and civil society development, leading initiatives on religion, development and LGBTQ+ rights.

Kate Bayliss is Senior Research Fellow at the University of Sussex, Brighton, UK and Research Associate at SOAS, University of London, UK. Kate has worked extensively on privatization, financialization and social equity in the UK and the Global South. Her main focus is on the nature and effects of changing paradigms surrounding private sector engagement in the provision of essential services.

Kathryn Cheeseman is a researcher, graphic designer and project manager currently based at the Institute of Development Studies, Brighton, UK. Kathryn has worked on the implementation of the Coalition for Religious Equality and Inclusive Development programme since 2019, and she is also Director and Co-founder of Wilding Network, a rewilding not-for-profit working to establish wildlife corridors across the UK. Kathryn has an MSc in Climate Change, Development and Policy from the University of Sussex, Brighton, UK.

Nighat Dad is Founder and Executive Director of Digital Rights Foundation. A feminist activist and lawyer, she has been working on issues of gender, technology and law for well over a decade. She is currently serving on the Oversight Board for Meta.

W. Cole Durham, Jr is Professor of Law and Founding Director of the International Center for Law and Religion Studies, J. Reuben Clark Law School, Brigham Young University, Provo, USA. Cole is a founding Editor-in-Chief of the *Oxford Journal of Law and Religion* and is a graduate of Harvard College and Harvard Law School, Cambridge, USA. Cole co-chairs the Organization for Security and Cooperation in Europe Advisory Panel of Experts on Freedom of Religion or Belief, and previously served as vice president of the International Academy for Freedom of Religion and Belief.

Becky Faith is Research Fellow and Leader of the Digital and Technology cluster at the Institute of Development Studies, Brighton, UK. Becky's professional experience and research interests encompass gender and technology, mobile communication studies, human computer interaction and technology for social change. After a career working in digital rights organizations, she completed a PhD on the use of mobile phones by women in low-income communities in the UK. In the digital cluster, her work focuses on digital inequalities, gender and technology, and the future of work.

Francesca Giliberto is Research Fellow on Heritage for Global Challenges at the University of Leeds, UK. In the past ten years, Francesca has carried out interdisciplinary and comparative research and professional projects on urban heritage conservation and management, heritage for sustainable development and urban policy evaluation. Her work bridges research, policy and practice. It facilitates the implementation of international frameworks at local levels, including UNESCO's Historic Urban Landscape Recommendation, the United Nations' Agenda 2030, the New Urban Agenda and UNESCO's Policy on World Heritage and Sustainable Development.

Mary Gill is a human rights lawyer, activist and political leader. She is the founder of Sweepers Are Superheroes, a first-of-its-kind campaign aiming to raise awareness of sanitation workers' plight and advocates for their right to dignity, safety and social protection. For her tireless work on the rights of sanitation workers, she was awarded the French government's Human Rights Prize 2021 and Sweden's prestigious Anna Lindh Memorial Fund 2020.

Kevin Hernandez is Research Officer at the Institute of Development Studies, Brighton, UK. He has worked on a large portfolio of projects and publications focusing on digital inclusion and digital inequalities, including a widely cited paper titled *Leaving No One Behind in a Digital World*. His other areas of expertise include digital governance, the future of work and the potential impacts of emerging technologies on the development sector and societies at large.

Amro Hussain is a political activist who has previously worked in finance as a consultant for various investment banks, and international development, providing oversight and support for the delivery of millions of dollars' worth of humanitarian and religious tolerance projects in Iraq, as well as gender equality projects in rural Honduras. As Director of the UK All-Party Parliamentary Group for Freedom of Religion or Belief, Amro played a vital role in influencing UK government policy on freedom of religion or belief (FoRB) and helped to guide and support the 100+ parliamentarian members of the All-Party Parliamentary Group to raise FoRB issues at home and abroad.

Nitya Jacob is a policy and advocacy practitioner in water, sanitation and hygiene, working as a consultant with international organizations. Nitya has researched and written two books on sanitation programmes and traditional water practices, and was formerly head of policy at WaterAid India and the water programme director with the Centre for Science and Environment, New Delhi, India. Nitya is the Coordinator for the India

Chapter of the Sustainable Sanitation Alliance, and has a master's degree in mass communication and an advanced certificate in integrated water resources management.

Amen Jaffer is Assistant Professor of Sociology at the Lahore University of Management Sciences, Pakistan. His research is located at the intersection of religion and urban studies with a particular focus on sociality, community and infrastructure in neighbourhoods, markets and Islamic institutions in South Asia. His first monograph, which is currently under preparation, is provisionally titled, *Making Islam Real: The Social Space of Sufi Shrines in Urban Pakistan* and examines the coming together of Islam and the city in Pakistan's Sufi shrines. He is the co-editor of *State and Subject Formation in South Asia*, published by Oxford University Press.

Devangana Kalita is pursuing a PhD in women's studies from Jawarharlal Nehru University, New Delhi, India. She is a feminist activist associated with the women students' collective Pinjra Tod (Break the Cage). She spent 13 months in Delhi's Tihar Jail No. 6, from May 2020 to June 2021, framed under 'terror' charges by the state for participation in protests against the discriminatory Citizenship Amendment Act.

Mayya Kelova is a multimedia expert and researcher, focusing on human rights, international relations and marginal identities. She joined the Minority Rights Group in November 2021. Mayya formerly worked for the United Nations, private companies, non-governmental organizations and media outlets in the USA, Europe and Eurasia. She holds an MA in Human Rights from the Department of Legal Studies of the Central European University, Vienna, Austria and a BA in Journalism and Mass Communications from the American University, Blagoevgrad, Bulgaria.

Surbhi Kesar is Lecturer in the Department of Economics at SOAS University of London, UK. She received her PhD in Economics from South Asian University, New Delhi, India and has been a Fulbright Fellow at the University of Massachusetts, Amherst, USA. She is also a visiting faculty member at Azim Premji University, Bengaluru, India. Her research interests are broadly in the fields of political economy and economic development, particularly focusing on issues of informality and exclusion, processes of structural transformation and capitalist transition, issues of identity and approaches towards decolonizing the economics discipline.

Shmyla Khan is Research and Policy Director at Digital Rights Foundation. She is a lawyer by training. Shmyla has also worked as a lecturer in law, technology, gender and privacy at various universities.

Elizabeth M. King is a non-resident senior fellow at the Brookings Institution, Washington, DC, USA, Editor of the *Journal of Development Effectiveness* and Adjunct Professor at Georgetown University's School of Foreign Service, Washington, DC, USA. She serves on the executive and advisory boards of international non-governmental organizations and multinational organizations. Elizabeth was formerly the World Bank's global director for policy and strategic issues in education, and has published journal articles, books and book chapters on human capital and gender. Her latest book, *Human Capital and Gender Inequality in Middle-Income Countries*, has been published under Routledge's Development Economics Series (2022). She received her PhD in Economics from Yale University, New Haven, USA.

Chris Kwaja is Senior Lecturer and Researcher at the Centre for Peace and Security, Modibbo Adama University Yola, Adamawa State, Nigeria. Chris is also a member of the United Nations Working Group on the Use of Mercenaries. His research has focused on security sector reform in transition societies, the privatization of security, the politics of identity in Africa, civil society, elections and democratization, as well as conflict, peace and security analysis.

Haidar Lapcha is a programme management professional working at the United Nations in the field of international development, with expertise in preventing and countering violent extremism (PCVE), social cohesion, new technologies and strategic communications. Haidar is currently focusing on the implementation of the Global PCVE Programme as part of the mandate to implement the Global Counter-Terrorism Strategy. His career with the United Nations has seen him coordinate, manage and deliver projects in Europe, Africa, the Middle East, and Central and South-East Asia.

Philip Mader is a political economist and sociologist. He is a Research Fellow at the Institute of Development Studies, University of Sussex, UK. His research often focuses on the politics of credit and debt in development contexts. He is author of *The Political Economy of Microfinance: Financializing Poverty* (2015) and co-editor of *The Routledge International Handbook of Financialization* (2020) as well as author of numerous articles on financialization, microfinance, water and market inclusion.

Yusra Mahdi managed the implementation and monitoring, evaluation and learning systems for the Coalition for Religious Equality and Inclusive Development programme in Iraq, focusing on freedom of religion or belief, religious education reform in primary and secondary schools, curricula development, participatory research methods and training of teachers. With a background in journalism and media production, Yusra has in-depth knowledge about problems on the ground pertaining to ethnic and sectarian conflicts, press freedom, displacement and poverty. Yusra speaks English and Arabic and has an MA in Human Rights and International Relations from Roehampton University, London, UK.

Kishan Manocha is Head of the Tolerance and Non-Discrimination Department at the Organization for Security and Cooperation in Europe Office for Democratic Institutions and Human Rights (ODIHR) in Warsaw, Poland and was formerly ODIHR's Senior Adviser on Freedom of Religion or Belief. Kishan has worked as a barrister and a psychiatrist, and also served as Director of the UK Bahá'í Office of Public Affairs. He is Research Fellow at the Religious Freedom and Business Foundation, Annapolis, USA, the Centre for Religion and Values at Dublin City University, Ireland and the Religious Life and Belief Centre at the University of Surrey, UK. He is also a member of the Global Steering Committee of the United Nations Plan of Action for Religious Leaders and Actors to Prevent Incitement to Violence that Could Lead to Atrocity Crimes, and of the International Religious Freedom or Belief Alliance's Global Council of Experts.

Andrea Mari is an informed, reflective monitoring, evaluation and learning practitioner knowledgeable in statistical analysis and passionate about participatory approaches. Andrea's activity is grounded in evidence and academic theories but is also flexible and realistic. He has experience working with non-governmental organizations and academic institutions on education, livelihoods and freedom of religion or belief across Asia, the Middle East, Europe and Africa. Andrea is currently working as a monitoring, evaluation and learning specialist at the Institute of Development Studies, Brighton, UK.

Rachna Mehra is Assistant Professor in the Urban Studies Program in the School of Global Affairs, Dr B.R. Ambedkar University Delhi. Rachna is a historian by training and her research interests include studying the impact of partition on the Indian subcontinent and tracing the urban history of small towns and cities.

Lyla Mehta is Professorial Fellow at the Institute of Development Studies, Brighton, UK. Her work focuses on water and sanitation, forced displacement and resistance, climate change, scarcity, rights and access, resource grabbing, and the politics of environment, development and sustainability. Lyla trained as a sociologist at the University of Vienna, and has a PhD in development studies from the University of Sussex, Brighton, UK.

Ghazala Mir is Professor of Health Equity and Inclusion at the University of Leeds with research interests in health and social inequalities, including religious and ethnic minorities. Her research focuses on the experience of people underserved by health and other public services. Ghazala leads the multidisciplinary Inequalities Research Network and the international Partnerships for Equity and Inclusion, which bring together academics, advocacy organizations, public services practitioners and policy makers to help reduce the inequalities that affect disadvantaged groups. Her research has been published by the United Nations Research Institute for Social Development and as case studies of good practice by the Chief Medical Officer and the Economic and Social Research Council.

Albashir Mohamed is President of the Grand Synergy Development Initiative and supported the establishment of the Civil Society Reference Group in Kenya, a membership network advocating for the protection of civic space and an enabling environment for civil society engagement. Albashir also co-founded the Eastern Africa Civil Society Network, supporting civil society collaboration with the African Union on continental early warning and conflict anticipation/prevention. Albashir is passionate about inclusive development and good governance and supports community-led research and action for evidence-based advocacy for minority communities.

Omar Mohammed is a historian from Mosul, Iraq, known until recently only as 'Mosul Eye'. He is the host of the podcast series *Mosul and the Islamic State*, which tells untold stories from inside the Islamic State's reign of terror, the pursuit of justice in its aftermath and the enduring struggle of the people of Mosul for a better future. Omar teaches Middle East History and Cultural Heritage Diplomacy at Sciences Po University, Paris, France. His focus has now shifted to the advocacy of social initiatives for the people of Mosul, including the international effort to re-supply the Central Library of the University of Mosul.

Moses Muhumuza is a graduate teacher by profession with a focus on nature conservation. His research interests include human nature interactions and what drives pro- or anti-conservation behaviours. Moses' academic approach is interdisciplinary, often combining both the natural and social sciences. For the last 16 years, his research has focused on critical perspectives on local communities and conservation of natural resources through the creation of national parks. His work has hitherto been focused on the African rural context. Moses is currently based at the Universal Institute of Research and Innovations, Mountains of the Moon University and Uganda Wildlife Research and Training Institute, all located in Western Uganda.

Somnath Mukhopadhyay is Chair of Paediatrics and Joint Head of the Department of Clinical and Experimental Medicine at the Brighton and Sussex Medical School, UK. In the clinical domain, he works as an

NHS consultant in children's allergy, asthma and respiratory medicine at the Royal Alexandra Children's Hospital. Somnath's research explores the gene environment, including pharmacogenomics, mechanisms underlying allergy-related diseases in childhood and seeks to develop novel, personalized management pathways that are likely to be more effective than current 'one size fits all' approaches. He feels that, beyond medical interventions, 'tailored' cultural approaches may also have important implications for health and wellbeing, particularly in culturally diverse populations.

Jill Olivier is Associate Professor at the University of Cape Town, School of Public Health and Family Medicine, Health Policy and Systems Division, South Africa. Jill teaches on health systems research and convenes the Masters in Public Health programme. She is the Principal Investigator of several multi-country studies conducted in Africa, Asia–Pacific and the Americas, and comes from a humanities and social science background with a particular interest in interdisciplinary areas of 'intersection'.

Salam Omer has over 20 years' experience in the media and business sectors, and has been involved in various successful media, education and business projects in Iraq, particularly in Iraq's disputed territories, Kirkuk, Ninewa, Diyala and Salahadin. Salam is Editor-in-Chief of the independent media outlet KirkukNow.

Maji Peterx is Alternatives to Violence Project (AVP) Lead Facilitator, Coordinator of Carefronting Nigeria and Senior Fellow of the Global Center on Cooperative Security, New York, USA. Maji has facilitated over 300 AVP, trauma and other peace promotion-related workshops in Nigeria and beyond and has been working in the field of preventing and transforming violent extremism for over a decade. Maji is a trauma awareness and resilience practitioner and has also taken the first and second level Eye Movement Desensitisation and Resilience training.

Simone Schotte is a development economist focusing on inequality, social stratification and labour market research. She holds a PhD from the University of Göttingen, Germany and has been a Research Associate and Visiting Researcher at the United Nations University World Institute for Development Economics Research in Helsinki, Finland. Previously, she worked at the German Institute for Global and Area Studies and was a consultant to the World Bank.

Bariya Shah works with Hive Pakistan as a programme support officer, engaging socio-religiously marginalized communities directly in social-action programmes and overseeing project delivery as part of Hive's monitoring and evaluation team. She is also an active member of a feminist activist group in Islamabad and has been part of the Aurat March Islamabad Organizing Committee for several years.

Shilpi Srivastava is Research Fellow at the Institute of Development Studies, Brighton, UK. A political sociologist with interdisciplinary training in political science, law and governance, and development studies, Shilpi has worked extensively on the cultural politics of water and climate change. Her current research explores the politics of decision making and preparedness under radical climatic uncertainty. She draws on qualitative and participatory methods to explore the everyday encounters of marginalized communities with the changing climate as they intersect with wider issues in political economy. She is also the series co-editor of the Palgrave Pivot series on Global Challenges in Water Governance.

Sadiqa Sultan is a research and development practitioner and peacebuilder based in Quetta, Pakistan. Her work focuses on human rights, community building, access to justice, social inclusion, gender equality and the intersectionality of marginalization. She studied Peace and Conflict Studies at the University of Otago, New Zealand. Through her work, Sadiqa envisions a world with more love, hope, peace and justice.

Mariz Tadros is Professor of Politics and Development at the Institute of Development Studies, University of Sussex, Brighton, UK. She specializes in the politics and human development of the Middle East. Areas of specialization include democratization, Islamist politics, gender, sectarianism, human security, and religion and development. Mariz is Director of the Coalition for Religious Equality and Inclusive Development, Principal Investigator of a British Academy grant that explores the relationship between heritage and sustainable development and Principal Investigator of an initiative that preserves oral heritage under threat in Egypt, Syria and Iraq. Her latest publication is *What about Us? Global Perspectives on Redressing Religious Inequalities* (2022).

Knox Thames is former US Special Adviser on Religious Minorities, serving during the Obama and Trump administrations at the Department of State. He is a Senior Visiting Expert at the US Institute of Peace, Washington, DC and a Senior Fellow at the Institute for Global Engagement, Arlington, USA. The views expressed here are his own.

Katharine Thane is a human rights, peacebuilding and development policy coordinator and advisor currently working with the Joint Initiative for Strategic Religious Action through Tearfund and with the International Panel of Parliamentarians for FoRB. Katharine was previously Senior Researcher and Policy Advisor to the United Nations Special Rapporteur on FoRB. She has an MA in Human Rights and Cultural Diversity from Essex University, UK and a BA in Philosophy and Theology from Durham University, UK.

Claire Thomas is Deputy Director of Minority Rights Group (MRG). During over 25 years at MRG, with her passion and dedication to building more inclusive societies, Claire has ingrained a collaborative and solutions-led approach. To effectively challenge injustice, she focuses on long-term solutions that respond to real needs on the ground, achieve maximum impact and use participation. She developed the innovative minority inclusion audit approach and has a special interest in advocacy strategies and techniques, gender, intersectional discrimination, as well as the importance of data disaggregation in relation to the Sustainable Development Goals.

Rifqah Tifloen is a researcher and connector with several years' experience in challenging roles covering research and advocacy, multimedia content curation and social movement building. She has also partnered with various civil society organizations in advocacy and in grassroots capacity-building projects on food systems and agricultural biodiversity. Rifqah is a master's candidate at the Desmond Tutu Centre for Religion and Social Justice (University of Western Cape, Cape Town, South Africa), and her research, entitled 'Constructing and Conserving the Urban Sacred: A Decolonial-Feminist Exploration of Urban Sacred Natural Sites', focuses on the political ecology of the sacred.

Kate Ward (publishing under a pseudonym for security reasons) is CEO of the Gender and Religious Freedom network, which connects practitioners and advocates and facilitates training and research with a gender-specific religious focus. She is currently completing a master's in gender and development at the Institute of Development Studies at the University of Sussex, Brighton, UK.

Michael Woolcock is Lead Social Scientist in the Development Research Group at the World Bank, Washington, DC and part-time Lecturer in Public Policy at Harvard University's Kennedy School of Government, Cambridge, USA. His current work focuses on strategies for assessing complex interventions and understanding transformations in social institutions during the development process.

Dilmurad Yusupov is a PhD candidate in the Participation, Inclusion and Social Change Cluster at the Institute of Development Studies, University of Sussex, Brighton, UK. His current research focuses on applying ethnographic and participatory methods to analyse the marginalization of people with disabilities and promote inclusive development in Uzbekistan.

Syed Ali Abbas Zaidi is a multi-award-winning activist, researcher and development professional with over 15 years of experience in designing, implementing and evaluating community-based projects, awareness campaigns and programmes. He is one of the ten young leaders handpicked by Kofi Annan for the global anti-extremism campaign Extremely Together. He is the founding Executive Director of Hive Pakistan, a social impact organization working to address issues of extremism and marginalization in Pakistan.

Confronting Poverty, Prejudice and Religious Inequality: Ensuring No One Is Left Behind

Mariz Tadros, Philip Mader and Kathryn Cheeseman

This book documents how poverty and uneven development often reflect religious prejudice and inequality, which is often overlooked in development practice and scholarship. Religious inequalities refer to the differences created between individuals and groups on account of their religious affiliation, which intersect with other sources of inequality. The term religious inequality points to deficits regarding freedom of religion or belief (FoRB), not only experienced at the individual and collective level, but also in terms of how individuals and groups interact with one another.

Although the effects of religious inequality and lack of FoRB can take forms as extreme as systematic physical violence and even genocide, they also permeate the everyday lives of people and societies. The job a person can have, the quality of education their children receive, how clean and reliable their water supply is, how likely they are to become a target of online hate speech or sexual violence, whether their ancestral heritage is threatened or protected and how well their family can access vaccines and other healthcare: all these depend to significant extents on whether they are perceived to be a member of the majority or the minority religion in contexts where religious diversity is not taken for granted.

The Sustainable Development Goals (SDGs) were designed by the United Nations (UN) to provide a global framework for addressing poverty, uneven development and the need for a sustainable future. Yet they omit religious affiliation as a basis for discrimination, and this undermines the delivery of the SDGs' mantra of 'leave no one behind'.

In fact, the SDGs, which were established in 2015 and are intended to be achieved by 2030, mention religion only once, namely as the second target of Goal 10 ('Reduce inequality within and among countries'), which is to 'empower and promote the social, economic and political inclusion of all, irrespective of age, sex, disability, race, ethnicity, origin, religion or economic or other status'. The omission of FoRB in the envisioning of a world where no one is left behind is all the more problematic in view of the widespread suffering experienced by religiously marginalized people, which is widely known about and reported. At the beginning of the twenty-first century alone, we have already witnessed a genocide of the Yazidis, Christians, Sabean-Mandeans, Kakais, Shabak and other minorities in Iraq (Tadros, Shahab and Quinn-Graham 2022) by the so-called Islamic State of Iraq and Syria (ISIS), a genocide of the Rohingya Muslims by the army in Myanmar, and crimes against humanity against the Uyghurs in China by the Chinese Communist Party (CCP), to mention only some major instances.

Yet the significance of the intersection of religious marginality, and political and socio-economic exclusion often lies in day-to-day suffering:

> About 5 per cent of the people in Lahore are Christian. However, in this city of about 12 million people, almost 100 per cent of solid waste management workers are Christian. These workers, in most instances, live in segregated neighbourhoods that are deprived of basic amenities … Inequality in water and sanitation access interlocks with religious inequality, producing a toxic mix of negative social outcomes. (Gill and Aqeel, this volume)

To take another example, the Khoisan, the original inhabitants of South Africa, have been forced to resist encroachment and assaults on the beliefs and land that they hold to be sacred. In July 2021, developers Liesbeek Leisure Properties Trust began construction on land that is sacred to the Khoisan, the first people in Southern Africa. The Khoisan are skilled hunter-gatherers and nomadic farmers, whose opposition has aimed to safeguard cultural heritage, biodiversity, and stop the capture and destruction of green space by private capital. However, despite the indigenous protest and an interim interdict of March 2022 to halt this development, construction has commenced at the sacred natural site.

As experienced first-hand by one of our contributors, who was falsely framed under terror charges and imprisoned in Delhi's notorious Tihar Jail, South Asia's largest prison complex, the disproportionate percentage of members of religious minorities occupying the prisons of India raises questions as to whether citizens from a non-Hindu background have equal access to justice: 'While Dalits, Adivasis and Muslims are overrepresented in prisons, survivors of crimes who belong to these communities find it extremely difficult to even register criminal cases or gain a fair investigation into incidents of attacks against them based on their caste, gender or religious identity' (Kalita, this volume).

As these examples, and many more throughout the book, show, religious prejudice and religious inequality breed poverty and reinforce other forms of inequality in societies. Disadvantaged people generally experience prejudiced attitudes and practices from the non-poor (Lemieux and Pratto 2003). In the example outlined, the sewage workers of Pakistan face extreme stigmatization and vilification from other members of society because of their profession, their caste and their religious affiliation. Additionally, in bitter irony, they themselves are excluded from sanitation services. Poverty amplifies the experience of those who face religious prejudice because the opportunities for accumulating economic, social and cultural capital – to use Pierre Bourdieu's (1984) sociological framework[1] – and of converting one form of capital into another, are significantly diminished. In the example from India, the intertwining of inequalities, being a numerical minority and being poor, severely obstructs the ability of religiously profiled incarcerated Indians from drawing on any economic resources in their community to assist with the legal costs of lawsuits. When an individual, group or community are both religiously and socio-economically marginalized, the intersection of these inequalities amplifies their experiences of exclusion because of their perceived religious identity. These inequalities can be heightened further when intersecting with other factors, such as gender, ethnicity, profession, location and so forth.

This is not to suggest that the compounding of inequalities renders individuals or communities entirely powerless; agency is exercised in important ways, both as individuals with multiple identities, and as collectives with multiple repertoires of affirmation. For example, Adivasi tribal groups in India find the tools to subtly resist economic exploitation and reclaim historic land rights in their spiritual-religious repertoires (Mader 2022). This is also evident in the example from South Africa (Tifloen, this volume), where the Khoisan people are simultaneously defending their right to freedom of belief in practising what constitutes the sacred and their right to be involved in decision making governing the land of their ancestors. Religiously marginalized communities can, at times, successfully use the

---

[1]   Bourdieu proposed that people's unequal status in society reflects the uneven distribution of three main forms of capital – *economic* (the value of people's money and assets), *social* (the value of people's networks of contacts) and *cultural* (various forms of knowledge, skills and behaviours which signify belonging to a social group) – alongside other forms that are less present or noticeably absent in most people's lives.

'weapons of the weak' (Scott 1985) to resist oppression, claim rights and turn development initiatives to their advantage.

Freedom of religion or belief and the Sustainable Development Goals

The aim of this book is to render visible the developmental inequities experienced by those who have been marginalized on account of their perceived religious affiliation or background, or, as in the case of the Khoisan, what they hold to be sacred. By rendering visible religious inequality as a dimension of exclusion, we hope not only to highlight that inclusive development remains elusive without the inclusion of the realities experienced by the religiously marginalized, but also, conversely, how the achievement of any development goals – be they the SDGs or a future, post-2030 framework – are enhanced when the resources and repertoires of those same individuals and groups are brought in.

International development is deeply contested and expansive in its meaning (Nederveen Pieterse 2010), and the SDGs, on which this book focuses as the site of its analysis, are themselves a contested framework at the heart of contemporary international development policy (Weber 2017). The UN development goals frameworks, beginning from the eight 1990–2015 Millennium Development Goals (MDGs), and continuing with the 17 post-2015 SDGs, have been lauded for focusing the attention of political leaders and policy makers on key goals and achievable targets (Sachs 2012). But they have also been criticized for narrowing development agendas and not addressing structural power imbalances (Amin 2006). Proponents argue that the SDGs have opened up the space for development to become more universal, both in the sense of covering the whole world, rather than 'developing' countries only, and being more encompassing in terms of including goals related to environmental sustainability, inequality and human rights (Jolly 2017). Yet critical voices contend that they are simultaneously too broad and not broad enough: so broad as to be internally inconsistent by simultaneously aiming for economic growth (as a way to address socio–economic goals) and environmental goals (Spaiser et al 2017); and too narrowly having followed dominant voices and mainstream economic discourses in their articulation, to the detriment of 'unheard voices' and the competing values, representations and problem–solution frames they could have advanced (Briant Carant 2017).

The post-2015 development agenda formulation process, that led to the definition of the SDGs and their 231 associated indicators, was led by a UN-appointed high-level panel and hashed out in a series of consultations with government, private sector and civil society actors (United Nations 2013). This process, which ran over four years, from 2012 to 2015, was markedly more open and transparent than the MDG process and involved intense multi-stakeholder consultations under the UN umbrella, led by member states rather than UN agencies (Fukuda-Parr and McNeill 2019). This enabled a shift in the conception of development in the passage from the MDGs, and made the SDGs more universal, complex, broad and integrated. Nonetheless, the process privileged certain types of knowledge and ideas, which led to a 'slippage of ambition and vision' (2019: 12): in terms of perspectives on development, with some goals ending up conceptualized in vague terms without ambition for radical change; and in terms of the chosen indicators, which frequently narrowed down the goals, distorting their meaning. Specifically, the inequality goal materialized primarily in a frame of addressing poverty and exclusion, rather than tackling extreme inequality, which would have entailed paying greater attention to income and wealth accumulation; it emerged without a target for actually reducing unequal distribution. Although we cannot say for sure why religious inequality and FoRB did not enter into the goals, the framing of reducing inequality in this way in the SDGs, instead of in the more radical, relational terms of tackling the uneven distribution of rights and resources between different individuals and communities, undoubtedly contributed.

Regardless of their merits and demerits, the SDGs have become a touchstone not only in the development discourse but the discourse on human wellbeing more generally and cannot be ignored. Moreover, they explicitly pay attention to inequality, with both SDG10 ('Reduce Inequalities') and other SDGs having inequality entwined with them in various ways, even though, as Stewart (2015) has highlighted, the goals remain silent on how economic structures need to change to actually reduce inequality and enable sustainability. The attention given to inequality (usually in an economic sense) in the SDGs is as heartening as the relative inattention to social and cultural inequality in general, and inequalities related to religion and belief in particular, is disappointing.

This book is the progeny of the Coalition for Religious Equality and Inclusive Development (CREID), a consortium that brought together academic, human rights and development leaders and organizations from secular and faith-based backgrounds to make development more aware of and responsive to intersecting inequalities on the basis of religion, class, ethnicity, gender, geographic location and political orientation (CREID 2022). The book endeavours to redress the blind spot of religious inequalities in poverty reduction, social justice and inclusive development. The chapters collected here reflect on a wide range of global case studies demonstrating how religious inequalities impact development. A conscious effort has been made to foreground the practical experiences of actors working directly to redress religious inequalities, and to interrogate their implications for policy makers.

There is a rich scholarship on religion and development more broadly – as opposed to FoRB and religious inequalities – in relation to the SDGs (Cochrane 2016; Sidibé 2016; Tomalin et al 2019). Such scholarship is indicative of the presence of a small but growing movement in international development that has been gaining momentum since the late twentieth century. These advocates have sought to give more prominence to the positive role of faith, faith leaders and faith institutions in contributing to wellbeing in development thinking, policies and practices. However, the promotion of FoRB is very different to the incorporation of religion in development in its theory of change, focus and activities (see Tadros 2022a).

The scholarship specifically on FoRB or religious equality in relation to the SDGs is virtually non-existent. The exceptions are analyses of the SDGs through a human rights lens – unsurprisingly, given that FoRB as a concept is grounded in international human rights, founded upon Article 18 of the Universal Declaration of Human Rights (UDHR), and Article 18.3 of the International Convention on Civil and Political Rights (ICCPR), which encompasses 'freedom of thought, conscience, religion or belief' (Ghanea 2012; Bielefeldt et al 2016; Thane 2022). Ahmed Shaheed, former Special Rapporteur on FoRB, dedicated his interim report to the 75th session of the UN General Assembly to the SDGs and FoRB, cautioning that religiously marginalized persons were at risk of 'being left behind', jeopardizing the successful implementation of the 2030 Agenda for Sustainable Development (Shaheed 2020: 2).

The UN Special Rapporteur's findings are informed by submissions made by civil society and 21 states related to the achievement of FoRB in relation to SDG16, in which states are called on to 'promote peaceful and inclusive societies for sustainable development, provide access to justice for all and build effective, accountable and inclusive institutions at all levels'. While the report places the greatest emphasis on Goal 16 with respect to safeguarding FoRB, it also refers to ending poverty (Goal 1), ensuring food security (Goal 2), health (Goal 3), education (Goal 4), gender equality (Goal 5), decent work and economic growth (Goal 8) and reducing inequalities within countries (Goal 10). Shaheed notes that FoRB is absent from the SDGs' global indicator framework, and the report's key recommendation to safeguard FoRB in the SDGs is for the advancement of indicators that can then be adapted at a country level for identifying gaps in inequalities and formulating measurable, time-bound objectives for addressing them (2020: 2).

Also approaching the SDGs from within a human rights framework, Marie Juul Petersen (2022) undertook a number of consultations with civil society leaders and organizations of different backgrounds for the FoRB Leadership Network. From these consultations and wider human rights literature, the review shows how the experience of people experiencing

FoRB violations is relevant for the achievement of SDGs 2, 3, 4, 5, 10, 13 and 16. The recommendations on advancing FoRB in relation to the SDGs are primarily addressed to parliamentarians and faith leaders, given that these are the main constituency of the FoRB Leadership Network, and draw on the synergies between articles in international human rights declarations and the SDGs. One of the major contributions of the report is the emphasis on FoRB being

> closely intertwined, interrelated and mutually interdependent with other human rights. To enjoy FoRB fully, several other rights must also be protected – and the other way around. FoRB is also related to other human rights in the sense that discrimination on the grounds of religion or belief rarely concerns only restrictions of religious practices and manifestations, but also entails violations of other rights. (Petersen 2022: 3)

The report explicates how the upholding of FoRB cannot serve as the premise for violating other rights, such as gender equality or freedom of expression. However, while the work of Petersen and Shaheed draws on a human rights framework in making the case to take FoRB more seriously in the SDGs, international development frameworks have been silent on FoRB (Tadros and Sabates-Wheeler 2020).

There are several challenges to the inclusion of religion as an axis of inequality in development. One of the most critical is the misconception that redressing inequalities along religious lines is commensurate with defending religion. There is, however, a consensus that it is the freedom of the person and not the religion that is at the heart of FoRB (see for example, Petersen 2022; Bielefeldt and Schirrmacher 2017; Tadros 2022b). In the words of Heiner Bielefeldt, a former UN Special Rapporteur for FoRB, at the centre of FoRB are 'believers rather than beliefs' (Bielefeldt and Schirrmacher 2017: 168). In redressing religious inequalities, we do not seek to equalize the position or status of different religions or beliefs. Rather we focus on how inequalities affect communities and individuals. Those that we consider religiously marginalized include: members of religious minorities living in contexts where state, society and/or non-state actors deny them equality; members of a religion, whose interpretation or practices are incongruent with those of the religious authority or mainstream society; those who engage with religion syncretically in contexts where the dominant ideology is oriented towards homogenization; as well as those who hold as sacred beliefs or practices that do not constitute a religion in the traditional sense (see Tadros 2022b). Development policy makers and practitioners should, in theory, be able to engage with persons marginalized by their association with religion, if religion or belief is treated as an axis of inequality.

Another challenge to the incorporation of religious inequalities in development has been a tendency to subsume religion under ethnicity or other such identifiers. In other words, where multiple drivers of inequality are in force, ethnicity is highlighted, but not religion, which becomes subsumed or 'eclipsed' under other factors (Petri 2022). For example, in CREID's own work, there were occasions in which the treatment of Christians and Hindus in Pakistan as sources of 'pollution' or 'uncleanliness' is exclusively attributed to their caste (being considered as Dalits) as opposed to the intersection of caste with belonging to a despised religious minority. By failing to recognize ideology driving inequality in intersection with other factors, the sources of inequalities are inadequately addressed.

A core challenge to redressing the intersection of religion with other inequalities is the concern that national governments consider matters pertaining to religion to be highly sensitive, political and securitized (Petersen and Marshall 2019; Tadros and Sabates-Wheeler 2020). For example, one of the key features of the SDGs is that indicators need to have data to allow for the measurement of progress. Most countries have taken measures to collect gender disaggregated data to varying degrees of accuracy and rigour; however, the same does not apply to the collection of data on demographics for religiously marginalized populations. Very few countries collect such data, in large part because it is considered to be of a very sensitive nature. The political sensitivities around engaging with a realm where international intervention is conventionally unwelcome may discourage development actors from actively seeking to engage with religious inequality, especially when termed 'freedom of religion or belief' or 'religious persecution' (Petersen and Marshall 2019: 13).

Engaging religious inequalities through the SDGs: impetus, rationale and approach of this book

The lack of a FoRB-sensitive lens onto development does not make the SDGs *in principle* irredeemable from a FoRB perspective. For the SDGs to become more aware of and responsive to religious inequalities on the ground, we may need to interrogate how inclusive the current framework is, and what needs to be reconfigured to truly leave no one behind with respect to people whose experience of marginalization is informed by the intertwining of religion or belief with other drivers of inequality. The fact that the SDG Agenda 2030 does pay attention to gender, age, disability, ethnicity and a whole range of other identity indicators that are correlated with exclusion and marginalization suggests that there is a recognition that inequalities are intersecting and involve many axes. Nonetheless, such recognition of identity indicators does not extend to religion and belief. In the SDGs themselves, SDG 10.2 on reducing inequalities is the only indicator which recognizes religion as a possible ground for discrimination, and religion is mentioned along with other axes of inequality, such as gender. The fact that the only mention of FoRB in the SDGs is under SDG10 (the theme of redressing inequality) reflects the appropriateness and relevance of the idea of 'religious inequalities' as a development framing of the issue. Accordingly, articulating a FoRB-sensitive development agenda in terms of religious inequality may be most congruent with the language and framing of international development. The use of the term 'equality', moreover, allows development actors to distance themselves from the politicization of the term FoRB in the foreign policy of Western governments when they inconsistently and haphazardly critique Southern countries' violations of FoRB, which Southern countries understand as a hidden agenda to encroach on their domestic sovereignty (Hurd 2017).

When religious equality is explored in relation to other equalities, it provides an analytical framework through which power dynamics are explored in a relational manner. This is critically important, since who religious minorities are depends on the context. Individuals who are discriminated against in one context on account of their religious affiliation may in another be considered followers of the majority religion (for example, Hindus in Pakistan and Muslims in India). In extreme cases, it is possible a religious minority can be persecuted in a given context while constituting a majority elsewhere and being complicit in the persecution of others.[2] Moreover, religious equality allows for an engagement with intra- and intergroup dynamics, which have often been overlooked, even in scholarship on understanding and measuring FoRB (Petri 2022). This is critically important as different members of religiously marginalized populations do not experience religious inequality in the same way since they are not a homogenous group. Individuals and communities have a differentiated status and divergent experiences of how religious inequality intersects with other factors, such as race, ethnicity, socio-economic status, gender and so forth. FoRB and religious inequality are at times used interchangeably in this book. However, an inequalities lens has proven to be highly relevant for examining the nexus of religious affiliation, socio-economic exclusion and other identifiers across all the SDGs, not only SDG10.

---

[2]   For example, the Uyghurs are an ethnic group who are majority Muslim and are severely persecuted in China. However, some members have joined ISIS in Syria/Iraq where they have been involved in religious cleansing operations of non-Sunni Muslims in both countries. See Dodwell et al (2016) and Clarke (2017).

The book builds on the resources mobilized by CREID's global network, drawing insights from the wide range of experiences which CREID's affiliates have encountered in working with and for religious minorities, directly or indirectly, to reshape the politics of religious inequality and FoRB. The mainstreaming of FoRB – or religious equality – in development was one of the aims of the CREID programme. However, as the SDGs had been adopted three years before the creation of the programme, there was little opportunity then to shape the agenda and redress its FoRB-blindness, and it could not serve as the overarching framework for informing CREID's quest to understand the nexus of socio-economic exclusion and religious inequality.

The opportunity of linking the SDGs with CREID's programme emerged organically from the programme's engagement with development challenges in the six countries it worked in, including during the COVID-19 pandemic, which many of the chapters reflect. Pursuing a participatory action-research approach involved the implementation of development initiatives in multiple countries, while researching and documenting power dynamics as they unfolded throughout the action process itself, not only in its aftermath. From these experiences, we were able to inductively identify evidence that would be particularly relevant to examining issues and themes featuring in the SDGs and to speaking to the FoRB-shaped gaps in the SDGs.

As the selection of partners who could contribute insights to this book was often based on where the consortium had already built legitimacy, trust and long-standing relationships, this shaped the selection of empirical material. Not all chapters are from the CREID programme, however. We invited a wide array of contributors whose insights and experiences could present evidence from other contexts or backgrounds. That said, further case studies from sub-Saharan Africa, and especially Central or South America, would have enriched the volume further, and the hope is that future work will cover these regions.

In conceptualizing the book, we realized that attempting to cover all 17 SDGs in an 'encyclopaedic' way (each in equal depth) would lead to an outsized tome and risk repetition across chapters. Hence, we decided to treat some SDGs as stand-alone FoRB issue areas, while addressing others as thematic clusters, in a total of ten thematic sections, as shown in Table 1.1. We also decided that SDGs 1 and 2, as fundamental goals that intersect with all other SDGs – and which are, moreover, intrinsically intertwined with one another – did not require the same coverage as, for instance, the (subtle yet profound) ways in which religious inequality shapes people's access to water and sanitation, or the ways in which cities and communities unequally reflect different groups' heritage. For members of religious minorities, poverty and hunger are not often directly the result of religious inequality, but usually a

Table 1.1: Thematic bundling of the Sustainable Development Goals in this book

Thematic cluster	SDG (full name)		Covered by
Fundamentals	1	End poverty in all its forms everywhere	Introduction Epilogue
	2	End hunger, achieve food security and improved nutrition and promote sustainable agriculture	
I Health and wellbeing	3	Ensure healthy lives and promote wellbeing for all at all ages	Opening chapter: Olivier. Pulse-checkers: Omer; Thomas, Kelova and Mohamed; Mir. Policy synthesis: Mukhopadhyay and Abul-Eis.
II Education	4	Ensure inclusive and equitable quality education and promote lifelong learning opportunities for all	Opening chapter: King. Pulse-checker: Lapcha and Mahdi. Policy synthesis: Thames.
III Gender	5	Achieve gender equality and empower all women and girls	Opening chapter: Tadros. Pulse-checkers: Sultan; Ward. Policy synthesis: Mari and Cheeseman.
IV Water and sanitation	6	Ensure availability and sustainable management of water and sanitation for all	Opening chapter: Bayliss. Pulse-checkers: Zaidi and Shah; Gill and Aqeel. Policy synthesis: Jacob.
V infrastructure and the economy	7	Ensure access to affordable, reliable, sustainable and modern energy for all	Opening chapter: Hernandez and Faith. Pulse-checkers: Dad and Khan; Kwaja. Policy synthesis: Kesar and Abraham.
	8	Promote sustained, inclusive and sustainable economic growth, full and productive employment and decent work for all	
	9	Build resilient infrastructure, promote inclusive and sustainable industrialization and foster innovation	

(continued)

Table 1.1: Thematic bundling of the Sustainable Development Goals in this book (continued)

Thematic cluster	SDG (full name)	Covered by
VI Inequalities	10 Reduce inequality within and among countries	Opening chapter: Schotte. Pulse-checkers: Thomas and Gill; Yusupov. Policy synthesis: Woolcock.
VII Cities and communities	11 Make cities and human settlements inclusive, safe, resilient and sustainable	Opening chapter: Giliberto. Pulse-checkers: Mohamed; Mehra. Policy synthesis: Jaffer.
VIII Climate and nature	12 Ensure sustainable consumption and production patterns	Opening chapter: Srivastava and Bachina. Pulse-checkers: Muhumuza; Tifloen. Policy synthesis: Mehta.
	13 Take urgent action to combat climate change and its impacts	
	14 Conserve and sustainably use the oceans, seas and marine resources for sustainable development	
	15 Protect, restore and promote sustainable use of terrestrial ecosystems, sustainably manage forests, combat desertification, and halt and reverse land degradation and halt biodiversity loss	
IX Peace and justice	16 Promote peaceful and inclusive societies for sustainable development, provide access to justice for all and build effective, accountable and inclusive institutions at all levels	Opening chapter: Durham. Pulse-checkers: Peterx; Kalita. Policy synthesis: Thane.
X Partnership	17 Strengthen the means of implementation and revitalize the Global Partnership for Sustainable Development	Opening chapter: Hussain. Pulse-checkers: Manocha; Battcock. Policy synthesis: Tadros.

Source: Authors' own, drawing on sdgs.un.org

result of intermediating causal relationships, such as unequal access to health (3), education (4), jobs (8) or unequal justice systems (16). Hence, we have not allocated SDGs 1 and 2 a separate section.

Each of the thematic sections contains three types of chapters. It starts with an opening chapter that explores what is known about the linkages of the particular SDG (or cluster of SDGs) with religious inequality and FoRB based on a state-of-the-art review of research. Most of these opening chapters have been written by academic researchers. They are followed by (typically two) chapters that 'take the pulse' of the issue on the ground, as experienced by members of a particular community or practice organization. Many of these pulse-checker chapters focus on describing and examining the effectiveness of specific approaches to creating change for marginalized groups. They have been written by activists or researchers with deep contextual knowledge, from development practitioners to trauma therapy specialists, journalists to lawyers. Finally, each section ends with a policy synthesis chapter, whose purpose is to reflect on learnings about how policy and practice could change to enable more effective progress on sustainable development by better integrating FoRB and attention to religious inequalities. These chapters have been written by authors from a mix of practice, policy-making and academic backgrounds with deep expertise, including senior civil servants working for the British government and physicians working in hospitals.

Finally, a note on what this book is and what it is not may be helpful. As a book aimed at a multiplicity of audiences, reflecting the fact that no 'FoRB and development' community as such yet exists, we hope the different chapters will speak (to inevitably different extents) to people hailing from a diverse set of communities of practice (development, social justice and specific SDG issue areas), the world of SDG- and FoRB-related policy making and politics and the academic worlds of relevant disciplines. Because we intend for the book to be accessible to practitioners and community organizers located around the world, we have tried to avoid academic jargon as far as possible, and to adapt (or, one might say, falsify) as little as necessary the authentic words of those contributors who are 'taking the pulse' and reporting from the world of policy and practice. Many of the chapters in this book foreground lived experiences, situatedness and practical thinking, which we hold to be a strength of the book, in view of the fact that key audiences are activists and practitioners who may be able to use insights from others' work as inspiration or impetus for new ways of working and thinking at the interface of FoRB with sustainable development. In order to ensure the evidence these chapters present ends up being more than anecdotal and case-specific, the sections are designed to connect them to the opening chapters' more rigorous type of analysis that we hope will facilitate knowledge transfer across contexts and more generalized understandings of how FoRB interacts with each (cluster of) SDG. The reader will notice that there is no single narrative integrating each of the different components (academic anchoring, case studies and policy perspectives). The design of the chapters was purposefully multivocal, presenting multiple narratives with the view of showing the myriad ways in which FoRB and the SDGs intersect, rather than presenting one reified, reductionist account.

Content of the book

Part I of this book explores SDG3, ensuring healthy lives and the promotion of wellbeing for all at all ages. The opening chapter by Jill Olivier highlights the challenges stemming from the severe lack of data to explain where religious inequalities form barriers to the availability, acceptability and accessibility of healthcare. Salam Omer explores how the COVID-19 pandemic impacted religious minorities in Iraq, and how KirkukNow, an independent media outlet operating in Iraq's disputed territories, helped to redress disparities in access to healthcare for internally displaced persons (IDPs) from the Yazidi, Christian and Kakai religious minorities. Claire Thomas, Mayya Kelova and Albashir Mohamed explore how attention to ethnic, religious and linguistic diversity in vaccination awareness campaigns significantly influenced uptake among Christian, Muslim and Somali minorities in northeast Kenya. Ghazala Mir presents a global review of the literature on the impact of religion or belief on healthcare provision. Somnath Mukhopadhyay and Haitham Abul-Eis conclude this section with a reflection on the implications for health policy from their own experiences working as doctors in the UK National Health Service, and how greater awareness of belief systems could deliver improved patient care.

Part II explores SDG4, ensuring inclusive and equitable quality education and the promotion of lifelong learning opportunities for all. In the opening chapter, Elizabeth King highlights how measures of religiosity reveal correlations with educational attainment and gender equity outcomes, suggesting that policy should emphasize mitigating factors confounding educational attainment among disadvantaged groups, such as poverty and the cost of schooling. Haidar Lapcha and Yusra Mahdi present the case study of Al-Khoei Foundation's project working with primary school teachers to reform Iraq's religious education curriculum in order to promote pluralism and the principles of FoRB in a context of deep sectarian divides. Concluding this section, Knox Thames outlines the importance of tolerance education as part of core curricula provision, an area where many educational systems still fall short of providing the necessary resources, and the empowerment of teachers to make a difference in the delivery of SDG4 for the advancement of FoRB.

Part III looks at SDG5, achieving gender equality and empowerment of all women and girls. Mariz Tadros argues how a FoRB-sensitive perspective would enhance the interpretive framework for redressing intersecting inequalities facing women on the margins. Sadiqa Sultan reveals how the religious and gender identities of Hazara Shias returning home to Pakistan from pilgrimages to holy Shia cities in Iran intersected to enhance their experiences of marginalization at quarantine centres on the border. Kate Ward reflects on the need to recognize that religion is part of the majority of women's lived experiences, necessitating that religious inequality and restrictions placed on people's beliefs be recognized and included as standard as part of gender equality indicators. Andrea Mari and Kathryn Cheeseman consider the challenges of involving women in FoRB-related policy and practice, drawing on the experiences of the CREID programme.

Part IV investigates SDG6, ensuring the availability and sustainable management of water and sanitation for all. Kate Bayliss introduces the political nature of water provision, and how access to water has been used as a tool for control in conflict, with water scarcity, including due to climate change, also dictating changing patterns of land use, leading to increasing vulnerability for minorities at the intersection of poverty and religious marginality. Syed Ali Abbas Zaidi and Bariya Shah present a case study of how, in Pakistan, deliberate oversight and discrimination against religious minorities shapes access to clean water, and how the establishment of a water filtration plant in Joseph Colony, a predominantly Christian minority neighbourhood in Lahore, addressed intersecting inequalities beyond access to clean water and sanitation. Mary Gill and Asif Aqeel review how the World Bank's Pakistan Poverty Alleviation Fund (PPAF), which ran between 2009 and 2015, entirely overlooked religious minorities, despite the intersection of poverty and religious marginality in Pakistan, particularly in access to clean water. In conclusion, Nitya Jacob reflects on the discrepancy in access to clean water and sanitation services among Muslim, Dalit and Adivasi communities in India when compared with the services provided to upper Hindu castes. Jacob outlines how discomfort with 'targeted programming' has undermined the provision of universal water and sanitation provision, leaving behind the most marginalized communities.

Part V investigates: SDG7, ensuring access to affordable, reliable, sustainable and modern energy for all; SDG8, promoting sustained, inclusive and sustainable economic growth, full and productive employment and decent work for all; and SDG9, building resilient infrastructure, promoting inclusive and sustainable industrialization, and fostering innovation. Kevin Hernandez and Becky Faith explore how digital exclusion and disconnection risk exacerbating the socio-economic exclusion of already marginalized groups. Nighat Dad and Shmyla Khan present learnings from digital safety and literacy workshops delivered to religious minorities by the Digital Rights Foundation (DRF) in Pakistan, while Chris Kwaja explores the intersection of religious and economic inequality in Nigeria, as perpetuated by segregated settlement patterns, mutual suspicion between Christian and Muslim communities exacerbated by Boko Haram attacks and unequal access to social services and basic amenities. Surbhi Kesar and Rosa Abraham conclude with an evaluation of how religious inequalities intersect with caste-based inequalities in the Indian labour market, emphasizing how the transformation of India's economic structure is translating into differential opportunities for Hindus and Muslims.

Part VI interrogates SDG10, reducing inequality within and among countries. Simone Schotte introduces this section with a discussion of how social exclusion on the grounds of religion translates into economic gaps, widening income inequality within countries. Claire Thomas and Mary Gill explore work to redress discrimination against sanitation workers in Pakistan, who are predominantly poor Christian and Hindu religious minorities. Dilmurad Yusupov analyses the intersecting marginality experienced by deaf Jehovah's Witnesses in Uzbekistan based on their disability and religious identity. Michael Woolcock concludes by reviewing the challenges and opportunities for development policy when seeking to address intersecting inequalities, highlighting the importance of protecting free and open spaces for deliberative discussion for accountable consensus building.

Part VII examines SDG11, making cities and human settlements inclusive, safe, resilient and sustainable. This SDG has a target to 'protect and safeguard the world's cultural and natural heritage'. Francesca Giliberto introduces the key role of heritage in fostering the meaningful participation of religious minorities in the development of sustainable urban governance. Omar Mohammed evaluates how intangible heritage has a role alongside the tangible in shaping Iraqi identity, and the role of theatre and cinema in helping people to reimagine their past and transform their futures in Mosul after the destruction wrought by Daesh. Rachna Mehra examines how the naming and renaming of places in Indian cities impacts religious minorities, serving to rewrite history and promulgate Hindutva ideology. Amen Jaffer concludes by showcasing how governance issues, including a lack of effective representation and issues of patronage, have exacerbated inequalities for Pakistan's Christian minorities and highlights policy implications for dealing with minority enclaves in urban development.

Part VIII evaluates the four climate and nature-focused goals: on SDG12, ensure sustainable production and consumption, SDG13, taking urgent action to combat climate change and its impacts, SDG14, protect life below water and SDG15, protect life on land. Shilpi Srivastava and Vinitha Bachina introduce how religious inequalities are exacerbated by environmental change and diverse forms of procedural, distributive, recognitional and cognitive injustices. Moses Muhumuza explores how the eviction of indigenous people from their lands and disregard for indigenous beliefs in the establishment of national parks has become a common practice in Africa, to the detriment of the land and its people, in the case of the Batwa in Uganda. Rifqah Tifloen explores the contested development of Amazon's Africa headquarters in the Two Rivers Urban Park (TRUP) area of Cape Town on land sacred to the indigenous Khoisan. Lyla Mehta concludes that the SDGs' failure to mention religion or culture, despite the fact that recipients of overseas aid overwhelmingly identify with a religious or belief system, severely limits the potential for effective and inclusive climate and environmental policy.

Part IX evaluates SDG16, promoting peaceful and inclusive societies for sustainable development, providing access to justice for all and building effective, accountable and inclusive institutions at all levels. W. Cole Durham Jr. introduces how freedom of religion or belief constitutes a vital part of the foundational architecture of SDG16, despite its absence as an explicit focus in the goal's formulation. Maji Peterx explores the experiences of the Preventing and Transforming Violent Extremism (PTVE) project in Borno and Yobe states in northern Nigeria, highlighting how facilitating spaces for the expression and processing of trauma for marginalized communities who have suffered at the hands of Boko Haram can promote recovery above retaliation. Devangana Kalita reflects on her own experiences as an inmate framed under terror charges and kept in Delhi's infamous Tihar Jail, South Asia's largest prison, evaluating how the criminal justice and prison system in India continues to reproduce colonial legal apparatuses that criminalize and disadvantage Dalits, Adivasis, Muslims and other religious minorities. Katharine Thane concludes with a reflection on the continuing blindspots of thinking around peacebuilding and what needs to be addressed to ensure the promotion of FoRB for all.

Part X concludes with a focus on SDG17, strengthening the means of implementation and revitalizing the Global Partnership for Sustainable Development. Amro Hussain introduces the importance of partnerships for religious equality, reflecting on his experiences as the former Director of the UK All-Party Parliamentary Group (APPG) on International Freedom of Religion or Belief, and providing recommendations for overcoming crucial barriers to promote religious and belief equality. Kishan Manocha outlines the importance of mutual literacy between the religious and policy-making sectors and the need to seek common ground, while Mike Battcock reflects on his experience convening the UK Aid Connect programme at the Foreign, Commonwealth and Development Office (FCDO), highlighting the importance of co-creation for inclusive, FoRB-sensitive partnerships. Mariz Tadros concludes with a reflection on the experiences of the Coalition for Religious Equality and Inclusive Development (CREID) in establishing and deepening partnerships for the promotion of inclusive processes of change.

A short epilogue reflects on key learnings from this collection and for recasting the post-2030 development framework.

References

Amin, S. (2006) The Millennium Development Goals: A critique from the South, *Monthly Review* 57.10: 1–15.

Bielefeldt, H. and Schirrmacher, T. (eds) (2017) *Freedom of Religion and Belief: Thematic Reports of the UN Special Rapporteur 2010–2016*, Eugene, OR: Wipf & Stock Publishers.

Bielefeldt, H., Ghanea, N. and Wiener, M. (eds) (2016) *Freedom of Religion or Belief: An International Law Commentary*, Oxford: Oxford University Press.

Bourdieu, P. (1984) *Distinction: A Social Critique of the Judgement of Taste*, Cambridge, MA: Harvard University Press.

Briant Carant, J. (2017) Unheard voices: A critical discourse analysis of the Millennium Development Goals' evolution into the Sustainable Development Goals, *Third World Quarterly* 38.1: 16–41.

Clarke, M. (2017) Is China's Uyghur challenge changing its calculus on Syria?, *The Diplomat*, 7 December, https://thediplomat.com/tag/uyghurs-in-syria/ (accessed 21 December 2022).

Cochrane, J. (2016) Religion in sustainable development, *The Review of Faith & International Affairs* 14.3: 89–94.

CREID (2022) Who we are, Coalition for Religious Equality and Inclusive Development. https://creid.ac/about-us/

Dodwell, B., Milton, D. and Rassler, D. (2016) *The Caliphate's Global Workforce: An Inside Look at the Islamic State's Foreign Fighter Paper Trail*, New York: United States Military Academy.

Fukuda-Parr, S. and McNeill, D. (2019) Knowledge and politics in setting and measuring the SDGs: Introduction to special issue, *Global Policy* 10: 5–15.

Ghanea, N. (2012) Are religious minorities really minorities? *Oxford Journal of Law and Religion* 1.1: 57–79.

Hurd, E. (2017) *Beyond Religious Freedom: The New Global Politics of Religion*, Princeton, NJ: Princeton University Press.

Jolly, R. (2017) Broadening the development agenda for the SDG world, in P.A. van Bergeijk and R. van der Hoeve (eds) *Sustainable Development Goals and Income Inequality*, Cheltenham: Edward Elgar Publishing, pp 20–31.

Lemieux, A.F. and Pratto, F. (2003) Poverty and prejudice, in S.C. Carr and T. Sloan (eds) *Poverty and Psychology: International and Cultural Psychology Series*, Boston, MA: Springer.

Mader, P. (2022) 'We put God and drums in the front': Spirituality as strategy in an Adivasi self-empowerment movement, in M. Tadros, (ed.) *What about Us? Global Perspectives on Redressing Religious Inequalities*, Brighton: Institute of Development Studies, pp 115–144.

Nederveen Pieterse, J. (2010) *Development Theory*, 2nd edn, Los Angeles, CA: Sage.

Petersen, M.J. (2022) Freedom of religion or belief and the Sustainable Development Goals, Briefing Paper 1, Copenhagen: Danish Institute for Human Rights.

Petersen, M. and Marshall, K. (2019) *The International Promotion of Freedom of Religion or Belief: Sketching the Contours of a Common Framework*, Copenhagen: The Danish Institute for Human Rights.

Petri, D.P. (2022) The tyranny of religious freedom rankings, *The Review of Faith & International Affairs* 20.1: 82–88.

Sachs, J.D. (2012) From Millennium Development Goals to Sustainable Development Goals, *The Lancet* 379.9832: 2206–2211.

Scott, J.C. (1985) *Weapons of the Weak: Everyday Forms of Peasant Resistance*, New Haven, CT: Yale University Press.

Shaheed, A. (2020) Interim report of the Special Rapporteur on freedom of religion or belief, A/77/514, Delivered to 75th session of the UN General Assembly, Geneva: United Nations.

Sidibé, M. (2016) Religion and sustainable development, *The Review of Faith & International Affairs* 14.3: 1–4.

Spaiser, V., Ranganathan, S., Swain, R.B. and Sumpter, D.J. (2017) The sustainable development oxymoron: Quantifying and modelling the incompatibility of Sustainable Development Goals, *International Journal of Sustainable Development & World Ecology* 24.6: 457–470.

Stewart, F. (2015) Horizontal inequalities: A neglected dimension of development, CRISE Working Paper 1, https://assets.publishing.serv ice.gov.uk/media/57a08cba40f0b652dd0014fa/wp1.pdf (accessed 1 June 2021).

Tadros, M. (2022a) Religious equality and FoRB International Development's blindspot, *Review of Faith and International Affairs*: 96–108.

Tadros, M. (ed) (2022b) *What about Us? Global Perspectives on Redressing Religious Inequalities*, Brighton: Institute of Development Studies.

Tadros, M. and Sabates-Wheeler, R. (2020) Inclusive development: Beyond need not creed, CREID Working Paper 1, Coalition for Religious Equality and Inclusive Development, Brighton: Institute of Development Studies.

Thane, K. (2022) Falling between the cracks? How freedom of religion or belief is considered in development and peacebuilding approaches, literature and practice, in M. Tadros (ed) *'What about Us?': Global Perspectives on Redressing Religious Inequalities*, Brighton: Institute of Development Studies.

Tomalin, E., Haustein, J. and Kidy, S. (2019) Religion and the Sustainable Development Goals, *The Review of Faith & International Affairs* 17.2: 102–118.

United Nations (2013) A new global partnership: Eradicate poverty and transform economies through sustainable development, The Report of the High-Level Panel of Eminent Persons on the Post-2015 Development Agenda, New York: United Nations.

Weber, H. (2017) Politics of 'leaving no one behind': Contesting the 2030 Sustainable Development Goals agenda, *Globalizations* 14.3: 399–414.

PART I

Health and Wellbeing

2

The Intersection of Religion with the Health and Wellbeing Sustainable Development Goal

Jill Olivier

Introduction

At first, 'religion' and 'health' seem to be an easy match, and therefore religion and religiously affiliated and motivated entities and efforts[1] would seem to carry obvious potential towards the achievement of the massive third Sustainable Development Goal (SDG3): ensure healthy lives and promote wellbeing for all at all ages, as well as the array of other health-related SDG targets and indicators.

From the dawn of religious practice, religions have promoted spiritual, psychological and physical wellbeing – and many such practices would later have secular descriptors in global health and be linked to the SDG targets. For example, food edicts in scripture became known as diet and health guidelines; the promotion of cleanliness through ritual became water, sanitation and hygiene (WASH) promotion; prayer and meditation became mental health mindfulness practices; religious counselling became psychosocial support; congregational and interreligious connections became community system strengthening; providing medical care as religious expression and outreach became non-state health provision; and religious response to emergencies became humanitarian aid (Balboni et al 2022). However, there is always a flip

---

[1] Even the term 'religion' is contested, and there are variations in whether this encompasses more traditional beliefs and alternative practices. There are also multiple terms for religiously affiliated entities (for example, 'faith-based organizations', congregations, 'faith-inspired institutions').

side, in this case the acknowledged potential negative health effects related to religion, such as religious 'healing' practices that have a negative impact on mental or physical health; religious interpretations motivating the rejection of biomedical interpretations and solutions, such as religious motivations for vaccination refusal; or religiously motivated bias and discrimination resulting in the refusal of care to others not of the same religious identity (Karam et al 2015).

This dualism has resulted in hesitancy on the part of the health and development sectors towards engaging with 'religion'. However, secularization has not taken hold in development contexts as predicted, where religion continues to flourish in varied forms and practices. Global migration has also ensured that the effects of religion on population health continue to be felt even in more secularized societies. The global health and development sectors continue to get regular reminders of the importance of religion to agendas and goals (Tomalin et al 2019). For example, in 2003, it was reported that a group of Islamic clerics from northern Nigeria single-handedly halted a regional polio campaign, and there are continued accounts of religious minority groups being refused access to health services on account of their religious identity, especially in health services run by other religious groups. However, a continued barrier to engagement on religion and health in development is the complexity and diversity of the terrain, which spans *all* issues of life, death and wellbeing, where classification is confounded by complex plural health-seeking behaviours and varied religio-cultural practices that are always context-specific – all of which generally defies 'measurement' at the scale demanded for intervention (Olivier 2016). Of course, the health-related SDGs reflect similar complexity, combining a mix of vertical-disease and horizontal-systemic goals; massive cross-cutting targets such as universal health coverage (UHC); and complex socio-cultural-politico concerns, such as environmental health, violence prevention and improvements in sexual and reproductive health.

This chapter considers whether and how 'religious inequality' might affect progress on the health-related SDGs. In a recent paper relating to improvements for monitoring the health-related SDGs, Asma et al (2020: 243) note that, 'the global community is in a virtual impasse on inequality tracking for the SDGs' and that while the SDG framework does emphasize the importance of addressing inequalities, 'examinations of [health-related SDG] inequalities across indicators like socio-economic status or minority groups (for example, race, ethnicity and religion) have yet to widely occur, largely because these data are simply not available' (Asma et al 2020: 243). Even more challenging is the realization that the health sector has struggled to develop the intellectual tools to conceptualize religious inequality and the causal links between this and health concerns. One of the main confounding factors is that 'religion' (as a label, or behavioural identifier) is *always* intertwined with other factors, such as ethnicity, culture, race, poverty, education or gender, and is particularly difficult to separate in large-scale population health research of the type being tracked for the SDGs, especially when trying to parse out causality (Olivier and Wodon 2015; Gyimah et al 2006). For example, it often indicated that a particular cluster of Muslim women in a particular context might exhibit lower access to a particular health service than their counterparts – however, such studies are usually inconclusive as to whether it is the women's religious identity which is the primary reason for that lack of access, or whether it is other prevalent factors, such as lower education or higher poverty rates. A further challenge is that measuring religious identity and 'religiosity' is notoriously difficult at a population scale – both because of the plurality of religious identity and also because responses to questions such as 'How frequently do you attend services?' (a common religiosity measure) have been shown to be flawed and do not often relate causally to health decisions (Olivier and Wodon 2015). Finally, religious inequalities are also extremely context-specific. What is a minority religion in one region of a country might be a majority in another region of that same country, necessitating the development of nuanced national or population-scale maps of religious inequalities and routinely tracking how these might be affecting health-related SDG targets.

The theme which most obviously relates to systemic marginalization in relation to health is 'access', an important cross-cutting issue for the health-SDGs, which has been defined as the 'empowerment of an individual to use health care' according to the dimensions of 'availability', 'affordability' and 'acceptability' (McIntyre et al 2009).

Access to health and how it might be hindered by (religiously driven) systemic oppression

The affordability of healthcare is one of those issues where factors of religious inequality connect closely with related patterns of poverty and socio-economic marginalization. There is surprisingly little literature which directly links lack of financial access to *religious* identity (Mhina 2019). While there are many studies which indicate that certain religious communities face financial barriers to healthcare, often as a result of financial marginalization, it is rare to see conclusions that it is primarily their religious status which resulted in this barrier. For example, Tackett et al (2018) reviews Muslim women's access barriers and gives examples of surveys of Muslim women living in the United States (US) with reduced utilization of preventive health services because they do not have health insurance. Similarly, Ransford et al (2010) note that Latino immigrants can experience a negative reception accessing public care, but this was mainly linked to their uninsured status, not their religious identity. Neither example correlates religious identity with lack of health insurance. However, the lack of evidence does not indicate that religious inequalities might not relate to lack of financial access; rather, this is an area needing synthesis of existing evidence.

With regard to availability, in the SDG declaration it is noted that to achieve the overall health goal, we must achieve UHC and access to quality healthcare (World Health Organization 2017). Consideration of coverage and availability of services has multiple aspects. There are anecdotes of religious minorities being refused access to public sector care as a result of their religious identity in certain fragile and conflict-affected contexts, even if legally it should be accessible (for example, persecution of Christian Sudanese by Muslim majorities, or persecution of Muslim minorities by Christians in the Central African Republic). However, again, there is little published about this. There is some evidence of where religious–gender inequalities resulted in limitations of physical access, for example, where Muslim women are discouraged or outlawed from driving (as a Muslim religious and sometimes legal edict), therefore limiting availability of healthcare and referral options (Tackett et al 2018).

How religious inequality connects with the geographic architecture of health systems, and the public–private mix, could also be viewed as a form of systemic oppression. For example, in Ghana, there is a significantly higher density of public and private health facilities available in the Christian-dominant central and southern regions of the country, while there are fewer facilities in the Islamic-dominant northern regions. The reason for this systemic inequality in terms of physical availability of services is historic, with roots in Anglo-colonial health administration and policies favouring Christian missions (Grieve and Olivier 2018). The result is a contemporary health system design that provides more availability (choice and specialist referral) to Christians in the more densely populated central and southern regions. This demonstrates the complexity of understanding religious inequalities at a national or population scale. The dominant mainstream Christian health service sector (operating around 30 per cent of the health sector in Ghana) has a close relationship with the state, with agreements in place governing sharing of resources. In contrast, the much smaller Islamic health sector (operating around 2 per cent of services) is often left out of collaborative engagements and has a much less formalized relationship with the state, and less access to state resources for health (Grieve and Olivier 2018).

One of the more controversial issues that becomes relevant here is availability in relation to the services provided by religious-health services (facilities owned by religious groups, where healthcare is provided). There are persistent anecdotes describing access barriers for patients of different religious identities in these institutions, or proselytization creating a barrier to care. This is a particular concern in development settings where religious-health services are still strongly present (for example Ghana, Uganda or

Nigeria) and often the only service available. However, empirical studies have shown little evidence supporting these anecdotes – to the contrary, the studied institutions do not evidence any discrimination on service-entry based on religion, and proselytization has been systemically discouraged since closer agreements with the state were forged (Mhina 2019). Of course, some religious facilities might present an availability barrier if they do not provide a certain *type* of care, such as a particular form of sterilization or abortion treatment – although again, what evidence there is shows a more complex reality, where certain treatments might not be available in policy, but are often still 'quietly' available, or where robust referral systems have been put into place (Olivier 2016). This is a controversial issue, and care should be taken with any general statements about the access denied/provided by religious-health facilities.

One of the more prominent observations in the literature is that access is often limited for religious communities, not because the institution refuses entry/care, but rather because of dominant *perceptions* about that facility. However, there is another major evidence gap on cultural acceptability of health services (public and private), and responsiveness of health services to religious minorities relating to experiences of treatment, rudeness and dignity. Acceptability is perhaps *the* central issue relating to religious minorities and the health-related SDGs. There are multiple examples of religious communities and individuals being discouraged from accessing care because of religious motivations, such as religious leaders forbidding congregants from accessing a certain type of reproductive service, or inhibiting the uptake of vaccinations (Smith and Kaybryn 2013). This can be considered as a type of acceptability barrier *and* a form of systemic oppression. In such cases, the 'religious' then imposes the 'inequality'. However, again, there are complexities. For example, analysis of the Nigerian polio outbreak in 2003, which began publicly as a result of Muslim clerics denouncing the vaccine, was shown to have been driven by an array of socio-political concerns (Antai 2009). Similarly, as many access barriers are described, there are equal numbers of examples of religious leaders motivating their communities *towards* care. There are even examples of migrants (sometimes having fled religious persecution) accessing 'religious capital' in their new settings by linking to local religious communities and thereby overcoming access barriers (Sheikh-Mohammed et al 2006).

Conclusion

The task ahead is two-fold. First, we will need to become better at parsing out and explaining what is 'religious' about certain inequalities which inhibit the health-related SDGs – and develop better conceptualizations and compound indicators that can track progress on these at a population scale, which can also be persuasive for SDG engagement. Second, a 'systems lens' is important going forward – taking a step further than the religious behaviours and beliefs of individuals to prioritize the consideration of meso (institutional) and macro (architectural) ramifications of inequalities present within health systems, and the ways we might work to counter these.

References

Antai, D. (2009) Faith and child survival: The role of religion in childhood immunization in Nigeria, *Journal of Biosocial Science* 41: 57–76.

Asma, S., Lozano, R., Chatterji, S., Swaminathan, S., de Fátima Marinho, M., Yamamoto, N. et al (2020) Monitoring the health-related Sustainable Development Goals: Lessons learned and recommendations for improved measurement, *The Lancet* 395: 240–246.

Balboni, T.A., Vanderweele, T.J., Doan-Soares, S.D., Long, K.N., Ferrell, B.R., Fitchett, G. et al (2022) Spirituality in serious illness and health. *Jama* 328: 184–197.

Grieve, A. and Olivier, J. (2018) Towards universal health coverage: A mixed-method study mapping the development of the faith-based non-profit sector in the Ghanaian health system, *International Journal for Equity in Health* 17: 97.

Gyimah, S.O., Takyi, B.K. and Addai, I. (2006) Challenges to the reproductive-health needs of African women: On religion and maternal health utilization in Ghana, *Social Science & Medicine* 62: 2930–2944.

Karam, A., Clague, J., Marshall, K. and Olivier, J. (2015) The view from above: Faith and health, *The Lancet* 386: 22–24.

McIntyre, D., Thiede, M. and Birch, S. (2009) Access as a policy-relevant concept in low-and middle-income countries, *Health Economics, Policy and Law* 4: 179–193.

Mhina, C. (2019) *Patient Cost of Access to HIV Care in Tanzania: A Comparative Analysis of State and Non-state Healthcare Providers*, Cape Town: University of Cape Town.

Olivier, J. (2016) Hoist by our own petard: Backing slowly out of religion and development advocacy, *HTS Theological Studies* 72: a3564.

Olivier, J. and Wodon, Q. (2015) Religion, reproductive health, and sexual behavior in Ghana: Why statistics from large surveys don't tell the whole story, *The Review of Faith & International Affairs* 13: 64–73.

Ransford, H.E., Carrillo, F.R. and Rivera, Y. (2010) Health care-seeking among Latino immigrants: Blocked access, use of traditional medicine, and the role of religion, *Journal of Health Care for the Poor and Underserved* 21: 862–878.

Sheikh-Mohammed, M., Macintyre, C.R., Wood, N.J., Leask, J. and Isaacs, D. (2006) Barriers to access to health care for newly resettled sub-Saharan refugees in Australia, *Medical Journal of Australia* 185: 594–597.

Smith, A. and Kaybryn, J. (2013) *HIV and Maternal Health: Faith Groups' Activities, Contributions and Impact*, London: Joint Learning Initiative on Faith and Local Communities.

Tackett, S., Young, J.H., Putman, S., Wiener, C., Deruggiero, K. and Bayram, J.D. (2018) Barriers to healthcare among Muslim women: A narrative review of the literature, *Women's Studies International Forum* 69: 190–194.

Tomalin, E., Haustein, J. and Kidy, S. (2019) Religion and the Sustainable Development Goals, *The Review of Faith & International Affairs* 17: 102–118.

World Health Organization (2017) Background paper for the regional technical consultation on: Monitoring the Health-Related Sustainable Development Goals (SDGs), 9–10 February, New Delhi: World Health Organization, Regional Office for South-East Asia.

3

How the Pandemic Impacted Religious Minorities in Iraq, and How Inclusive Journalism Helped

Salam Omer

In 2020, a lack of specialized doctors and medicines obliged Andy Joseph, a resident of Alqoush, a primarily Christian-inhabited sub-district in northern Iraq, to take his mother to the city of Duhok for treatment.

'In 2020, only one doctor was available in Alqoush and we had to buy medicines from outside the health centre. My mom suffered hypertension and we already knew there is only one doctor here and we will eventually need to buy her medications from outside, therefore we decided to take her directly to Duhok.'

Andy's mother is 45 years old, and when she suffered hypertension last summer, they decided to take her to Duhok, 40 km away, because the Alqoush health centre also closes at 2 pm.

'It was around 3pm when my mother's health deteriorated. Fortunately our car was available, so we immediately rushed her to Duhok. On the way we were afraid that she might have a heart attack, therefore my dad was driving fast and we arrived in Duhok in half an hour, thanks to God that we arrived in time at the hospital, she received treatment and her blood pressure was controlled.'

KirkukNow, an independent media outlet working in the disputed territories of Iraq, has interviewed a dozen of the citizens of Alqoush sub-district, and several of them spoke of their discontent with the health services provided in the area but asked to remain anonymous. The head of the health centre insists that its standard of service is not lower simply because it mainly serves a religious minority. However, Andy and others in the area disagree. Another Alqoush resident, who spoke to KirkukNow on condition of anonymity, said: "the Iraqi government has neglected not only Alqoush, but all the areas populated by Christians and other religious minorities. Whatever we say it will make no difference, we only have God who can fix the situation."

COVID-19: an extra burden on top of displacement and marginalization

The majority of internally displaced persons (IDPs) in Iraq come from Ezidi, Christian, Kaka'i and other religious minorities. Recently, the livelihoods of these IDPs were severely impacted due to the COVID-19 crisis. Only minimal health services are available in IDP settlements. For example, in one northern, primarily Christian-inhabited sub-district of Alqoush, 40 km north of Mosul, there is only one doctor per 5,000 residents. To give another example, the government has employed only three general practitioners and provided one ambulance for the 30,000 Ezidis living in the centre of Shingal District. The difference is stark when compared to the majority groups' districts, such as Bardarash district centre, south-east of Duhok, where a population of 40,000 has ten physicians and 12 ambulances.

KirkukNow's work focuses on IDP camp residents and the home regions of Ezidis, Kaka'is, Christians, Shabaks and Armenians in the Nineveh Plain and other areas disputed by the Iraqi federal government in Baghdad, and the Kurdish Regional Government (KRG) in the north. Large parts of these areas were left in ruins by the attacks by the Islamic State of Iraq and the Levant (ISIL) and the war to push out the group. Almost the entirety of Iraq's infrastructure, including medical centres, has been destroyed during the advance of the militants of ISIL. Iraq's minorities have been caught in the crossfire between Iraqi forces and the militants. Out of the 787,000 IDPs who reside within the KRG, 47 per cent are from minority religious groups. Food and personal protective equipment against COVID-19, such as masks and gloves, are lacking inside the IDP camps, and health facilities are inadequate. Facilities in IDPs' home regions are still in ruins, where hospitals, physicians and other health workers lack key necessities, including medical equipment.

Journalistic intervention as a solution

KirkukNow delivered the voice and demands of marginalized citizens through a number of reports between April and June 2020, delivered in partnership with Minority Rights Group and the Coalition for Religious

Equality and Inclusive Development (CREID) on the challenges that religious minorities in Iraq faced during the pandemic, championing their needs through reporting and direct advocacy.

Despite challenges to reporting the issues facing marginalized communities, such as limited access to information from government and administrative officials, as well as difficulties related to obtaining the views of minority groups due to a prevailing lack of trust in the media, KirkukNow's reporters were able to gain access as they are from minority communities themselves, helping to convey legitimacy, enable direct interviews and the gathering of statistics to inform cases. Reporters then later obtained statements from relevant officials to raise the profile of these stories.

After championing the needs of IDPs through reporting and direct advocacy, KirkukNow's work was highlighted by local community leaders and camp managers as having led to an increased supply of emergency provisions. Jalal Khalaf, Mayor of Ezidi-majority Tel Uzer sub-district, testified: "medical and preventive essentials reached us, and we distributed them among the residents ... that was made possible with the help of media outlets like KirkukNow, which constantly and accurately would report on the truth about the conditions people were living under during the COVID-19 outbreak."

The Iraqi Ministry for Immigration and Displacement was also made aware of the plight of the minorities and resumed sending monthly food aid. A number of camp managers stressed that since the publication of the reports, they received sanitizers, cleaning and preventive essentials from the ministry and a number of humanitarian NGOs, while the UNHCR distributed cash among 110,000 families in order to buy face coverings and other protective equipment. The media reports also helped to raise awareness about the plight of Ezidis, who were unable to travel to work due to pandemic-related restrictions. The authorities, on the condition of testing and quarantine, have now made exceptions for these workers to be able to travel, allowing Ezidis to regain their mobility and source of income.

Journalistic intervention as a solution

KirkukNow's work with marginalized religious communities, however, has faced problems. When religious minorities come under constant pressure and face injustice, it is normal for them to reduce their relationships with outsiders, such as the media, as a way to protect themselves from potential threats. A problematic result of this is that if minority communities do not speak out, their voices are not heard, and authorities are less likely to deliver services. Without communities exercising voice, the government may not even know about the needs of such communities. KirkukNow has developed strategies to deal with these challenges, including building trust through objective reporting, building closer ties with the local communities and giving them priority and voice in reporting. In this way, KirkukNow has been able to help religious minority communities to open up and allow different voices, even conflicting ones from within the same community, to speak on a common platform and to understand each other's concerns.

Having deep knowledge of the environment and people you are working with is essential for anyone who works with marginalized and disadvantaged groups to make a positive difference in terms of progress on sustainable development. In KirkukNow's work to address the health crisis that religious minorities in Iraq have faced, deep and context-specific knowledge, as well as the media outlet's network within such communities, were critical in reaching out to them, reporting accurately and putting pressure on authorities to respond to the needs of these marginalized groups.

Meanwhile, specifically in conflict contexts, to be able to help effectively, it is crucial to avoid being labelled as biased towards any ethnic, religious and political groups. This is fundamental in the Iraqi context, as the media is sharply divided along ethnic and religious lines. It is very unlikely that people will talk to any media affiliated with other religious or ethnic groups. However, as an independent media outlet, KirkukNow was able to reach out to all ethnic groups, regardless of their political views, to enable objective reporting about their living conditions.

Inclusive reporting is a significant tool in highlighting inequalities in the provision of health services to the unheard communities of Iraq. The Iraqi mainstream media deals with underprivileged groups as numbers, not as human beings. Inclusive and objective reporting privileging the voices of minorities will greatly contribute towards exposing injustice, holding local officials accountable in healthcare provision. Eventually, objective and inclusive reporting will help to empower Iraq's minority communities, enhancing solidarity across Iraq's diverse communities.

4

Religion and Confidence in COVID-19 Vaccination: The Trust Deficit

Claire Thomas, Mayya Kelova and Albashir Mohamed

Fatma,[1] a 32-year-old nurse serving in a government health facility in Marsabit County in northeast Kenya, shares her experience of participating in the COVID-19 vaccine roll-out: "it is very discouraging waking up in the morning with an intention of saving the population from the pandemic through administering vaccines, but returning with almost 60 per cent of our daily target completed and unused doses."

Although Fatma is Muslim and the community she was serving is also largely Muslim, ethnic differences complicate relationships and add complexity to building trust between health providers and the populations they serve. "I remember one time I visited a location and before distributing the vaccine I was asked to introduce myself properly, I was forced to mention my tribe and eventually asked to leave with my vaccines because I belong to an ethnic community they did not like."

While, for us as researchers, it would be neater if we could clearly distinguish the impacts of ethnicity and religion, in reality, these are two highly interdependent facets of any individual's culture and identity. Where religious and ethnic influences inter-mingle and cross-fertilize each other, as is the case in Kenya, aiming to single out any one and attribute effects or issues to it alone is a futile and ultimately misleading exercise.

Marsabit and Mandera are two counties in northern Kenya with primarily pastoralist and rural populations. Marsabit's population of around 450,000

---

[1] Name changed for security reasons.

is approximately 50 per cent Muslim. Mandera has between 900,000 and 1.2 million people, of whom an estimated 75 per cent are Muslim (Statista 2022). Both are far from Nairobi and close to the borders with Ethiopia and Somalia, with low levels of infrastructure. In recent years, both counties have faced many challenges, including ongoing drought. Inter-community/ clan local low-level conflicts erupted in 2020.

Health workers in the area are low-paid and have low job and personal security and difficult working conditions. Before the COVID-19 pandemic, a series of demonstrations and strikes left many facilities closed. Thus, the sector was unprepared for the pandemic. Not all the nurses were whole-heartedly behind the vaccination campaign, with some having personal hesitancies about its safety or effectiveness. This is the context in which the COVID-19 vaccine roll-out needs to be understood.

Vaccination prevalence reflects patterns of trust

In March 2022, Marsabit and Mandera were the counties of Kenya with the lowest proportion of adults fully vaccinated against COVID-19, both at around 10 per cent; less than half the national average, 22 per cent (Ministry of Health Kenya 2022). By contrast, in Nyeri County, 52 per cent of the adult population had been vaccinated. Nyeri is close to Nairobi, has good infrastructure, and has a primarily agrarian, settled and Christian population, many of whom belong to the ethnic group of Kenya's president (Kikuyu).

How has this disparity been allowed to happen? Rather than being unique, it follows established patterns. An internationally recognized survey, the Demographic Health Survey (DHS), shows that Somalis, who make up over 75 per cent of the population of Mandera, are also the least vaccinated ethnic group when it comes to almost all the routine childhood vaccinations. If you ask a Kenyan national whether he or she has ever had a vaccination, almost one quarter of ethnic Somali (and Muslim) Kenyans will say no, compared to a national average of only 6 per cent.

Is the problem one of infrastructure and managing the refrigeration chain needed to preserve vaccines? This account suggests that it is not. Instead, the problem is one of a fundamental breakdown in the relationship of trust between the community, health workers, health and broader political authorities. While trust is an issue for all communities, in settings like Mandera and Marsabit, problems of trust may be deeper and more likely to affect the behaviour of substantial numbers of people.

What are some factors that contribute to such a trust breakdown? All too often, vaccine awareness campaigns are designed and run according to a 'one size fits all' logic (Tadros and Thomas 2021). Ethnic, religious and linguistic diversity in the target population may be ignored as inconvenient, costly or an inessential distraction. In many countries, health messages are not translated into local languages. This leaves speakers of minority and indigenous languages (who are often also religious minorities) at higher risk of believing disinformation.

Reaching out and listening

Minority Rights Group (MRG) is a human rights organization focused on countering discrimination and persecution of ethnic, religious and linguistic minorities. Together with Grand Synergy Development Initiative (GSDI), a media and rights organization based in northern Kenya, MRG wanted to understand more about why vaccination rates in Marsabit were so much lower than elsewhere in Kenya. The most cost-effective way of getting more information was to use 'social listening', whereby the team would aim to 'scrape' data from social media conversations about the vaccine while coding comments and posts. The team used names, language, as well as geolocation to identify content from Somalis and Muslims (almost all Somalis are Muslim, but not all Kenyan Muslims are Somali, with notable Muslim populations in coastal areas particularly, as well as north-eastern Kenya).

Because a large share of households in Marsabit/Mandera do not own a smart phone, especially the poorest, and would be missed out using this method, we also simultaneously ran a series of radio talk shows on local radio stations. (Almost all households have access to a working radio.) As the content of the shows was informed by what was revealed through social media listening, they not only began to address the misinformation that was circulating but also allowed us to capture and code the call-in comments from members of the public after the show and compare them to the data scraped from social media.

What we found

Levels of confidence in vaccines were low among identifiably Christian, Muslim and Somali social media users. Similarly, half of radio show callers had either 'low' or 'no' confidence, with 'low' prevailing (Christian 43 per cent, Muslim 37 per cent, Somali 47 per cent), whereas 'no' confidence reached 7 per cent among Christians and Somali participants. However, Muslims were twice as likely to mention no confidence.

'Doubt over vaccine safety' was a dominant reservation across the three communities in both social media and radio talk show data (32 per cent vs 23 per cent). In radio talk shows, members of the Somali community were the most concerned about safety of the vaccine (32 per cent). There were other reservations, such as the vaccine not being real (that is, people were being injected with saline solution), or conspiracy-related fears (that is, vaccinations as a plot to cause sterility among certain groups), but these were less likely to be expressed in radio talk shows than on social media.

Despite the known infrastructural limitations, comments about obstacles to access were rare. However, on both social media and radio shows, Muslim and Somali communities commented on this more frequently (9 per cent vs 3 per cent among identified Christians). When it comes to distrust in authorities, individuals identified as Christian, Muslim and Somali expressed equally high levels of distrust in the government actions in social media (over 95 per cent of all members of all groups made references to distrust) and radio talk shows, although in the latter it was less frequent, with just over 70 per cent of all comments including a reference to distrust.

Conclusion

The method was partially successful although social media scraping had limitations concerning partial mobile phone penetration and differential willingness to make open statements. Linking social media content with religion or ethnicity was more difficult and time-consuming than anticipated. While major health surveys routinely provide data on who is vaccinated and who is not, they are unable to tell us why, and participatory action research is essential to uncover the reasons and address them.

It is important to note that religious affiliation does not imply that there is a religious driver behind rejection of the vaccine among religious groups. As was evident from the research, the main obstacle to vaccination was not based on religious grounds or as a result of discrimination linked to religion, but on a lack of trust, shared across religious and ethnic groups, as well as geographic locations.

References

Ministry of Health Kenya (2022) COVID-19 Vaccination Program – daily situation report: as date: Monday 21 March, 2022, Nairobi: Ministry of Health.

Statista (2022) Muslim population in Kenya as of 2019. www.statista.com/statistics/1199572/share-of-religious-groups-in-kenya/

Tadros, M. and Thomas, C. (2021) Evidence review: Religious marginality and COVID-19 vaccination – access and hesitancy, *Social Science in Humanitarian Action Platform*, Brighton: Institute of Development Studies.

5

Religious Inequality and Health: Taking the Pulse through a Global Review of the Literature

Ghazala Mir

Despite the attention paid in policy making and research to health inequalities, there has been little attention paid to religious identity or the impact of this on health or healthcare provision. Indeed, attempts to introduce such attention to religion into health service frameworks may be met with hostility and resistance (Mir and Sheikh 2010; Mir et al 2015). UN action on the Sustainable Development Goals has similarly paid little in-depth attention to religious exclusion, despite the overrepresentation of religious and ethnic minorities among the poorest communities (Ostry et al 2014; Roser and Ortiz-Ospina 2018).

For minority religious communities, much of the evidence on how to address religious–health inequalities has been subsumed into studies of ethnicity and health, in which religion is subsumed within ethnicity (Mir and Sheikh 2010). Ethnic inequalities are often linked with religious discrimination (Mir and Sheikh 2010; Mir et al 2012), which has been associated in various global contexts with the rhetoric of nationalist groups and ruling political parties (Pew Research Centre 2018; Obadare 2005). A focus on religious identity has, for example, been recognized in the concentration on Muslim communities as an imagined 'other' in UK government policies on cohesion and security (Younis and Jadhav 2020).

This chapter draws on some of the results of a systematic global evidence review on strategies for the social inclusion of minority ethnic and religious communities (Mir et al 2020). The review focused on four public service areas – education, health, local government and police services – as key arenas in which social exclusion, that is, restriction of full social participation or citizenship, operates (Gerometta et al 2005). Fifty-six publications, mostly conducted by Western academics, often in Western contexts, were identified as relevant to the following research questions:

- What strategies exist for the social inclusion of ethnic and religious minorities within public institutions?
- What evidence exists in relation to their success, effectiveness or sustainability?
- What gaps in the current evidence need to be filled to inform future policy and practice?

Drivers of exclusion

Our analysis found that the social exclusion of minority ethnic and religious communities is created and operationalized at three distinct but interconnected levels of society. At the macro- or socio-political level, structural inequities are maintained by competition for resources, power imbalances, racism, stereotypes and misconceptions (Fesus et al 2012; Goodkind et al 2010). These connect with meso-level (institutional) failures to recognize and appropriately respond to the needs of minority groups, which produces barriers to access and inequities in service provision and outcomes (Anderson et al 2003; Davy et al 2016; Kehoe et al 2016). These barriers in turn connect to community and micro-level factors, such as: poverty; lower understanding of public service systems; greater fear and mistrust of service providers; disempowerment; and lower literacy, capacity, social and cultural capital among disadvantaged ethnic and religious groups (Eakin et al 2002; Alam et al 2008; Lakhanpaul et al 2014).

Strategies for inclusion

We mapped initiatives identified from the review, most of which related to health or education services, to these three levels. At the macro level, socio-economic inequalities, lack of representation in decision making and social stigma can be, for example, addressed through initiatives such as financial assistance or other incentives; correcting power imbalances through instituting participatory decision making; and changing social norms through removing ethnically segregated education and targeting provision at those experiencing disadvantage.

Meso-level strategies for inclusion seek to ensure equitable service provision through targeting staff or communities. For example, 'managed care protocols' reduced the use of staff discretion in provision of healthcare, which might be discriminatory, by standardizing best practice. Increased access to health services was also associated with the development of a more representative service workforce, educating and training professionals within institutions and actively recognizing and meeting the service needs of excluded groups. Revising institutional policies and adapting or changing service practice in collaboration with excluded groups also helps ensure they are more culturally acceptable. Meso-level strategies could also involve partnerships with communities to make the provision of services more responsive to their needs and to effect changes in behaviours, such as community mobilization and changes to living conditions, including improvements in how safe residents of an area perceived their neighbourhood to be.

Strategies to address the micro-level causes of public service exclusion aim to increase individual capacity and cultural capital, for example through skills development in education, changing individual health behaviour and reducing negative perceptions of health services through health promotion that recognizes the value of community engagement. Initiatives such as behaviour change training also had the potential to improve patients' understandings of systems and outcomes (see Table 5.1).

The problem with the evidence base is that there is not much strong evidence on what works for addressing social inequality, particularly in health. The few robust studies available showed that service access and participation could be improved through the cultural adaptation of treatments, the use of motivational interviewing, more engagement with excluded minorities and their involvement in the development of new or adapted services.

Very few studies focused on macro-level initiatives or activities that could work across the continuum of social exclusion; those that did related to education, a key determinant of health (Solar and Irwin 2010). We also noticed, across the studies, a common lack of attention to how wider socio-cultural environments created and helped to maintain social exclusion and the historical and social processes that produced these inequities. For example, interventions would often focus on changing the behaviours of disadvantaged ethnic and religious communities, rather than addressing the mechanisms of service provision or policy gaps. Similarly, training service users on 'how to be a patient', for example, or providing community advocates, were not found to be effective solutions, especially where these strategies were responses to the challenges of navigating very complicated care systems.

Collaborative approaches through intergroup dialogue may be effective at improving services and making them more inclusive. For example, more effective partnerships between Australian Aboriginal and dominant ethnic group partners were created through explicit reflection on the process and relational elements of these partnerships, and the use of partnership assessment tools that enabled transformative or iterative evaluation procedures. The effectiveness of school-based obesity interventions targeting minority children can also be improved by inclusion of the family and home

Table 5.1: Drivers of exclusion and strategies for inclusion

Context	Driver of exclusion	Inclusion strategy
Macro: socio-economic/ political	• Competition for resources • Power imbalances • Racism, stereotypes, misconceptions	• Financial assistance or other incentives • Participatory decision making • Removing segregated education • Targeting provision at those experiencing disadvantage
Meso: institutional/ practice	• Failure to recognize/meet needs/poorer service • Non-representation barriers to service provision • Inequities in service and outcome	• Revising institutional policies; adapting or changing service practice • Development of a representative service workforce • Actively recognizing and meeting the service needs of excluded groups • Partnerships with communities • Protocols to standardize best practice and reduce use of staff discretion • Educating and training professionals
Micro: individual level	• Lower system understanding • Mistrust/fear of services • Lower literacy/capacity/ social and cultural capital	• Behaviour change training • Health promotion • Skills development

Source: Adapted from Solar and Irwin (2010)

environment as well as explicit operationalization of behavioural theories; incorporation of systematic process evaluation and long-term follow-up of intervention outcomes. Responding to the multiple social disadvantages that impact on patients' participation in shared decision making and tailoring patient decision aids to address these is helpful in cancer care.

One issue with many initiatives, however, is poor acknowledgement of the intersectional nature of disadvantage, such as the additional layers of exclusion associated with gender, age, migration status, the overlap between religious and ethnic identity or geographical location. Studies rarely took account of the additional barriers experienced by women or young people from disadvantaged ethnic and religious groups, for example. These groups appeared to be consistently excluded from research, even within countries with policies to address these issues.

Despite the lack of explicit discussion within included papers of underlying theories that informed interventions, our analysis identified three overarching considerations that could usefully inform the development of strategies to achieve greater equity for minority ethnic and religious groups in public services:

1. There needs to be more attention to the influence of social context on the production of inequities – in relation to how power and privilege is generated and maintained, and the impact of internalized racism.
2. Multiple strategies are needed to achieve system reform, which might require a reconfiguration of existing provision across multiple sites or multifaceted approaches, such as targeting interventions at different stages of service provision.
3. Tailored solutions involving collaboration with affected communities are required, which could include power-sharing partnerships and structured communication processes that provide guidelines for intergroup dialogue.

Conclusion

Religious and ethnic exclusion from health services is a global phenomenon. Public services have the potential to act as a mechanism for social change and improve the lives of people from disadvantaged religious and ethnic groups. The global evidence review provided by this chapter shows that much more evidence on effective strategies for reducing health inequalities related to religious and ethnic inequalities is needed. Much about what could work is not yet known, particularly about how structural disadvantage can be addressed alongside institutional, community and individual factors. What we do know, however, is that non-representation, power imbalances and unequal distribution of resources between more disadvantaged and more socially included populations are key issues to address simultaneously for inclusive health policies and healthcare delivery. The need is not just for healthcare institutions to deliver more inclusive provision, but for the policy processes behind these to be equitable and inclusive of people from religious minorities.

References

Alam, R., Singleton, L. and Sturt, J. (2008) Strategies and effectiveness of diabetes self-management education interventions for Bangladeshis, *Diversity in Health and Social Care* 5.4: 269–279.

Anderson, L.M., Scrimshaw, S.C., Fullilove, M.T., Fielding, J.E., Normand, J. and Task Force on Community Preventive Services (2003) Culturally competent healthcare systems: A systematic review, *American Journal of Preventive Medicine* 24.3: 68–79.

Davy, C., Harfield, S., McArthur, A., Munn, Z. and Brown, A. (2016) Access to primary health care services for Indigenous peoples: A framework synthesis, *International Journal for Equity in Health* 15.1: 163.

Eakin, E.G., Bull, S.S., Glasgow, R.E. and Mason, M. (2002) Reaching those most in need: A review of diabetes self-management interventions in disadvantaged populations, *Diabetes/Metabolism Research and Reviews* 18.1: 26–35.

Fesus, G., Ostlin, P., McKee, M. and Adany, R. (2012) Policies to improve the health and well-being of Roma people: The European experience, *Health Policy* 105.1: 25–32.

Gerometta, J., Haussermann, H. and Longo, G. (2005) Social innovation and civil society in urban governance: Strategies for an inclusive city, *Urban Studies* 42.11: 2007–2021.

Goodkind, J.R., Ross-Toledo, K., John, S., Hall, J.L., Ross, L., Freeland, L. et al (2010) Promoting healing and restoring trust: Policy recommendations for improving behavioral health care for American Indian/Alaska Native adolescents, *American Journal of Community Psychology* 46.3–4: 386–394.

Lakhanpaul, M., Bird, D., Manikam, L., Culley, L., Perkins, G., Hudson, N. et al (2014) A systematic review of explanatory factors of barriers and facilitators to improving asthma management in South Asian children, *BMC Public Health* 14.1: 403.

Mir, G. and Sheikh, A. (2010) 'Fasting and prayer don't concern the doctors … they don't even know what it is': Communication, decision-making and perceived social relations of Pakistani Muslim patients with long-term illnesses, *Ethnicity & Health* 15.4: 327–342.

Mir, G., Salway, S., Kai, J., Karlsen, S., Bhopal, R., Ellison, G.T. et al (2012) Principles for research on ethnicity and health: The Leeds Consensus Statement, *The European Journal of Public Health* 23.3: 504–510.

Mir, G., Meer, S., Cottrell, D., McMillan, D., House, A. and Kanter, J.W. (2015) Adapted behavioural activation for the treatment of depression in Muslims, *Journal of Affective Disorders* 180: 190–199.

Mir, G., Karlsen, S., Mitullah, W. V., Bhojani, U., Uzochukwu, B., Okeke, C. et al (2020) Achieving SDG 10: A global review of public service inclusion strategies for ethnic and religious minorities, Occasional Paper 5, Sweden: United Nations Research Institute for Social Development.

Obadare, E. (2005) A crisis of trust: History, politics, religion and the polio controversy in Northern Nigeria, *Patterns of Prejudice* 39.3: 265–284.

Ostry, M.J.D., Berg, M.A. and Tsangarides, M.C.G. (2014) *Redistribution, Inequality, and Growth*, Washington, DC: International Monetary Fund.

Pew Research Centre (2018) Global uptick in government restrictions on religion in 2016, www.pewresearch.org/religion/2018/06/21/global-uptick-in-government-restrictions-on-religion-in-2016/ (accessed 20 July 2022).

Solar, O. and Irwin, A. (2010) *A Conceptual Framework for Action on the Social Determinants of Health*, Geneva: World Health Organization.

Younis, T. and Jadhav, S. (2020) Islamophobia in the National Health Service: An ethnography of institutional racism in PREVENT's counter-radicalisation policy, *Sociology of Health & Illness* 42.3: 610–626.

6

Health and Wellbeing Alongside Belief Systems at the Patient Care Coalface: How Does Policy Fit In?

Somnath Mukhopadhyay and Haitham Abul-Eis

Belief systems profoundly influence people's health and wellbeing and shape how patients, nurses and doctors engage with health questions and healthcare systems. This is something we authors – both children's doctors in the UK, and both first-generation immigrants (from India and Iraq) – have learnt first-hand and deal with within our day-to-day work and research.

Yet how religious and spiritual belief systems matter in the interactions between healthcare professionals and patients from many different cultural backgrounds, often in heart-breaking life-and-death scenarios, is not always fully appreciated by policy makers. With this short chapter, which cannot do justice to the full complexity of the issue, our aim is to provide an opportunity for reflection. Unrestrictedly infusing our own views, we draw on experience from several decades working at the 'coalface' of medicine in our home and adopted country settings.

Encounters and moral–health dilemmas

From our observations as doctors, the healthcare system in the UK is often reactive when it comes to religion and belief. The system's reaction is usually entirely patient-driven, and religion and belief only come into discussion when there are crises, especially when patients and families demand special arrangements while receiving healthcare. A number of brief examples can illustrate the challenges that can arise when healthcare professionals need to attend to the very different faiths and communities that live together in the area covered by their hospital:

- The urgent need for giving blood transfusion to patients who are Jehovah's Witnesses has prompted health providers to create policy that guides health workers in such recurring scenarios. It is well known among medical professionals that Jehovah's Witness patients will not accept blood products but not very clear if they might accept derivatives of primary blood components like albumin or immunoglobulins. Most of these patients and families now carry a 'No Blood' card which is an 'Advance Directive' absolutely refusing blood; this also releases clinicians from any liability. The hospital policy is important as it would cover all possible eventualities, for example, if the patient is unconscious or when the patient is not mentally capable.

- A child from an Orthodox Jewish family was required to stay in hospital on Saturday (Shabbat) for medical reasons. This led to disagreement and discussion about the best ways to accommodate the family's need, in order not to break its religious duties. We involved their local Rabbi to facilitate the child's stay in the hospital. The family needed to have reassurance from a religious authority that there are exceptions for such situations that are allowable. As this was possible, they agreed to hospital admission, so all parties were happy in the end, with a good outcome for the health of the child.

- A Muslim family who lost a loved one was reluctant to agree to post-mortem examination where the medical professional felt it was necessary. This may be, for example, for determining the cause of death and sometimes additionally for medico-legal reasons. These decisions are not solely made by medical professionals, and cases, on occasion, are referred to the coroner's office for the ultimate decision. From the perspective of Muslims, the body remains sacred after death and should be buried as soon as possible. However, parents often agree for samples like blood, urine and cerebrospinal fluid (obtained by lumbar puncture) to be taken immediately after death. From the medical perspective, such samples may often be sufficient to conclude regarding the cause of death. A policy change based on better understanding of belief systems could lead to clearer instructions that, if there are no criminal or safeguarding investigations, the coroner should take this into account and respect the wishes of the parents.

- A vegan atheist woman complained because her preterm new-born baby received surfactant soon after birth to help his breathing. She discovered later that this product was derived from animals; no one discussed this with her in advance. This example illustrates that patients and carers who do not practise any religion, accounting for over a third of the UK population, may still have strong beliefs, and could be extremely upset when these beliefs are violated through ignorance in healthcare. Unfortunately for child and family, it was too late to rectify the situation, and the reason provided to the family was that this situation was an emergency with not enough time to think widely. Often, the devil lies in the detail, as some medics might think that as long as animal products are not eaten or given via the oral route, it should be OK.

In all these cases, blindness or inattention to the patients' cultural, religious or spiritual beliefs risks the patients receiving sub-optimal care, and this potentially puts their lives at risk, or risks their deeply held beliefs being violated. Yet, when met with understanding, compassion and respect for their beliefs, we could see in some cases how sensitivity for patients' beliefs could shape their decision at critical points where a medical team has to respond quickly, without compromising care. We have to acknowledge here the time and effort spent by a busy medical team in managing these scenarios, and the importance of building in this training within nursing and medical education and the training of all healthcare staff.

Medical professionals and their beliefs

One of us was raised in a predominantly Hindu cultural context in India and began practising medicine in Kolkata, whereas the other practised medicine for some time in the city of Al-Najaf, in Iraq, which is known as a very religious city and a spiritual capital of Shia Islam, and feels deep cultural ties to this religion. For us doctors, reflecting on how our patients' beliefs shape their health choices has also led us to reflect on whether we can share our approaches to culture, religion and beliefs with our patients.

All medical specialties see a large percentage of patients with chronic illnesses, including cancers. One of us feels the initial consultation after diagnosis often contains the following approach:

'we don't know for sure what caused your illness, and there are a few theories, but none stand out. We can't cure your disease but we hope to keep it under control. We might need to try different treatment modalities before we achieve this goal. We could not predict how your disease will progress, the prognosis is uncertain.'

Sometimes it feels like it could help to add, 'whatever I told you, remember God made a specific plan for you', as a way to mitigate uncertainty and help patients deal with the question of meaning through submission to God. The non-religious background of the other author, influenced by the Upanishads and similar readings, together with reflective practice, would lead him to encourage the patient not to identify with the illness but carefully observe and thus create distance from thoughts, as thinking ('worrying') primarily generates the 'stress' in disease. This latter approach is entering clinical practice through 'mindfulness' and other techniques. The key issue, however, is that of tailoring advice according to the cultural and religious background, and this may not happen in clinical care in the West.

Both of us did our training in the UK, and as junior doctors rarely saw any of the seniors talk to patients about beliefs and religion, or ask about it, unless patients (or parents) brought it up. Clinical training in the UK encourages us not to do this. Apart from avoiding imposing one's own beliefs on patients, in a diverse society like the UK, which also includes many people with no religious affiliation, not bringing up religion or beliefs is one way to avoid unpredictable reactions or comments. Working in a busy setting with limited time, this can feel safer. But it has also meant leaving out belief, faith or religion at times when it may have felt helpful.

One of us observes that working in Al-Najaf was very different from the UK, in that colleagues and patients would seek reassurance with religion-based phrases and recognized the positive emotional impact such words could have on patients. While healthcare providers need to be inclusive of all religions, it also sometimes feels like, in leaving religion and belief out, something goes missing from doctor–patient relationships. Healthcare personnel often feel they may be able to help the distressed person in this regard, but we do not know how patients will receive such help. There may of course be a difference in acceptance among individuals, although children might be more receptive. Instead of shutting it out, the NHS could consider developing a framework within which such help can be offered, and it is possible that this will be welcomed by some, although possibly rejected by others.

Can we bring culture, belief and religion back into health and wellbeing?

Policy, regulations and protocols that are enshrined in parliamentary laws do not allow any leeway for health professionals to use their own cultural strengths to support the patient in distress. Good Medical Practice from the General Medical Council UK states 'you must not express your personal beliefs (including political, religious and moral beliefs) to patients in ways that exploit their vulnerability or are likely to cause them distress' (GMC 2022). This approach is intended to protect against 'proselytising' (Department of Health 2009). There is a risk of disciplinary action if these codes are violated. The result is that doctors and nurses are trained at every level to steer clear of any reference to personal beliefs.

However, real-life experiences encountered in hospitals, such as those just described, must be better understood, otherwise management of health and wellbeing will remain straightjacketed by an ignorance of the role belief systems can play in addressing the needs of the individual patient. This challenge exists in most societies in the world. Regrettably, the current 'one size fits all' approach also misses out on the unique cultural strengths of an incredibly diverse workforce within healthcare in many countries, and in the UK in particular. This diversity could be used to deliver better interactions with patients, acting flexibly (where appropriate) to deviate from the 'modern' Western European model of patient–doctor interactions, in which healthcare professionals seek to keep religion and belief at bay rather than include it actively in patient care. 'Proselytising' is very rare, and an overwhelming majority of doctors and nurses speak with the good of the patient in distress foremost in their minds. We feel that the vast majority of patients want this too, and qualitative studies must be adequately designed to capture this evidence from the healthcare 'coalface' to drive policy for practice that is more attuned to the views and beliefs of the individual patient or carer.

References

Department of Health (2009) *Religion or Belief: A Practical Guide for the NHS*, London: Equality and Human Rights Group, Department of Health.

GMC (2022) Religious and personal beliefs, General Medical Council, https://www.gmc-uk.org/education/standards-guidance-and-curric ula/guidance/religious-and-personal-beliefs#:~:text=Good%20medi cal%20practice-,Para.,likely%20to%20cause%20them%20distress (accessed 6 May 2023).

PART II

Education

7

Religion, Religiosity and Educational Progress

Elizabeth M. King

This chapter reviews the patterns and trends of the degrees of religious freedom, religious diversity and religiosity across countries. Instead of focusing on specific religions, it examines whether the degree of religious freedom, diversity and religiosity in a country provides the supportive environment for higher and more equal education. Data and the findings of previous studies indicate that it is religiosity, the strict adherence to traditional beliefs and attitudes, rather than religious affiliation, that is negatively associated with gender equality in education.

Whither religious freedom, diversity and religiosity?

The majority of countries worldwide profess a commitment to freedom of religion, a freedom that is recognized as a constitutional right – but many countries also declare a preferred religion. According to a Pew Research Center report (Pew Research Center 2017), Islam is the most common government-endorsed faith, with 27 countries, mostly in the Middle East and North Africa region, officially choosing it as their state religion. A smaller number, just 13 countries, including nine European nations, designate Christianity or a particular Christian denomination as their state religion. An additional 40 governments unofficially favour a particular religion, with a branch of Christianity being preferred in 28 of those countries and receiving preferential treatment, such as subsidies. The rest of countries worldwide do not favour any one religion (Barro and McCleary 2005; Barro et al 2010). The share of people who are unaffiliated – that is, those who self-identify as atheists or agnostics and those who say their religion is nothing in particular – has been growing, especially in North America and Europe (Hackett et al 2015).

The Pew Research Center Religious Diversity Index (RDI) is a measure of the concentration of religions in 232 countries. That index uses a scale of 0 to 10, with ten signifying maximum possible diversity if each of eight religious groups constitutes an equal share of the population.[1] Figure 7.1, which divides the distribution of the RDI into ten ranges, shows that a large majority of countries have a low RDI value of less than three and only a small minority have a value of seven. Six of the 12 most religiously diverse countries are in East Asia, with Singapore topping that list. Asian countries also have among the highest education levels and the best academic performance (using standardized international student tests such as the Programme for International Student Assessment (PISA)) in the world, thus helping to drive the positive relationship between religious diversity and schooling shown in the right panel of Figure 7.1.

An individual in any country, however, may have a different view of his or her actual freedom to choose and practise a religion, so the measure of freedom of religion in a country, if defined as how people see or experience it, is not necessarily the same as a country's official declaration of whether there is or isn't freedom. It is important to distinguish between religious freedom as a constitutional right and religious freedom *as experienced* by individuals, and further, between religious affiliation and religiosity.

Data for 2000, 2010 and 2019 from the World Development Indicators (WDI) show that freedom of religion has worsened over the past decade, since 2010 (Figure 7.2). The data capture the views expressed by randomly selected samples from country populations rather than the legal or constitutional provision in each country. The average and median values for the indicator across countries declined considerably between 2000 and 2019, as illustrated by the curve for 2019 lying below the curves for 2000 and 2010 and by the scatterplot in the right panel which lies below the diagonal line that would indicate no change between 2010 and 2019. Although constitutional or legal provisions about religion do not change from year to year, these data demonstrate that the perceptions of people about their experienced level of freedom of religion do. Similar cross-national data on the degree of repression of religious organizations also indicate that repression has increased in the past two decades, and support the view that religious freedom has declined.[2]

---

[1] The Religious Diversity index is a version of a Herfindahl-Hirschman Index of concentration. The religions used are Buddhists, Christians, folk religions, Hindus, Jews, Muslims, other religions considered as a group and the religiously unaffiliated (Pew Research Center 2017).

[2] Grim and Finke (2007) find that social and government regulation of religion tends to lead to religious persecution. They analyse data from 143 countries using the 2003 International Religious Freedom Reports.

Figure 7.1: Religious diversity index and education, 2010

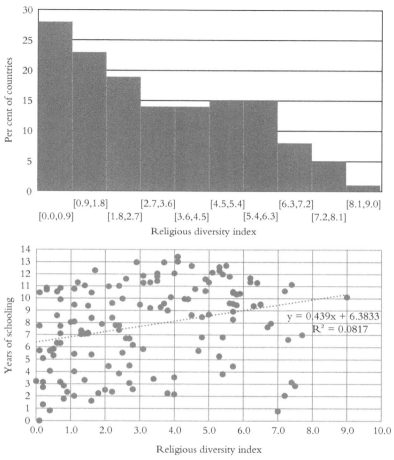

Source: Author's own, based on Pew Research Center (2014) and Barro-Lee education database on average completed years of schooling for adults aged 25–64 (2013)

The gap between the official view of a country's religious freedom and people's view of their religious freedom – and what factors might account for the deterioration over time in people's views about their religious freedom – are worthwhile topics for further research. One possible factor of change over time is people's increased educational levels, punctuating the point that the relationship between religion and educational progress goes both ways: religion can affect beliefs about the benefits of formal education, and education can affect the adoption and practice of religious beliefs. Country-level data estimate a positive correlation of 0.34 between views about freedom of religion and educational

Figure 7.2: Distribution of countries by reported degree of religious freedom, 2000–2019

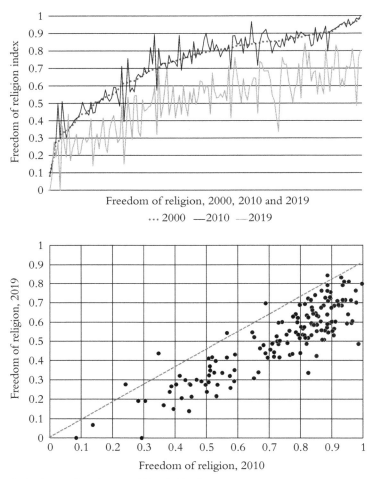

Source: Author's own, based on World Bank (2022)

attainment across 130 countries.[3] This is not a strong correlation, but since many other factors determine completed years of schooling in a country (for example, education policy and expected economic returns to education), a correlation of this magnitude nevertheless suggests an important relationship.

---

[3]   We use data from the World Development Indicators (World Bank 2022) and the Barro-Lee education database on average completed years of schooling (2013).

Religion, religiosity and gender inequality in education

SDG4 and 5 extol the critical importance of gender equality in education for economic and poverty reduction. Education opens doors of opportunities for young women, especially when they cannot count on family wealth, property or business connections. Women with more years of schooling are more likely to find employment, earn higher wages and operate farms or firms. There has been significant progress in closing the gender gap in education, but there remain hotspots in the world where girls are either not entering school or dropping out too early. The widest gender gaps in education are in the poorest countries. Many countries in Africa, the Middle East and South Asia are still working to enrol all girls in primary schools and to close the gender gaps at the primary and secondary levels – and countries that have successfully enrolled girls in primary and secondary education are nonetheless trapped in low-quality learning, struggling to ensure that students master foundational skills (King and Winthrop 2015).

Lewis and Lockheed (2007) argue that multiple and intersecting factors – gender, poverty and ethnolinguistic minority status – are barriers to girls' and women's education. Country data indicate only a weak correlation between freedom of religion, religious diversity and women's average completed years of schooling. Other factors besides religion are at work. However, the scatter plots in Figure 7.3 suggest that religious freedom and religious diversity are positively associated with a measure of gender equality in education, the absolute difference between men's and women's average completed years of schooling – the countries with higher religious freedom and religious diversity tend to have a smaller education gender gap.

Why is there a link between religion and gender equality in education?

Studies that estimate the relationship between religion and education using multivariate analysis provide some support for this positive association. Norton and Tomal (2009), for instance, examine the link between major religions and female educational attainment using a sample of 97 countries, controlling for colonial heritage, urbanization, labour force participation and young adult mortality. Their estimates show powerful negative associations between female educational attainment and the gender gap in schooling, on the one hand, and the proportion of the population who are Hindu and Muslim adherents in each country, on the other. In Nigeria, Kazeem, Jensen and Stokes (2010) and Osagiobare, Oronsaye and Ekwukoma (2015) conclude that parents' cultural and religious beliefs negatively influence their educational aspiration for daughters because of the belief that a daughter who is educated is more likely to dominate her husband, thus diluting her

Figure 7.3: Freedom of religion, religious diversity and gender equality in education

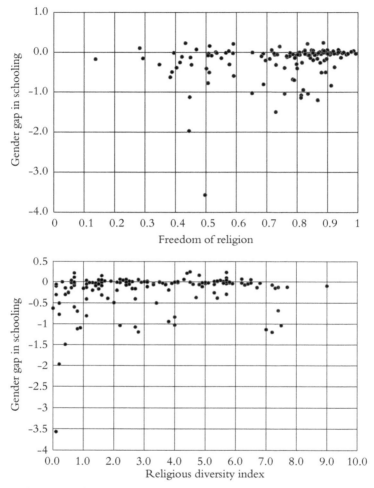

Source: Author's own calculations based on Pew Research Center (2014) and Barro-Lee database on completed years of schooling (2013)[4]

marriage prospects. In Kenya and Malawi too, the culture of patriarchal lineage, authority and control is associated with a preference for sons and lower education for daughters (Buchmann 2000). In Pakistan and northern Nigeria, Bano (2019) finds that girls who attend secular educational institutions rather than religious institutions tend to pursue more progressive

---

[4] Gender equality is denoted as zero difference in the average schooling levels of men and women.

Table 7.1: Distribution of responses to the question 'the basic meaning of religion is …', by level of education

	Lower	Middle	Higher
… to follow religious norms and ceremonies	33.5	27.8	27.4
… to do good to other people	66.5	72.2	72.6
Number of observations	27,906	29,759	25,959

Source: World Values Survey, Wave 7 (2017–2021)[5]

interpretations of Islamic rulings to advance their professional careers and are influenced by their household characteristics and urban exposure, and not only by religious conviction.

Here then is the importance of distinguishing between religious affiliation and religiosity. *Religiosity* is about the level of consistent adherence, in belief and practice, to the rules and regulations of one's religion. Conservative believers differ from liberal believers in that they are more likely to adhere to such rules and regulations. While evidence indicates that formal religious institutions shape cultural norms, social rules and behaviours, and can have a measurable impact on the rigidity of gender roles and attitudes (Seguino 2011), religious affiliation is not equivalent to the degree to which members of that religion believe or actively practise its tenets and rituals. Panjwani (2017) observes that many who call themselves Muslims do not actually share religion as a predominant 'identity-attribute' for themselves and would rather refer to themselves as secular or cultural Muslims. Likewise, Protestants would differ according to whether they are mainline, evangelical or liberal Protestants, as well as whether they belong to different Protestant denominations (Lehrer 2004). Glas, Spierings and Scheepers (2018) argue that 'women and men might "live" their religion differently and have the ability to bargain with their religion and interpret it in ways that deviate from the dominant patriarchal mainstream'.

Cross-country data indicate that religiosity and education are negatively associated. According to the responses to the World Values Survey (Wave 7, 2017–2021) fielded in 59 countries, respondents with less education are more likely to answer that the basic meaning of religion is to follow norms and rituals rather than to do good to other people (Table 7.1). These patterns are consistent with the findings of previous studies.

A study of the Second Industrial Revolution (1870–1914) in France that uses a multivariate analysis concludes that more religious locations experienced lower economic development after 1870 (Squicciarini 2020).

---

[5]   A lower of education pertains to primary education; middle education pertains to lower secondary level; and higher education pertains to upper secondary education and beyond.

The more religious areas adopted a technical curriculum in primary schools more slowly, pushing instead for religious education and slowing the industrial development in those areas 10 to 15 years later, when those schoolchildren were entering the labour market. Bénabou, Ticchi and Vindigni (2015) attribute the link between religion and development to the relationship between religiosity and views about innovation. Using data from the World Values Survey (1980 to 2005), they conclude that individuals' openness to innovation, such as attitudes toward science and technology, is negatively associated with measures of religiosity (as separate from religious affiliation), controlling for usual sociodemographic variables and religious affiliation.

Does policy matter?

Religion is part of people's socio-cultural and economic environments in most societies. It affects beliefs, attitudes and practices related to all spheres of life. One's religious affiliation, however, is not the same as one's religiosity (the degree of adherence to a religion's tenets and practices). Whether or not religious affiliation stifles educational progress and development depends on how strongly communities persist to protect its cultural traditions and resist change (Inglehart and Baker 2000; Solt et al 2011; Seguino 2011). Can policy support educational progress despite restrictive religious beliefs? Cooray and Potrafke (2011) find that it is political institutions rather than culture and religion that explain gender inequality in education in 157 countries over the 1991–2006 period.

Compulsory education laws, if enforced and supported by government programmes, have been shown to lead to higher schooling levels and more gender equality in education. When parents or guardians and students are not aware of, or are not convinced about, the social and economic returns to education, compulsory laws and programmes that reduce the costs associated with schooling can sway the decision to send children to school, especially girls. In several African countries, for example, attempts to abolish school fees as part of compulsory education laws succeeded in expanding enrolment rates of boys and girls (Lincove 2009; Nguyen and King 2022). In Canada, more education reduces levels of religious affiliation and religiosity later in life (Hungerman 2014), and in India, parents' education mediates the role of religion on children's education – that is, where parents are literate, the effects of religion and caste on children's schooling are negligible, but where parents are not literate, those effects are significant (Borooah and Iyer 2005).

In sum, this chapter examines the trend and patterns in religious freedom and religious diversity across countries, but argues that it is the degree of religiosity, that is, one's adherence to a religion's traditional beliefs and practices, that affects educational attainment and, thus, development.

More studies estimating causal relationships – from religion and religiosity to education and development, and from education to religion and religiosity – are needed. By mitigating the impact of factors such as the cost of schooling, poverty and low returns to education facing disadvantaged populations, policy can reduce the power of traditional religious beliefs to counter development.

References

Bano, M. (2019) Religion and female empowerment: Evidence from Pakistan and northern Nigeria, *Canadian Journal of Development Studies/Revue canadienne d'études du développement* 40.2: 163–181.

Barro, R. and Lee, J.W. (2013) A new data set of educational attainment in the world, 1950–2010, *Journal of Development Economics* 104: 184–198.

Barro, R. and McCleary, R.M. (2005) Which countries have state religions? *The Quarterly Journal of Economics* 120.4: 1331–1370.

Barro, R., Hwang, J. and McCleary, R. (2010) Religious conversion in 40 countries, *Journal for the Scientific Study of Religion* 49.1: 15–36.

Bénabou, R., Ticchi, D. and Vindigni, A. (2015) Religion and innovation, *American Economic Review* 105.5: 346–351.

Borooah, V.K. and Iyer, S. (2005) Vidya, Veda, and Varna: The influence of religion and caste on education in rural India, *The Journal of Development Studies* 41.8: 1369–1404.

Buchmann, C. (2000) Family structure, parental perceptions, and child labor in Kenya: What factors determine who is enrolled in school? *Social Forces* 78.4: 1349–1378.

Cooray, A. and Potrafke, N. (2011) Gender inequality in education: Political institutions or culture and religion?, *European Journal of Political Economy* 27.2: 268–280.

Glas, S., Spierings, N. and Scheepers, P. (2018) Re-understanding religion and support for gender equality in Arab countries, *Gender & Society* 32.5: 686–712.

Grim, B.J. and Finke, R. (2007) Religious persecution in cross-national context: Clashing civilizations or regulated religious economies? *American Sociological Review* 72.4: 633–658.

Hackett, C., Stonawski, M., Potančoková, M., Grim, B.J. and Skirbekk, V. (2015) The future size of religiously affiliated and unaffiliated populations, *Demographic Research* 32: 829–842.

Hungerman, D.M. (2014) The effect of education on religion: Evidence from compulsory schooling laws, *Journal of Economic Behavior & Organization* 104: 52–63.

Inglehart, R. and Baker, W.E. (2000) Modernization, cultural change, and the persistence of traditional values, *American Sociological* Review: 19–51.

Kazeem, A., Jensen, L. and Stokes, C.S. (2010) School attendance in Nigeria: Understanding the impact and intersection of gender, urban-rural residence, and socioeconomic status, *Comparative Education Review* 54.2: 295–319.

King, E.M. and Winthrop, R. (2015) Today's challenges for girls' education, Global Economy and Development Working Paper 90, Washington, DC: Brookings Institution.

Lehrer, E. (2004) Religiosity as a determinant of educational attainment: The case of conservative Protestant women in the United States, *Review of Economics of the Household* 2.2: 203–219.

Lewis, M.A. and Lockheed, M.E. (2007) *Exclusion, Gender and Education*, Washington, DC: Center for Global Development.

Lincove, J.A. (2009) Determinants of schooling for boys and girls in Nigeria under a policy of free primary education, *Economics of Education Review* 28.4: 474–484.

Nguyen, V.T. and King, E.M. (2022) Should school fee abolition be comprehensive? An evaluation of Mozambique, *International Journal of Educational Development* 88: 102513.

Norton, S.W. and Tomal, A. (2009) Religion and female educational attainment, *Journal of Money, Credit and Banking* 41: 961–986.

Osagiobare, O.E., Oronsaye, R.O. and Ekwukoma, V. (2015) Influence of religious and cultural beliefs on girl-child educational aspiration in Nigeria, *Journal of Educational and Social Research* 5.2: 165.

Panjwani, F. (2017) No Muslim is just a Muslim: Implications for education, *Oxford Review of Education* 43.5: 596–611.

Pew Research Center (2014) Global religious diversity, 4 April, www.pewresearch.org/religion/2014/04/04/global-religious-diversity/

Pew Research Center (2017) Many countries favor specific religions, officially or unofficially, 3 October, www.pewresearch.org/religion/2017/10/03/many-countries-favor-specific-religions-officially-or-unofficially/

Seguino, S. (2011) Help or hindrance? Religion's impact on gender inequality in attitudes and outcomes, *World Development* 39.8: 1308–1321.

Solt, F., Habel, P. and Grant, J.T. (2011) Economic inequality, relative power, and religiosity, *Social Science Quarterly* 92.2: 447–465.

Squicciarini, M.P. (2020) Devotion and development: Religiosity, education, and economic progress in nineteenth-century France, *American Economic Review* 110.11: 3454–91.

World Bank (2022) *World Development Indicators*, Washington, DC: World Bank.

8

Training Iraqi Teachers to Become Effective Promoters of Freedom of Religion or Belief Principles in Primary Education

Haidar Lapcha and Yusra Mahdi

In Iraq, the education curriculum has failed to acknowledge the country's ethnic and religious plurality and has excluded religious minorities from the religious education (RE) curriculum (Osman 2019). This contributes to the strengthening of stereotypes and the marginalization of individuals from minority religions (Lapcha 2019). The situation of religious minorities, such as Chaldeans, Assyrian-Syriacs, Yazidis, Sabean-Mandaeans, Shabaks and Turkmans in Iraq, considerably worsened during the war waged by the ISIS terrorist group; thousands lost their lives and parts of their cultural heritage (Hanish 2015).

At an education policy level, minorities in Iraq also saw their rights violated. Current state policy mandates that Islam is the official and only religion taught in the national school curriculum. While Muslim students attend and are graded on the subject of RE, minority students cannot attend classes. Instead, they are supposed to learn about their own religion outside of school, at home or in churches, temples or other places of worship. The lack of exposure to religious minorities in the RE curriculum's teaching content and methods contributes to limited awareness of the diversity of Iraqi society among students and teachers, which in turn contributes towards discrimination, intolerance and the eventual marginalization and exclusion of minority groups (Barany 2013).

Reforming the Iraqi curriculum

In December 2019, Al-Khoei Foundation, a consortium partner of the Coalition for Religious Equality and Inclusive Development (CREID), launched a project to reform RE with the aim of improving poor religious education standards. The project sought to foster pluralism, promote freedom of religion or belief (FoRB) and address religious inequalities in the national curriculum to contribute towards greater social cohesion and inclusivity in Iraq. The first project phase aimed to develop a new pro-pluralism curriculum for Iraqi primary schools based on the principles of religious equality through the engagement of religiously diverse stakeholders and the development of the competencies of teachers, learners and other stakeholders.

In March 2021, trainers conducted workshops with 43 RE teachers (31 females and 12 males) from primary schools in three Iraqi provinces, Dhi Qar, Anbar and Baghdad. The training aimed to facilitate teachers' acquisition of values of religious equality and translate these into their classroom practice; to empower teachers to become agents of change. The workshops combined concurrent online and in-person delivery and utilized participatory learning and action (PLA) and reflective practices. The new pro-pluralism RE curriculum, which has reached over 1,526 students, incorporates FoRB values such as diversity and pluralism, and the teachers were trained on the use of different pedagogical methods and educational learning theories.

The teachers were familiarized with the concepts and values of FoRB through interactive discussions. Subsequently, microteaching, a participatory training method which supports participants in translating theory into practice and acquiring the flexibility needed to teach in challenging and dynamic circumstances, was used to ensure that participants internalized the knowledge and skills acquired. The microteaching method provides teachers with pre-implementation experience and practical understanding of the teaching and learning process in a controlled environment (Özonur and Kamışlı 2019). The teachers participated in a micro-lesson planning group exercise, which involved developing short lessons making use of the newly acquired concepts and values, which helped to provide an in–depth understanding of the new methodology and the values it aimed to promote:

> The practical application of what we learned during the training, the workgroups that were formed, and the lessons that were implemented by the trainees had a great role in equipping us with the skills and knowledge needed to teach the new programme. (Teacher feedback in training)

> Inculcating values needs to be not just through textbooks … it needs to be through experience and practicality. (Teacher feedback in training)

As anticipated, it was the practical implementation and group learning which made a difference compared to other, more traditional, theoretical teacher training programmes. At the beginning, trainers used frontal lecturing to instruct teachers about the new pro-pluralism RE curriculum. However, frontal lecturing proved least effective in engaging stakeholders in the promotion of religious diversity. Traditional training and teaching methods, which focus on acquiring theoretical knowledge, are not effective in promoting and sustaining FoRB values in the education system. They often rely on repetition and reproduction of existing patterns that do not contribute to change. By contrast, PLA and reflective practices improve teachers' acquisition of practical knowledge through enabling reflection on personal experience (Benequista and Gaventa 2011).

Teachers used the STAR (situation, task, action, result) method to describe a scenario where they had to deal with a conflict associated with an act of discrimination against a minority student (DDI 2022). Teachers were encouraged to reflect on the significance of their role, of their impact on learners' behaviour, and most importantly, of their understanding of and position towards difference. This use of reflective practices enables teachers to recognize the assumptions, frameworks, and patterns of thought and behaviour that shape their thinking and action, which in turn can nurture greater self-awareness, imagination and creativity (Benequista and Gaventa 2011).

Rawa, a female teacher from Baghdad, presented a role-play based on her personal experience:

> 'Hello class, I want to share with you an incident that happened to one of your classmates and I want stress that it was wrong. Zainab, can you stand up? What did you say to your friend Saja? That she has dark skin and you made fun of her! Do you think this is right, class? Look how upset you made your friend Saja. We don't make fun of people just because they are different to us. We are beautiful because we are different. Now can you apologise to your friend Saja.'

Rawa said that she wanted to empower her student who had suffered from the incident by making her class leader and that Saja now had many friends, including the girl who had made fun of her.

Challenges and setbacks

The project faced many setbacks due to long bureaucratic processes, the suspension of RE teaching because of the COVID-19 pandemic and the challenge of working within the education system in Iraq, which is weak, outdated and not designed to accommodate innovation from within. Teachers and educators struggle to deliver quality education due to poor training and lack of professional development opportunities, and they are often left demoralized and unmotivated to explore solutions (Issa and Jamil 2010).

The practical participatory methods of microteaching and scenario-based sessions engaged, motivated and empowered teachers to take ownership of promoting the principles of religious diversity. However, we recognize that this is not enough to end the cycle of the systematic exclusion of religious minorities in education. Educators may be able to reflect on their own experiences and change some behaviours in their classrooms, by including stories which promote pluralism and diversity, but this alone will not solve the institutional discrimination which fails to provide a parallel religious education system for non-Muslim learners. Nevertheless, we believe that by improving teachers' knowledge and awareness of religious diversity, we can enhance action towards an inclusive and equitable education system that recognizes the rights of religious minorities in Iraq.

The participatory teacher training approach recognized teachers' key role in the provision of inclusive, equitable quality education and the promotion of lifelong learning and reflection. Bottom-up engagement, encouraging ownership of the new curriculum and the agency to shape it, has helped to directly contribute towards the change in the curriculum sought, with teachers themselves becoming agents of change working towards the Sustainable Development Goal of education for all.

References

Barany, L. (2013) Teaching of religious education in Iraqi state schools and the status of minorities in Iraq: A critical review, *International Journal of Arts & Sciences* 6.4: 451–466.

Benequista, N. and Gaventa, J. (2011) Blurring the boundaries: Citizen action across states and societies, Brighton: Institute of Development Studies.

Development Dimensions International (DDI) (2022) STAR Method.

Hanish, S. (2015) The Islamic State effect on minorities in Iraq, *Review of Arts and Humanities* 4.1: 7–11.

Issa, J.H. and Jamil, H. (2010) Overview of the education system in contemporary Iraq, *European Journal of Social Sciences* 14.3: 360–368.

Lapcha, H. (2019) CREID country scoping report, London: Coalition for Religious Equality and Inclusive Development and Al-Khoei Foundation.

Osman, K.F. (2019) *Sectarianism in Iraq: The Making of State and Nation since 1920*, New York: Routledge.

Özonur, M. and Kamışlı, H. (2019) Evaluation of pre-service teachers' views related to microteaching practice, *Universal Journal of Educational Research* 7.5: 1226–1233.

9

Advancing Freedom of Religion or Belief through Religiously Inclusive Education

Knox Thames

Education can be a powerful force for good, and diversity is an increasing reality for every society. To foster durable peace, international efforts supporting education must emphasize the benefits of pluralism and the importance of human rights, including freedom of religion or belief (FoRB). While domestic and international rights organizations regularly highlight human rights abuses, governments have often paid insufficient attention to the importance of systematically engaging the mentality that leads to violations in the first place. Promoting appreciation for pluralism and human rights is a long-term strategy to nurture peace and advance fundamental freedoms.

Faith everywhere, except in education

Surveys on global religiosity continue to demonstrate the salience of faith. The world is increasingly interconnected, with people from different religions, ethnicities and cultures intermixing as never before. The Pew Research Center reports that 84 per cent of people globally identify with a religious community (Hackett et al 2012). Moreover, the world is young. According to the World Bank, there is a 'youth bulge' in developing countries, with significant percentages of the population under 30 (Yifu Lin 2012). At the same time, Pew found that almost 60 per cent of the Earth's population live in countries with high restrictions on faith practices, either by governments or societal actors (Majumdar et al 2010).

With these demographic realities, it is crucial to prepare young people as students to live in a pluralistic, multi-ethnic, multi-religious world. To understand how to promote education about pluralism and human rights, the author, in his capacity as a Senior Visiting Expert at the US Institute of Peace (USIP), conducted dozens of interviews in 2021 on teaching multi-faith tolerance. USIP convened roundtables with organizations working on programmes to promote religious tolerance through education from Lebanon, Jordan, Pakistan, Iraq and the United States, among others. Numerous consultations were also held with practitioners, government and UN officials, the Organization for Security and Cooperation in Europe (OSCE), educators and other civil society organizations with the goal of better understanding how each approach their work.

The findings demonstrated how the reality of diversity in our globally connected world necessitates equipping students with the tools to participate in their pluralistic societies successfully and constructively. However, many education systems fail in this regard, while other voices promote fear or hatred of others. Teachers understand the need to do more. In USIP interviews, teachers and practitioners repeatedly emphasized the importance of teaching students about the benefits of pluralism through formal education and experiential learning. Doing so will make conceptual ideas relevant and help students develop skills to navigate diversity in any context. One practitioner stressed the importance of exploring identity with students on topics such as religion, race and gender, to help equip them to deal with biases, and build up to human rights. Or, as another participant said, to 'develop positive memories' about diversity.

Positive education about others

A positive, and not fearful, view of diversity is crucial. Irina Bokova, the former UNESCO Director-General, said it well: "Education should be about values, values of human rights, of mutual respect, of respect for the nature and of humanity, of living together. Teaching tolerance, respect for cultural diversity, and human rights is an essential part of bringing peace." The answer is apparent, but getting there will require hard work and long-term commitment.

Too many students around the world fail to receive basic education in reading, writing and mathematics. However meagre, even basic education in these subjects usually surpasses many times over what they receive regarding appreciation for pluralism or human rights. When attempting tolerance education, teachers are often unprepared and materials lacking. More often, curricula teach the opposite, diminishing minority faith communities' role in society or omitting mention of historic religious diversity. For instance, Iraqi minorities have complained to me for years about how textbooks treat them like guests to be tolerated instead of equal citizens who played key roles in Iraq's long history. In worst-case examples, some education systems explicitly or implicitly promote discrimination or even incitement to violence. At the same time, outside influencers actively promote prejudicial and violent world-views, creating a mindset that can lead to human rights abuses and instability, with few resources committed to pushing back.

Ignoring intolerance in education will only result in recurrent human rights abuses and instability, so the implications stretch beyond mere human rights issues to one of security and national stability. The value of teaching tolerance is made evident through academic research showing how it creates 'a commitment to pluralism [that] makes societies more secure' (Saya 2019: 69). Teaching about pluralism and a human rights approach to respecting diversity can protect youth from becoming susceptible to hateful ideologies, helping them to appreciate just and pluralistic societies. Such a mindset, if instilled, can help produce a string of other positive outcomes, including protecting human rights and religious freedom, creating resilient communities, and reduction of conflict and violent extremism.

Teachers value tolerance education

Interviews with practitioners during the USIP study repeatedly conveyed how crucial tolerance education is in preparing students to peacefully coexist with those from other cultural, religious and ethnic backgrounds. By learning about the benefits of pluralism, they can develop the skills to navigate diversity in any context. Several organizations explained how teaching the meanings of tolerance and benefits of pluralism is associated with healthier and more inclusive communities.

For instance, the work of the Alliance of Iraqi Minorities (AIM), which has been supported by USIP over the years, has focused on bringing about durable change through curricular reform, working to bring together Iraq's diverse groups who have been pitted against each other. AIM has 'focused on including more examples of multiculturalism and conviviality in the curriculum, a balanced compromise between the need for integration and minority concerns of assimilation' (Levkowitz and Abdulrahman 2021). As an example of the success of AIM's engagement, based on AIM's recommendation, the Ministry of Education in Baghdad 'will modify second-grade Islamic religious curriculum to highlight Armah, the seventh century Christian king of Abyssinia and Axum. The king was known for providing generosity and refuge to Muslim pilgrims in what is modern-day Ethiopia, serving as an example of religious coexistence' (Levkowitz and Abdulrahman 2021). While small, such change is an important first step.

But unfortunately, a constant refrain heard in USIP's study was the lack of government funding focused on teaching students to understand different belief systems and practices and instilling respect for the individual freedom of conscience. Research demonstrated the need to support new education efforts on respecting religious pluralism and protecting FoRB. For instance, several of the ministerial conferences to advance religious freedom, first launched by the United States in 2018, have discussed its importance, with several country delegations highlighting the need to do more. Subsequent interviews with diplomats from Europe and the United States further demonstrated an appreciation for the utility of tolerance education to prevent human rights abuses. The UN-sponsored 'Faith for Rights' framework, adopted in 2017, includes the commitment to 'refine the curriculums, teaching materials and textbooks wherever some religious interpretations, or the way they are presented, may give rise to the perception of condoning violence or discrimination' (OHCHR 2017: 31). In addition, the #Faith4Rights Toolkit offers 18 modules for facilitating peer-to-peer learning exercises to manage religious diversity in real-life situations (OHCHR 2020).

New funding to spur new efforts

Nevertheless, promoting religious tolerance through education is rarely given sufficient long-term funding by the international donor community. To durably meet this challenge, the international community must provide new resources to teach the benefits of pluralism, human dignity and equality for all. It is impossible to recommend one method or solution, as the needs of local communities are situation-specific. No 'one size fits all' approach exists for teaching multi-faith understanding, the benefits of pluralism, human rights and FoRB. An effective programme in Afghanistan will inevitably look very different from Nigeria or Brazil. Circumstances can vary radically from country to country, city to city and even between neighbourhoods. Many also stressed that central to successful and sustainable efforts is the investment in and support from local communities and stakeholders. Drawing on the values and traditions, including the religious communities who help to ground these in locally embedded and supported efforts, can be very powerful.

No time to lose

Teaching students about the importance of multi-faith understanding, the benefits of pluralism and human rights and FoRB should be a core component of any effort to support basic education. While teaching these subjects will take time and not immediately guarantee less conflict, it can foster greater respect for human rights and positively equip students to succeed in a globalizing world. Furthermore, doing nothing will undoubtedly ensure continued human rights abuses and instability.

References

Hackett, C., Grim, B., Stonawski, M., Skirbekk, V., Potančoková, M. and Abel, G. (2012) *The Global Religious Landscape*, Washington, DC: Pew Research Center.

Levkowitz, J. and Abdulrahman, S. (2021) In Iraq, advocates aim to reform education to build collective identity, United States Institute of Peace, 16 February, www.usip.org/blog/2021/02/iraq-advocates-aim-reform-education-build-collective-identity

Majumdar, S., Villa, V., Cooperman, A. and Fengyan Shi, A. (2010) In 2018, government restrictions on religion reach highest level globally in more than a decade: Authoritarian governments are more likely to restrict religion, Pew Research Center, 10 November, www.pewresearch.org/religion/2020/11/10/in-2018-government-restrictions-on-religion-reach-highest-level-globally-in-more-than-a-decade/

OHCHR (2017) *The Beirut Declaration and Its 18 Commitments on Faith for Rights*, Commitment XII, Geneva: United Nations High Commissioner for Human Rights.

OHCHR (2020) *#Faith4Rights Toolkit*, Geneva: United Nations High Commissioner for Human Rights.

Saya, N. (2019) Pluralism and peace in South Asia, *The Review of Faith & International Affairs* 17.7: 69–82.

Yifu Lin, J. (2012) Youth bulge: A demographic dividend or a demographic bomb in developing countries, *World Bank Blogs*, 5 January.

PART III

Gender

10

Interrogating the Gender and Religious Equality Nexus

Mariz Tadros

SDG5 is the stand-alone goal focused on the promotion of gender equality, while the expectation is that all other SDGs would also be gender-sensitive in their application. However, the relationship between women's right to gender equality and freedom of religion or belief (FoRB) in development hardly features in academic scholarship, though there is a vast scholarship on gender equality and religion more broadly which addresses the contribution of religious doctrine, leaders, religious-inspired political parties and movements undermining women's rights (Razavi and Jenichen 2010; Balchin 2011; Lodhia 2014). There is also a body of scholarship informed by different epistemic traditions, such as post-colonialist feminist and religion and development, that have shown that religion can have an empowering role in women's lives (Mahmoud 2012; Tomalin 2013). On account of this dearth of scholarship, this chapter makes use of grey literature and other relevant sources. The first part of this chapter will review some of the key academic and grey literature sources on the FoRB-gender equality nexus. The second part will then adopt a FoRB-lens onto gender equality with respect to the indicators drawn for SDG5, drawing primarily on the Coalition for Religious Equality and Inclusive Development (CREID) programme's scholarship.

Gender and freedom of religion or belief rights: intersections and divergences of rights and equalities

The overriding focus of scholarship published in the late 1990s and early 2000s in the area of FoRB has focused almost exclusively on the tensions between women's enjoyment of FoRB and rights. For example, Lindholm, Durham and Tahzib-Lie's seminal *Facilitating Freedom of Religion or Belief: A*

Desktop (2004) is one of the first scholarly explorations of the subject and contains five chapters exploring women and FoRB. Of those, four are primarily focused on the tensions between religion and women's equality (Borresen 2004; Denli 2004; King 2004; Sheen 2004). The crux of most of these important chapters is that women's equality is compromised as a consequence of power holders' formal and/or informal understandings of religion. The patriarchal, as well as paternalistic, nature of those who often exercise power in society has long been established, in particular as they often promote a gender exclusionary ideology (also see contributions in Tadros 2012 and Tadros 2020b for global perspectives). The majority of earlier work on FoRB was written from the vantage point of legal and human rights experts, and often pitched international human rights instruments as the measure of a religious ideology's deviance from women's equality.

Nazila Ghanea's (2017) *Women and Religious Freedom: Synergies and Opportunities* is one of the first attempts at considering, using legal instruments of human rights, the possibilities of reconciling women's rights and FoRB. Ghanea suggests that the international human rights framework, if taken in its totality, makes FoRB and women's equality reconcilable given that all human rights are indivisible, interdependent and interrelated. However, the prospects of finding synergies between FoRB and gender equality necessitate that we engage with individuals' right to exercise FoRB, rather than the rights of religion *per se*. This is especially since countries have used religion as a basis for reservations to ratifying the Convention on the Elimination of Discrimination against Women (CEDAW), as well as for the justification for the continuation of practices that undermine women's rights. This is elaborated further by Marie Juul Petersen, who argues that, in protecting individuals' and communities' right to have and practise a religion or belief, this 'includes women's right to interpret and practice their religion the way they believe is true, even when this challenges mainstream religious traditions and norms' (Petersen 2020). This is crucially important as women who follow mainstream religion(s) may also experience encroachments, and indeed enter into conflictual relationships with powerful formal and informal authorities as they defend their rights to freedom of conscience, challenging prevailing religious interpretations and practices (for an excellent example from Iran, see Mir-Hosseini 2011).

Also drawing on international human rights frameworks as a term of reference, Ahmed Shaheed, the former UN Special Rapporteur for FoRB, adds another dimension to the discussion in his report on gender and FoRB (Shaheed 2020). One of the fundamental issues challenging the reconcilability of gender equality and FoRB pertains to the use of the term 'gender'. While some consider gender equality as relating to challenging unequal power relations between women and men that inform patriarchal hierarchies, others conceive of gender equality in broader terms. Shaheed proposes that, by adopting a more fluid understanding of gender and sexuality, we can make FoRB more inclusive to also incorporate a wider set of identities, including LGBTQ+ persons.

A FoRB-sensitive reading of SDG5?

While the study of intersectionality has become very popular in gender and development, exploring the intersections of gender with several identifiers or social attributes, there is very little on the intersection of gender with religious affiliation in the analysis of SDG5. Pandey and Kumar's (2019: 155) review of UN Women's approach to engendering SDG5 highlights that 'Women's vulnerabilities due to intersections with other forms of discrimination, for example, age, disability, ethnicity, migration, economic status and so on, significantly enhance the burden of their disadvantage'. However, there is no mention in the report of vulnerability on account of the intersection of religious marginality and gender.

CREID's own research on FoRB and women's equality has specifically interrogated how gender inequality is exacerbated by inequalities on account of religious marginality, class, ethnicity and so forth. This chapter will focus specifically on those identifiers pertaining to SDG5's indicators. With respect to indicator 5.1, ending all forms of discrimination pertaining to legal frameworks that enable or hinder gender equality, CREID's research shows that the enforcement of legal frameworks that draw on religions different from those of the minority, as well as providing women with differential access to justice and rights according to their faith, is a major area of FoRB violation for women who are from religious minority backgrounds (see Tadros 2020a). In terms of the elimination of gender-based violence in public spaces (5.2) in particular, we see that women who belong to religious minorities and come from socio-economically deprived backgrounds can be vulnerable to differential experiences of sexual harassment in public spaces, both in terms of exposure and intensity (see Tadros 2020c; Tadros et al 2022). With respect to indicator 5.3 that addresses harmful practices such as early and forced marriage, for women who belong to religious minorities, in some contexts, coerced conversion can occur at the time of marriage to a member of the majority faith. In some of these cases, forced or coerced conversions associated with interfaith marriage circumscribes these women's freedom of conscience, and in some cases, deprives them of their families and communities (see Tadros 2021a; Kanwer and Mirza 2021).

While Goal 5.4 on recognizing the value of unpaid care and securing access to social protection is an issue that disproportionally affects socio-economically excluded women of all religious backgrounds (and no faith), religious marginality cannot be ignored. For example, in India, a citizenship law that undermines Muslims' ability to be recognized as citizens disproportionately affects Muslim women who lack papers (Hoda 2020). In the absence of paperwork, the right to make claims for rights, including social protection, are severely undermined.

Women's full and effective participation and equal opportunities for leadership at all levels of decision making in political, economic and public life (Indicator 5.5) is another area where women who belong to religious minorities and come from socio-economically deprived backgrounds are particularly likely to be excluded from formal political power. It is also important to note that access to healthcare, sexual and reproductive services, and economic resources (Indicator 5.6) is also often influenced by the nexus of poverty, religious marginality and gender in the lives of women from religious minority backgrounds (see Tadros 2020c, 2023; Tadros et al 2022). For example, in Egypt and Baghdad-administered parts of Iraq, women of non-Muslim religious background are denied the right to implement their own laws pertaining to gender parity in inheritance. The combination of patriarchal social mores, in addition to the legislative framework, means that their rights to land and asset ownership on a par with men are denied (see Tadros 2021b; Tadros et al 2022).

A FoRB-sensitive perspective can enhance our interpretive framework for redressing intersecting inequalities facing women on the margins. A FoRB-sensitive lens would allow us to ensure that women who are religiously marginalized are among those not left behind, both conceptually but also empirically. A FoRB-sensitive lens would enable the design and implementation of more gender-inclusive policies, transnationally, nationally and locally.

References

Balchin, C. (2011) Avoiding some deadly sins: Oxfam learnings and analysis about religion, culture, diversity, and development, Oxford: Oxfam.

Borresen, K. (2004) Religion confronting women's human rights: The case of Catholicism, in T. Lindholm, J. Durham, and B.J. Tahzib-Lie (eds) *Facilitating Freedom of Religion or Belief: A Deskbook*, Leiden: Martinus Nijhoff Publishers: 545–560.

Denli, O. (2004) Between Laicist state ideology and modern public religion: The head-cover controversy in contemporary Turkey, in T. Lindholm, J. Durham, and B.J. Tahzib-Lie (eds) *Facilitating Freedom of Religion or Belief: A Deskbook*, Leiden: Martinus Nijhoff Publishers.

Hoda, N. (2020) India's Muslim women are breaking free, *Asia Times*, 20 January.

Ghanea, N. (2017) *Women and Religious Freedom: Synergies and Opportunities*, Washington, DC: United States Commission on International Freedom.

Kanwer, M. and Mirza, J. (2021) 13-year-old Hindu girl Kavita is the latest victim of organised forced conversions in Sindh, *Briefing Note*, Coalition for Religious Equality and Inclusive Development, Brighton: Institute of Development Studies.

King, U. (2004) Hinduism and women: Uses and abuses of religious freedom, in T. Lindholm, J. Durham, and B.J. Tahzib-Lie (eds) *Facilitating Freedom of Religion or Belief: A Deskbook*, Leiden: Martinus Nijhoff Publishers.

Lindholm, T., Durham, J. and Tahzib-Lie, B.J. (2004) *Facilitating Freedom of Religion or Belief: A Deskbook*, Leiden: Martinus Nijhoff Publishers.

Lodhia, S. (2014) 'Stop importing weapons of family destruction!': Cyberdiscourses, patriarchal anxieties, and the Men's Backlash Movement in India, *Violence Against Women* 20.8: 905–936.

Mahmoud, S. (2012) *Politics of Piety, The Islamic Revival and the Feminist Subject*, Princeton, NJ: Princeton University Press.

Mir-Hosseini, Z. (2011) Beyond 'Islam' vs 'Feminism', *IDS Bulletin* 42.1: 67–77.

Pandey, U.C. and Kumar, C. (2019) *SDG5 – Gender Equality and Empowerment of Women and Girls*, Bradford: Emerald Publishing.

Petersen, M.J. (2020) *Promoting Freedom of Religion or Belief and Gender Equality in the Context of the Sustainable Development Goals: A Focus on Access to Justice, Education and Health. Reflections from the 2019 Expert Consultation Process*, Copenhagen: The Danish Institute for Human Rights.

Razavi, S. and Jenichen, A. (2010) The unhappy marriage of religion and politics: Problems and pitfalls for gender equality, *Third World Quarterly* 31.6: 833–850.

Shaheed, A. (2020) Gender based violence and discrimination in the name of religion or belief, Report of the Special Rapporteur on freedom of religion or belief, A/HRC/43/48, Geneva: United Nations Human Rights Council.

Sheen, J. (2004) Burdens on the right of women to assert their freedom of religion or belief, in T. Lindholm, J. Durham and B.J. Tahzib-Lie (eds) *Facilitating Freedom of Religion or Belief: A Deskbook*, Leiden: Martinus Nijhoff Publishers.

Tadros, M. (2012) *The Muslim Brotherhood in Contemporary Egypt: Democracy redefined or confined?*, Abingdon: Routledge.

Tadros, M. (2020a) Invisible targets of hatred: Socioeconomically excluded women from religious minority backgrounds, CREID Working Paper 2, Brighton: Coalition for Religious Equality and Inclusive Development, Institute of Development Studies.

Tadros, M. (2020b) Typology of women's collective agency in relation to women's equality outcomes: Case studies from Egypt and beyond, *European Journal of Development Research* 3: 1930–1951.

Tadros, M. (ed) (2020c) Violence and discrimination against women of religious minority backgrounds in Pakistan, Brighton: Coalition for Religious Equality and Inclusive Development, Institute of Development Studies.

Tadros, M. (2021a) Coercive consent: Unlocking the truth behind disappearing women in Pakistan, Blog, https://creid.ac/blog/2021/02/05/coercive-consent-unlocking-the-truth-behind-disappearing-women-in-pakistan/

Tadros, M. (2021b) The invisibility of women's faces in religious freedom-promoting high places, Coalition for Religious Equality and Inclusive Development, 8 March.

Tadros, M. (ed) (2023) Violence and discrimination against women of religious minority backgrounds in Nigeria, Brighton: Coalition for Religious Equality and Inclusive Development, Institute of Development Studies.

Tadros, M., Shahab, S. and Qulliam-Graham, A. (ed) (2022) Violence and discrimination against women of religious minority backgrounds in Iraq, Brighton: Coalition for Religious Equality and Inclusive Development, Institute of Development Studies.

Tomalin, E. (2013) *Religions and Development*, London: Routledge.

11

Dire Conditions for Hazara Shia Pilgrims during COVID-19 Quarantine in Pakistan

Sadiqa Sultan

This chapter explores whether the extended quarantine and poor treatment of Hazara Shia women pilgrims returning home to Pakistan after travelling to Iran in 2020 was due to their identity as Hazaras, an ethnic religious minority which already experiences violence and discrimination in Pakistan (Sultan et al 2020; Eggert et al 2022). This chapter further explores how the intersection of gender and religious belief enhanced experiences of marginality for the Hazara Shia women, who were kept in poor conditions and with little access to information, essential care or supplies. Due to the persecution Hazara Shias face, all names in this chapter have been changed to protect the women's anonymity.

> 'Why were we still subject to imprisonment and inhuman behaviour when we didn't show any symptoms of coronavirus, even after 40 days of being locked up? It was unjust, we did not deserve this. When traders and pilgrims who did not look like Hazaras were sent home shortly after they crossed the border, we understood it had to do something with [our Hazara identity].' (Saeeda)

Saeeda, aged 50, was one of hundreds of women who, in March 2020, returned from pilgrimages to the Shia holy city of Qom and Mashhad in Iran. She's an ethnic Hazara from Pakistan's least developed and poorest western province of Balochistan, which borders Iran. Iran, one of the first countries where COVID-19 spread, announced its first two deaths attributed to COVID-19 in February 2020, and there was concern about

Hazara and other Shia Muslims returning from Qom across the Pakistan border. Shia believers, about 10–15 per cent of the population of Pakistan (Minority Rights Group International 2022), are regarded as apostates by some extremist Sunni groups. Many face regular hostility from extremists and public calls for members to be killed. The most vulnerable are the sizeable Hazara population in Quetta. Hazaras are an ethnic group predominantly based in Afghanistan, but with a population of up to half a million living in Quetta, the provincial capital of Balochistan. As both an ethnic and religious minority, Hazaras face intersectional discrimination. The community already experiences persecution and their differential treatment during the pandemic (Tadros et al 2021) further eroded their already limited trust in authorities.

Hazara Shia pilgrims treated more harshly than other pilgrims returning from Iran

Pilgrims repeatedly mentioned that only Hazaras were subject to isolation and discrimination. They were initially quarantined in a tented camp at Taftan on the border, then transferred to Mia Ghundi on the outskirts of Quetta, and finally to either Haji Camp or Sheikh Zayed Hospital, both in Quetta itself. "Initially there were non-Hazara pilgrims as well with us at Taftan. [But] they were sent home soon after. Other non-Shias were not stopped at all for screening or testing for COVID-19 and were let go" (Nusrat, 45).

By not screening the non-Shias at the border, the message conveyed by authorities was that only Shia Hazaras were the likely carriers of the virus. This, the Hazara community argued, enabled the rest of the province to spread hatred and fear against Hazaras in general, and Hazara pilgrims in particular (Mirza 2020). "We were treated more harshly than non-Hazara Shias at Taftan – the authorities would not even talk to us in a normal way" (Saeeda). "My quarantine started upon arrival at Taftan on 3rd March and ended in Sheikh Zayed Hospital on 17th April – 44 days [later]" (Nusrat).

While most pilgrims were kept at Taftan camp without tests for 20 or more days, some tested negative within the first or second week, but were still kept at the camp for a couple more weeks, despite the global standard for quarantine for suspected infection, which was 14 days at the time.

Misinformation, dire facilities and inadequate care for those with medical conditions

Pakistani authorities were neither prepared nor able to facilitate proper isolation centres, and the lack of available washrooms and running water was identified as a particular challenge, with only one washroom provided for hundreds of users. Although there were separate toilet facilities for women in all the quarantine centres, they were in poor condition. This lack of facilities also affected women's observance of religious rituals and prayers. Saeeda said she would wake up as early as 3 am, two hours before morning prayers, to do her ablutions, given that 'around prayer time, it used to get crowded and even dirtier'. In Mia Ghundi, tent toilets were arranged and later the authorities brought in fibre plastic ones. However, Hafiza, 36, recalls that at Taftan, they were only provided with sanitary protection after they had asked for it several times: 'there were no bins for disposal either, causing embarrassment as some toilets were used by both men and women because of high demand'. Some women continued to use medication they'd taken with them to skip or delay their periods while on pilgrimage (because during them, they cannot perform certain rituals) to avoid awkwardness in the camp, but they ended up with infections and skin problems. Hameeda, 20, in Taftan with her mother and brother, said the washrooms were so bad she decided to starve herself so as not to have to use the toilets. Women would also go to the washroom in groups or with male family members because 'some women reported being followed when they went in the middle of night'.

In Taftan, Saeeda reported

'I could hardly sleep in the tent. I did not feel safe. There were instances when, in the middle of the night, I saw a shadow approaching our tent. Whoever it was kind of searched and tapped the tent with his hands from outside. I was about to shout but, luckily, he did not step in. It happened several times.'

She said she was sure it was not a Frontier Corps' security guard, as they were identifiable in their uniforms with guns patrolling around the tents. Nusrat, who was eventually moved to Sheikh Zayed Hospital, said, "usually two or three men would come at 12 or 1 am to clean our wards. We were scared of them coming around that time although we were in a group of eight to ten persons in a ward." Although three meals were provided daily, food at quarantine centres was also either not hygienic or inadequate: "food was hurled to us as if we were animals, or they would lock the door, pile up food behind the door and then would ask us to take it". Halima, 53, mentioned a woman with a child in a ward in Sheikh Zayed: "she was probably six months pregnant. The volunteer told me she was ill and not eating well. There was no special care or check-up facility for her." Halima also remembered a diabetic woman who was really sick. The sick woman's daughter made many efforts to get help for her, but all in vain. Eventually, the daughter gave up, but wanted to harm herself or someone else to get the hospital authorities to take notice.

Quarantined pilgrims felt withdrawn, fatigued and experienced suicidal thoughts

Suicidal thoughts among the women became common, particularly for the young girls. Nusrat recollected:

> 'we were on the third floor in Sheikh Zayed. Young girls, totally withdrawn and fatigued would, time and again, refer to jumping out of the window. What would you do if you were locked in for more than 40 days and treated like animals? We were careful though and calmed them down through engaging them in conversations and showing them entertaining videos with the limited data they had on their mobile phones.'

Nusrat's daughter, Fatima, 13, recalled:

> 'I was separated from my father in Mia Ghundi. I was told that I was being taken to Fatima Jinnah Hospital for a test and would be reunited with him. They brought me to Sheik Zayed Hospital instead. I asked them why they lied to me. I was worried and cried a lot, but nobody cared. If that day my mother and her friend [they were protesting at Sheik Zayed Hospital] did not see me getting out of the ambulance, I would surely have been shifted to a different ward from them.'

While there were some improvements to conditions due to the constant protests within and outside the quarantine centres, Hazara Shia pilgrims have been left with traumatic memories of their treatment: "I was released on 6th April and came home. My heart was bursting. I cried for hours as if I was released from prison – the quarantine centre was indeed a prison. Other than my immediate family, no-one came to visit."

This chapter reveals how the religious identity of the Hazara Shia pilgrims interviewed intersected with their gender to enhance the women's experiences of marginalization at the quarantine centres on the Iran/Pakistan border. Hazara Shias were particularly targeted for quarantine and seen to be the spreaders of the virus (Mirza 2020), while in the quarantine centres themselves, Hazara Shia women felt particularly unsafe, both in their tents and to use facilities on their own. The lack of provision of adequate and clean sanitation facilities further impacted women's health as they sought mechanisms to avoid using the toilets altogether, or to medically suspend their menstrual cycles. This illustrates the necessity of recognizing how intersecting inequalities on account of faith, belief, ethnicity, gender and other identifiers can deeply enhance experiences of marginalization in a given context, with detrimental outcomes for health and wellbeing, and how the SDGs need to be attentive to all forms of inequality to ensure no one is left behind.

References

Eggert, J., Kanwer, M. and Mirza, J.A. (2022) Responsiveness to religious inequalities in contexts of displacement: Evidence from providers of humanitarian assistance to Shi'a Hazara refugees from Afghanistan in Pakistan, CREID Working Paper 12, Brighton and Washington, DC: Coalition for Religious Equality and Inclusive Development and Joint Learning Initiative on Faith and Local Communities.

Minority Rights Group International (2022) Shi'a and Hazaras, World Directory of Minorities and Indigenous Peoples, https://minorityrights. org/minorities/shia-and-hazaras/ (accessed 23 November 2022).

Mirza, J.A. (2020) Pakistan's Hazara Shia minority blamed for the spread of COVID-19, *Institute of Development Studies*, 17 April.

Sultan, S., Kanwer, M. and Mirza, J.A. (2020) The multi-layered minority: Exploring the intersection of gender, class and religious-ethnic affiliation in the marginalisation of Hazara women in Pakistan, Brighton: Coalition for Religious Equality and Inclusive Development, Institute of Development Studies.

Tadros, M., Kanwer, M. and Mirza, J.A. (2021) Religious marginality, COVID-19 and redress of targeting and inequalities, *IDS Bulletin* 52.1.

12

The 'Messy' World of Women and Religious Inequality

Kate Ward

In the area of religious inequality and women's rights, there lies a complexity of compounded vulnerabilities. There appears to be no 'one size fits all' approach to both the interventions that need to be considered and to advocating in response to breaches of freedom of religion or belief (FoRB) and women's rights. Indeed, I would describe this interface as messy.

Anisha[1] was a member of a group in a project for women belonging to religious minorities. She lived in a region containing a diverse religious community. They faced significant restrictions and targeted abuses in a south Asian nation governed by a religious nationalist regime. Her story highlights intersecting vulnerabilities that she experiences day-to-day. Anisha was widowed when her children were young and expressed how fearful she was at her husband's death explaining, "I said to him, 'don't leave me, I don't know what to do'." At that point she was following the country's majority religion, yet she felt powerless due to her very low social position and the lack of resources available to her. She also believed she had a 'curse' in her house with her children getting sick. Due to her limited income, she prioritized feeding her children, leaving herself hungry with little energy to work. She met members from a minority religion and was supported and cared for by them, which inspired her to change her religion. Since that decision, she has been fearful of being raped when she walks alone but prays, in which she finds comfort, and says she feels protected. She remains extremely poor. However, she feels she has a new sense of belonging and that her situation has changed because her own mindset has shifted with a

---

[1] This is not her real name due to securing her identity within her context.

more positive attitude. This is despite the fact that she has been rejected by her own family in response to her religious conversion, and that her father has said that neither she nor her children will inherit the family land.

Anisha's story is not unusual. When I talked to other participants involved in skills workshops and self-help groups, women reported similar stories and stated they had suffered gender-based violence due to belonging to a religious minority as a woman. Many repeated stories of rejection by the local community and their wider family. "100 per cent face violence of that kind," one facilitator said.

Unravelling the mess

Anisha's example is amplified by millions of women who endure discrimination and abuses. The layers of complexity or 'messiness' need to be unravelled from within the context, driven by family expectations and societal norms, and from outside by perpetrator's actions or legal and state restrictions. Moreover, some communities face targeted attacks and then move into a 'recovery state', while others live with everyday discriminatory behaviours or restrictions. Working with women such as Anisha is *messy* to the international actors based in the Global North who can insist on precise frameworks for measuring outcomes that might become irrelevant, or follow policy recommendations which can quickly lack applicability due to the rapidly changing context. More importantly, if interventions are unable to address this level of challenge or messiness, they could contribute towards gender discrimination and increasing the gender gaps in development outcomes.

Do the Sustainable Development Goals contribute towards the messiness?

How much do those implementing the Sustainable Development Goals (SDGs) consider the compounded issues that religious minority women face? In a Bond review on SDG5 in 2015, they recommended that the UK government should 'Develop a clear strategy for better identifying, understanding, investing in and reporting on women and girls across various lived experiences of marginalization, including age, disability status, ethnicity, caste, education, geography, sexuality and/or LBTI identity, and child, early or forced marriage' (Bond 2019).

Although the list of 'lived experiences of marginalization' is broad, there was no mention of religion throughout the document, nor in any of the other recommendations. The same was true during my attendance at the United Nations Commission for the Status of Women in 2018 and 2019. Although my team contributed to presentations and first-hand testimonials on the intersection of FoRB and women's rights to side events, I did not witness any engagement with religion in the main plenaries, despite the fact that 83.4 per cent of women globally identify with a faith group, compared to 79.9 per cent of men (Pew Research Center 2016). This led me to wonder whether the secularization of the Global North has 'invisiblized' religion and belief so that international organizations exclude it from programming and the SDGs. Moreover, have those advocating, researching and implementing programmes in the area of religious and gender inequality excluded themselves from the field of women's rights due to assumptions on issues such as sexual and reproductive rights? If the goal is to represent religious minorities, are these women slipping off *a glass cliff*[2] because FoRB actors remain siloed in the FoRB arena, while not interacting with other human rights violations that occur concurrently and particularly affect them?

If the SDGs had greater interaction with goals to improve religious freedom, how might that change the outcome for women like Anisha? For example, the nation in which she lives is co-signatory to trade agreements with Western governments who appear to have avoided any discussion on breaches of human rights. They do, however, seem to be performing relatively well compared to other similar nations in the lower-middle-income group in their Strategic Development Goals without the inclusion of religious freedom in their targets.

Correcting past practices to change today's outcomes

My own views and practice have been radically transformed over three decades. I began my career based on a notion of 'respecting cultural norms'. I had assumed that women had to remain in the private sphere while men lived in the public sphere. But this dissipated when I began to gather more evidence and collaborate with indigenous partners and peers in the field. This ensured that harmful practice based on gendered social norms and assumptions were exposed and women's inclusion and representation in programme delivery and research became the norm. Now we are working closely across networks and in coalitions to challenge one another and bring critique to both social and cultural norms. This includes addressing how sacred texts are misinterpreted and used to support the patriarchy and abuses of power that are often seen in religious practices and justified through distorted beliefs and teaching. In addition, this approach contributed towards and shaped recommendations to the UK government in 2019 that highlighted intersectionalities, such as gender and FoRB, and called

---

[2]   *Glass cliff* is a term that is increasingly used to describe the position of female leaders given an impossible role or task that is bound to fail. They are often put there by those sceptical of their skills and wanting to prove that women are not always 'right for the job'.

for 'bolstering of research between the critical intersection of FoRB and minority rights' (Mountstephen 2019).

Returning to Anisha's context, a new challenge to donors has emerged with regard to inclusion. In her community, women expressed that they would be less vulnerable to abuse and traffickers if some of the women belonging to the majority religion joined their projects. That would create a greater sense of social cohesion, decrease suspicion and lead to gains through achieving shared goals. However, donor funding is often restricted to specific *beneficiaries*,[3] whereby they may insist they fund a minority group or adherents of the same religious identity as the donor. An unwillingness to change organizations' policies and practices leaves women more exposed and vulnerable because of their gender. When men change their religion in Anisha's context, they don't risk losing their children. They expect their wives to follow their beliefs and they move location if social hostilities emerge. Women do not have the power to do that. Funding targets should be gendered, avoiding masculine normativity, and consider the impact of gender-specific religious hostilities and oppression (Miller et al 2022).

In this chapter, I have highlighted some of the messiness which emerges with compounding religious inequality and religious minority women. In doing so, I have used Anisha's story as an example of the complex issues millions of women face living and surviving as a religious minority. Failure to understand or address these issues results in greater gender inequality, potentially reduced funding and resourcing and, invariably, the propping up of existing patriarchal structures. A new drafting of the SDGs, post 2030, should adopt new practices and advocate for policies that recognize religion as part of the majority of women's lived experience, and determine that religious inequality and restrictions placed on people's beliefs are recognized and included. As development practitioners and academics, we can be uncomfortable with what appears as disorder or messiness, yet if we anticipate, adapt and address some of those challenges, we can look forward to being a part of changing Anisha's story and the millions of women like her.

References

Bond (2019) The UK's global contribution to the Sustainable Development Goals: Progress, gaps and recommendations, www.bond.org.uk/wp-cont ent/uploads/2023/03/bond_the_uks_global_contribution_to_the_sdgs_ online_full_report.pdf (accessed 8 May 2023).

Bond (2022) Strategic Development Goal 5: Progress, gaps and recommendations, https://bond.org.uk/wp-content/uploads/2022/09/sdg5.pdf

---

[3] 'Beneficiaries', although accepted in programming terminology, can sound paternalistic, but I am intentionally using this language.

Miller E.L., Brown, E., Fisher, H. and Morley, R. (2022) Invisible: The Gender Report 2022, Oxford: Open Doors, www.opendoors.org/theg enderreport (accessed 16 December 2022).

Mountstephen, P. (2019) *The Bishop of Truro's Independent Review for the UK Foreign Secretary of Foreign and Commonwealth Office Support for Persecuted Christians. Final Report and Recommendations (2019)*, London: Christian Persecution Review, www.google.com/search?client=safari&rls= en&q=Bishop+of+truro+report&ie=UTF-8&oe=UTF-8 (accessed 16 December 2022).

Pew Research Center (2016) The gender gap in religion around the world, Washington, DC: Pew Research Center, www.pewresearch.org/religion/ 2016/03/22/the-gender-gap-in-religion-around-the-world/#:~:text= An%20estimated%2083.4%25%20of%20women,in%20192%20countr ies%20and%20territories. (accessed 16 December 2022).

13

Empty Chairs: Freedom of Religion or Belief's Gender Problem

Andrea Mari and Kathryn Cheeseman

This chapter speaks to the gender gap in women's representation in leadership, particularly leadership for freedom of religion or belief (FoRB). Target 5.5 of gender equality, the fifth Sustainable Development Goal (SDG5), aims to 'Ensure women's full and effective participation and equal opportunities for leadership at all levels of decision-making in political, economic and public life.'

The specific indicators of this sub-target are measures of:

- the proportion of seats held by women in national parliaments and local governments (5.5.1); and
- the proportion of women in managerial positions (5.5.2).

However, overlooked in these indicator measures is the extent to which the absence of FoRB affects women's full, effective and equal opportunities for participation and leadership, both at local and national levels. This chapter explores the experiences of women and men involved in the implementation and management of the Coalition for Religious Equality and Inclusive Development (CREID) programme in relation to gender justice. The chapter further explicates CREID's policy of championing gender equity and empowerment across its network and projects as a central pillar of its theory of change, recognizing the deep intersection of gender and religious marginality, and its impact on the attainment of gender equality in leadership.

Where are the women?

Only a handful of women (about eight out of 51) appeared in the official group photo of the high-ranking delegates and speakers at the Ministerial to Advance Religious Freedom in 2019, one of the most influential spaces created by the US government to champion FoRB. This deficit was replicated at the Alliance to Advance International Religious Freedom, another high-level governmental platform that convened for the first time in February 2020 in Poland, where there were only three women out of 26 participants seen to be sitting at the decision-making table (Tadros 2021).

Conscious of this bias in FoRB spaces, CREID actively sought to ensure that, at all levels of its programming, there would be opportunities for the assumption of power by, and for, women. This was a policy actively sought, rather than a position by default. CREID pursued this active opportunism to enhance women's representation through the following policy measures, ensuring women engaged:

- as speakers in its public-facing events;
- as managers of CREID's projects, locally and centrally;
- as delegates representing the programme across policy and public fora;
- as producers and critics of academic knowledge;
- in access to knowledge exchange and learning opportunities; and
- in access to publication platforms, as bloggers about FoRB violations as part of CREID's global bloggers network.

This active pursuit of gender equality measures went beyond the remit of the programme itself. The CREID programme refused to participate in external events where women (or men) were completely absent.[1] It was not enough to promote equal opportunism across the programme itself – this approach was applied across all of CREID's engagements. Given the dominance of men in FoRB spaces, and the intersection of inequalities meaning that, in many cases, women from religious minorities face additional barriers to participation and leadership (Tadros 2020; Tadros et al 2022), this approach had its challenges, but this also highlights why it was and is so very important to instigate change.

---

[1] Although each organization in the consortia and its leadership had the liberty to apply this when acting in their own independent capacity.

The Coalition for Religious Equality and Inclusive Development's golden rules

The practical recommendations that follow outline how everyone engaging in FoRB should approach gender equality – a means to (politely but firmly) ruffle feathers for equitable engagement:

- If you are invited to speak at, or otherwise participate in, an event, explain to event organizers why you will only participate if there is equal representation of women and men as speakers.
- If you are convening events, ensure to formulate achievable milestones for ensuring that all public-facing engagements reflect a commitment to inclusion.
- Think about women in relation to other axes of inequality, such as location, background, profession, age, ability/disability and ethnicity. CREID was keen to prioritize representation from the Global South when adopting a gender-sensitive approach as much as possible.

Of course, a critique of these could be that the programme perpetuates the phenomenon of 'token women'; that is, women who assume a public-facing role for window-dressing purposes, but do not enjoy real, substantive decision-making power. CREID was privileged to work with a wide pool of partners and organizations which fortunately meant that there was never a shortage of women of substance, calibre and capacity empowered and empowering others in leadership.

Inclusion matters, but so does legitimacy

For CREID, one of the few exceptions to the programme's strict policy of equal gender representation, management and engagement were the stakeholders consulted to develop the new pro-pluralism religious education curriculum in Iraq (see Lapcha and Mahdi, this volume). The project's aim was to develop a curriculum based on the criteria of religious pluralism and diversity, while maintaining an Islamic perspective. Among the people consulted, which included religious educators, academics, religious minorities and Islamic, community and tribal leaders, women were underrepresented – not by intention or design but by the very fact of entrenched, institutional marginalization in Iraqi society.

> 'From a total 32 people consulted, who were actively involved in the curriculum development … about ten per cent [four] were women … all from the academia. [I think] this is because in the … higher ranks, stakeholders are predominantly male … they tend to be in positions of authority … This was the case for the religious leaders we consulted

[and] the tribal leaders.' (Yusra Mahdi, former Al-Khoei Foundation Project Manager)

While efforts were made to redress this gender imbalance, it was not possible to find suitable female experts beyond the four identified to engage with the scope of the consultation. Despite best intentions, some things are beyond a project's control. In this instance, it is important to be clear on these limitations, and accountable for their source. "The woman who was in charge of [the curriculum project] was very much aware of this imbalance … she did try to bring on more women in the consultation process, but she said there wasn't enough expertise" (Yusra Mahdi, former Al-Khoei Foundation Project Manager).

However, where this part of the process was inequitable, the team sought to address the gender gap at other stages of the project. For example, addressing the practical and logistical obstacles to women teachers fully participating in the capacity-building workshops and ensuring that they felt sufficiently supported in public spaces to be able to articulate their ideas, thoughts and opinions, even in the presence of a large number of men.

Key reflections

Important reflections on enrolling women in high-ranking positions should be addressed at this stage, serving as guidance for future projects:

1. Ensuring that more women hold high-ranking positions does not mean that we ghettoize women's issues so that men don't take them seriously.

Ironically, engendering the topic sometimes has the reverse effect of making men's involvement in FoRB activities suddenly disappear. If the theme of an event is women and FoRB, often the room looks reversed in terms of representation – the majority are women, with only a handful of men. Therefore, the aim is not to replace a room full of men with women but to achieve equity and inclusiveness. Having events and projects attended and managed only by women misses the point of ensuring a plurality of voices to promoting inclusivity. There should be equal representation of men and women at all levels of projects, including when the topic is gender. In addition, gender should not be separated from other axes of inequality, such as age or ethnicity.

2. It is important to invest in the training of young women to become leaders, rather than just installing women with existing expertise into senior positions.

CREID undertook a proactive approach, understanding the concomitant need to empower young women to work their way up and assume managerial positions, as well as hiring women with existing skills into managerial roles. This dual approach is significant in helping to address the impact of intersecting inequalities, which may otherwise impede the advancement of women, and particularly women from religious minorities, into managerial positions.

3. Recognizing the impact of intersecting inequalities.

There are numerous challenges which women have to face when they decide to climb the career ladder. Some of these challenges apply to all women, regardless of their religious background or the position they occupy in a society.

> 'I think there are some stereotypes about women which also apply to non-religious women, [they apply] to women in general. [Stereotypes] which are deeply entrenched in many people's minds. So ... that there's less women who make it to the top than men generally.' (Yousif Abualqassim, Al-Khoei Foundation Director)

> 'It's a great challenge for every woman living in a patriarchal society to establish herself as a professional in any field, be it teaching, engineering, health, or activism. So, a gender-biased gender-segregated society is a challenge for any woman in general.' (Naumana Suleman, former Minority Rights Group South Asia Coordinator)

While it is true that all women experience hurdles and stereotypes, when gender intersects with other factors, such as belonging to a religious or ethnic minority, women's career paths become even more challenging.

> 'If you are from a religious minority [the problem] is compounded ... There are [more] inhibitions for women when you are in a religious setting.' (Yousif Abualqassim, Al-Khoei Foundation Director)

> 'When it comes to minority women, this adds more vulnerability because the religious bias also comes in, which may lead for example to a comparatively less welcoming attitude from the society than for other women ... When you are a minority woman, you need more energy to prove yourself because people don't recognise your hard work and commitment. Also, many believe that minority women are not suitable or able to occupy high-ranking positions.' (Naumana Suleman, former Minority Rights Group South Asia Coordinator)

The intersection of gender and religious background can impact women in the workplace, delaying their career advancement.

'[I knew it would have been harder to move up positions at work], especially as a minority as well as a female, a woman from a Muslim background working in [the field of] development. I felt it was very challenging … I had to work extra hard to get where I wanted, compared to my male colleagues … [I felt I had] constantly … to prove myself … I felt like we [women] have to step in and do everything … just so that we can be heard more … [In my previous job] male colleagues who were in my same position … were a lot quicker in getting promoted … Even a woman manager discriminated against me just because … she felt like my male colleague was more capable.' (Yusra Mahdi, former Al-Khoei Foundation Project Manager)

A gender-sensitive approach to participation and leadership

There was widespread awareness among CREID's management of the difficulties experienced by women who aim for high-ranking positions and how these are compounded when women belong to religious minorities. As part of the programme's commitment to gender sensitivity in participation and leadership, CREID undertook a gender audit to evaluate its engagement around the promotion of gender equality across its projects. However, male and female interviewees had different perceptions on what challenges women who want to pursue a career face. According to male interviewees, family matters are the main obstacle. Having children was described as problematic, taking up women's time and energy. On the other hand, female interviewees identified people's attitudes as the principal hurdle to their career progression. This included not being taken seriously, bullying, belittling, and the energy spent feeling the need to constantly prove themselves compared with their male colleagues. Yet hostile attitudes don't only come from men but cut across gender, age group, socio-economic status, religious belief and position held.

While CREID has achieved much in terms of gender equality in its strategy and implementation, it has only scratched the surface of the pathway to engendering FoRB. This necessitates equal representation of men and women at all levels of projects, including when the topic is gender. Having events and projects attended and managed only by women misses the point of ensuring a plurality of voices to promoting inclusivity. In addition, gender should not be separated from other axes of inequality, such as age or ethnicity. Finally, building leadership capacity from below while also ensuring women leaders requires a dual strategy; merely placing more women in high-ranking positions is not a guarantee of gender equality. An active, considered and intersectional approach is necessary to address FoRB's gender problem, and the empty chairs at the decision-making table.

References

Tadros, M. (ed) (2020) Violence and discrimination against women of minority backgrounds in Pakistan, Coalition for Religious Equality and Inclusive Development, Brighton: Institute of Development Studies.

Tadros, M. (2021) The invisibility of women's faces in religious-freedom promoting high places, Coalition for Religious Equality and Inclusive Development, 8 March.

Tadros, M., Shahab, S. and Quinn-Graham, A. (eds) (2022) Violence and discrimination against women of minority backgrounds in Iraq, Coalition for Religious Equality and Inclusive Development, Brighton: Institute of Development Studies, DOI: 10.19088/CREID.2022.025

PART IV

Water and Sanitation

14

Freedom of Religion or Belief and Access to Safe Water

Kate Bayliss

SDG6 aims to 'ensure availability and sustainable management of water and sanitation for all' by 2030, but progress is way off course. In 2020, 2 billion people (26 per cent of the world's population) lacked access to safely managed drinking water and 3.6 billion (46 per cent of the population) lacked access to safely managed sanitation (UN 2022). The impacts are devastating. Water is essential for life and a core element of most social and economic processes, for civilizations as much as individuals. Failings in relation to SDG6 impact all other SDGs, particularly gender equality, health, education and poverty reduction.

Progress in SDG6 is particularly hindered for groups that face discrimination, and religious bias intersects with other identifiers, such as gender and class, to compound disadvantage. Access to safe water is typically provided by physical infrastructures often involving networks of pipes and pumps. These are mediated by institutional and social structures and the way in which these are governed is inevitably imbued with political choices. The capacity of different groups to influence governance structures shapes the wider system, and access to water and other essential services can be used to exercise social power (Perreault 2014).

This chapter explores intersections between progress towards SDG6 and freedom of religion or belief along the following channels: first, religious bias has shaped infrastructure development in discriminatory ways in some places, although the way in which this occurs is complex across different actors in the process of water systems; second, inequalities in water access result from discrimination in the way that some religious faiths are located in more fragile situations that increase vulnerabilities; finally, increased water scarcity has led to changing patterns of land use, leading to increased vulnerability and conflict, in some cases along religious fault lines. Interventions to promote SDG6 will need to address complex and intersecting dimensions to religious bias in water access.

About water

Water has certain material properties and social associations that affect the way it is accessed and used. Water in its raw form comes from surface sources, such as rivers, and underground sources, via wells and boreholes, and rainwater harvesting. Water is heavy to transport and so tends to be consumed close to where it is sourced. However, in some cases, water courses are diverted via networks of dams and pipes from their natural sources to areas of economic activity (such as in South Africa). Water tends to be prone to leakiness and evaporation such that usage can be difficult to measure with precision. Across the world, water supplies are coming under increasing strain from pollution and climate change.

The governance of water is often managed by a range of institutions that connect raw water to end users. But the nature of this system varies hugely across contexts. In a rural area, water might be accessed by a simple borehole or rainwater storage. In urban areas, water reaches end users via an extensive range of actors from different state departments across water engineers, plumbers, tanker operators and bill collectors, and there may be private water providers involved. This will be embedded within a legal institutional framework. At each stage in the system of water provision, decisions are mediated by a set of agents. Decision making at different stages leads to observed outcomes in patterns of inclusion and exclusion which may have inherent biases (Mawani 2019). While water flows in one direction, finance often flows in the other so that providing water can be lucrative for some actors, while poor households may be excluded from safe supplies.

Patterns of access and exclusion in water are often also reflected in other deprivations such as poor housing and weak access to basic services such as healthcare, education, transport and economic opportunities. Furthermore, marginalized groups may share common features across different types of identity and social structures, such as caste, as well as class, income and political affiliations. For example, in India, religion intersects with caste and gender in discriminatory exclusion from water access (Dutta et al 2015; 2018). Achieving SDG6 will require identifying and addressing discriminatory practices across all levels of water systems, from the design of urban infrastructure through to the treatment of IDPs in refugee camps.

How is progress towards SDG6 affected by religious inequality?

Water is typically provided by networks of pipes and pumps (and sometimes trucks) so there tends to be a spatial element to segregated provision, with areas rather than individuals experiencing discrimination in water access on the basis of religion or ethnicity. Biases in provision tend to extend not just to water but to other essential services such as shelter, energy, health and education. In Pakistan, for example, Christian and Hindu communities face unequal treatment and 'otherization', with limited or lack of provision of fundamental infrastructure, decent accommodation and economic and social opportunities. This is exacerbated by 'dilapidated and non-functional health, sewerage, sanitation and water facilities' (HRCP 2019: 1).

In India, cities are locations of spatial segregation along religious, class and caste lines associated with differential access to living standards, including water services. Several studies find that Muslim towns and districts have weaker access to water than other areas and that the provision of public services is used as a political instrument (Das and Kar 2016; Adukia et al 2019).

Mawani (2019: 3) unpacks such segregation in detail with reference to the 'visibly stark differences' in housing and urban infrastructure between Muslim and Hindu areas in the city of Ahmedabad, which is often taken to be indicative of state-led discrimination. However, she cautions against reductive associations and highlights the complex 'journey' of a planning proposition, from formulation to implementation, involving actors with diverse interests intervening, mediating and influencing. Moreover, she highlights that political decisions take physical form via a range of 'material, physical and bureaucratic processes' (Mawani 2019: 3). Her detailed analysis shows that there are multifarious reasons why infrastructure has not been constructed, including, in part, resistance from influential Muslims who would lose out from the rezoning of agricultural land. Mawani suggests that while spatial divisions on the basis of religion may have influenced the origins of segregation, the pressures that lead to such divides being maintained may not be due to religious divides alone. Majority and minority groups are not necessarily homogenous and the boundaries between state and non-state are not clear-cut.

Inequalities in water access also arise from the location of minority groups in areas that are more precarious and difficult to serve. In South Asia, for example, Dalit communities are often concentrated in the least hospitable environments that are the most vulnerable, such as in the densely populated areas of the coastal Bay of Bengal region, which is increasingly prone to flooding, and marginalized communities are also often sidelined in emergency responses to natural disasters (MRG 2019). In rural areas too, ethnic minority households can fare worse than others. For example, in Vietnam, while minorities faced differential access rates to water across the country, this was particularly pronounced in mountainous areas (Huong et al 2020).

Levels of deprivation are particularly severe for refugees and internally displaced persons (IDPs) who have been the victims of ethnic- and religious-based violence. For example, those escaping violence from Boko Haram in northern Nigeria lack access to basic facilities in refugee camps (Mohamed 2018). The Yazidi in Iraq were subject to forced relocation in the 1970s into townships that initially lacked basic services, and the persistent absence of primary infrastructure is a major obstacle to return (UN Habitat 2015). Many remain in camps with poor access to water and sanitation, as well as housing, energy and other essentials (UNHCR 2019).

Climate change has intensified water scarcity and often this has penalized minority communities disproportionately. For example, according to the NGO Manthan Sanstha Kotri, minorities such as the nomadic and marginalized communities that live in the Ajmer and Nagua districts in Rajasthan, India, suffer extreme deprivation across multiple dimensions, including water. Conditions have worsened due to environmental stress on top of other pressing social, economic and political challenges (Manthan Kotri 2022). The water has become increasingly saline due to proximity to a lake and the saltwater clogs up the metal taps (Pal 2022). Water resources are also depleted by economic activity which has discriminated against ethnic minorities and indigenous communities, such as with mining activity in Brazil (Rodrigues 2022), hydro power in Guatemala (Viaene 2021) and oil production in Nigeria (Godwin 2021). These affected communities do not benefit from the infrastructure but instead see already fragile supplies of safe water depleted further.

Historically, water distribution has led to cooperation rather than conflict between countries but increased water stress is contributing to intra-country tensions (Cooper 2020; Gleic et al 2020; Water Conflict Chronology 2022). Growing scarcity can exacerbate religious conflicts. For example, in Nigeria and neighbouring countries, the land available for nomadic herders to graze and water their livestock has been eroded by increasing desertification and droughts as well as urbanization and the acquisition of land by large-scale farmers and private commercial interests. This is associated with an increase in violent conflict between the Fulani Muslim pastoralists and the mostly Christian local farmers and is linked to an increase in religious extremism (Gleick et al 2020). Sensitivity to religious belief and intersecting inequalities, then, plays a significant role in progress towards SDG6. Achieving water access for all requires not just addressing physical infrastructure needs but also unpacking the detailed ways in which discriminatory practices are played out. Growing scarcity looks set to exacerbate religious tensions.

Conclusion

Water and sanitation shortage tends to feature as one of a number of forms of deprivation. The vital nature of water means that it can be a significant tool of oppression, but the issues are complex. On one level, lack of access to safe water can be seen in terms of biased decision making regarding the distribution of infrastructure. The supply of water in some cases is used as an additional dimension to the oppression of certain religious beliefs. However, the issues may go further such that the geographical location of religious minorities can contribute to their vulnerabilities and persistent lack of water access. Ethnic violence has triggered displacement that makes water access more challenging for some communities. Increased water scarcity is set to increase inequalities in water access in ways that risk exacerbating tensions among ethnic groups and contributing to increased religious extremism. Achieving SDG6 will require a concerted effort to address religious bias in some locations in the supply of water. But attention is also needed to address the underlying conflicts and pressures that put those of certain faiths at severe disadvantage in vulnerable locations. Pressures from climate change are going to need greater attention, not just to the way water is distributed but the role it plays in shaping bias and discrimination.

References

Adukia, A., Asher, S., Novosad, P. and Tan, B. (2019) Residential segregation in urban India, Berkley, CA: University of California, https://cega.berkeley.edu/wp-content/uploads/2020/03/Tan_PacDev2020.pdf (accessed 26 August 2022).

Cooper, R. (2020) Water, climate change, and conflict, K4D Helpdesk Report No.895, Brighton: Institute of Development Studies.

Das, P.K. and Kar, S. (2016) Are religious minorities deprived of public good provisions? Regional evidence from India, *The Journal of Developing Areas* 50.1: 351–372.

Dutta, S., Behera, S. and Bharti, A. (2015) Access to drinking water by Scheduled Castes in rural India: Some key issues and challenges, *Indian Journal of Human Development* 9: 115–132.

Dutta, S., Sinha, A. and Parashar, A. (2018) Dalit women and water: Availability, access and discrimination in rural India, *Journal of Social Inclusion Studies* 4.1: 62–79.

Gleick, P., Iceland, C. and Trivedi, A. (2020) Ending conflicts over water: Solutions to water and security challenges, Washington, DC: WRI, www.wri.org/research/ending-conflicts-over-water (accessed 25 August 2022).

Godwin, A. (2021) Ogoni communities lack water, health facilities 1,000 days into cleanup, *The Guardian*, Nigeria, 7 October, https://guardian.ng/news/ogoni-communities-lack-water-health-facilities-1000-days-into-cleanup/ (accessed 25 August 2022).

HRCP (2019) Faith-based discrimination in Southern Punjab: Lived experiences field investigation report, *Human Rights Commission of Pakistan*, New Garden Town, Lahore: HRCP, https://hrcp-web.org/hrcpweb/wp-content/uploads/2020/09/2019-Faith-based-discrimination-in-southern-Punjab.pdf (accessed 25 August 2022).

Huong, L., Tuyet-Hanh, T.T., Minh, H.V., Ha, B., Anh, N.Q., Huong, N.T. et al (2020) Access to improved water sources and sanitation in minority ethnic people in Vietnam and some sociodemographic associations: A 2019 national survey, *Environmental health insights* 14: 1178630220946342.

Manthan Kotri (2022) About us, www.manthankotri.in/about-us/ (accessed 6 December 2022).

Mawani, V. (2019) Unmapped water access: Locating the role of religion in access to municipal water supply in Ahmedabad, *Water* 11: 1282.

Mohamed, J. (2018) Thousands displaced by Boko Haram languish in Abuja IDP camps, *Al Jazeera*, 26 March, www.aljazeera.com/features/2018/3/26/thousands-displaced-by-boko-haram-languish-in-abuja-idp-camps (accessed 26 August 2022).

MRG (2019) Minority and indigenous trends annual report: Focus on climate justice, London: Minority Rights Group International, https://minorityrights.org/wp-content/uploads/2020/08/2019_MR_Report_170x240_V7_WEB.pdf (accessed 25 August 2022).

Pal, P. (2022) Lived reality of the Bagariyas: Barely surviving amidst a water crisis, *The Sanitation Learning Hub*, 18 February, https://sanitationlearninghub.org/connect-share-learn/practitioner-voices/lived-reality-of-the-bagariyas-barely-surviving-amidst-a-water-crisis/ (accessed 25 August 2022).

Perreualt, T. (2014) What kind of governance for what kind of equity? Towards a theorization of justice in water governance, *Water International* 39: 233–245.

Rodrigues, M. (2022) Mining threatens isolated indigenous peoples in the Amazon, *EoS*, 25 January, https://eos.org/articles/mining-threatens-isolated-indigenous-peoples-in-the-amazon (accessed 25 August 2022).

UN (2022) *The Sustainable Development Goals Report 2022*, New York: United Nations, https://unstats.un.org/sdgs/report/2022/The-Sustainable-Development-Goals-Report-2022.pdf (accessed 25 August 2022).

UN Habitat (2015) Emerging land tenure issues among displaced Yazidis from Sinjar, Iraq, United Nations Human Settlements Programme in Iraq, https://unhabitat.org/emerging-land-tenure-issues-among-displaced-yazidis-from-sinjar-iraq-how-chances-of-return-may-be (accessed 25 August 2022).

UNHCR (2019) COI note on the situation of Yazidi IDPs in the Kurdistan region of Iraq, Geneva: UN High Commissioner for Refugees, www.refwo rld.org/docid/5cd156657.html (accessed 25 August 2022).

Viaene, L. (2021) Indigenous water ontologies, hydro-development and the human/more-than-human right to water: A call for critical engagement with plurilegal water realities, *Water* 13: 1660.

Water Conflict Chronology (2022) Water conflict chronology map, www. worldwater.org/conflict/map/ (accessed 6 December 2022).

15

How Clean Drinking Water in Joseph Colony Addresses Religious Inequalities and Sustainable Development Goals

Syed Ali Abbas Zaidi and Bariya Shah

Nasreen is a young Christian woman residing in Joseph Colony, a low-income informal settlement of Christians in Lahore, Pakistan. Like most of her neighbours, her family struggles economically and lives below the poverty line. She is a lactating mother of a one-and-a-half-year-old baby, who is often sick. Nasreen finds it difficult to access clean drinking water because the nearest filtration plant is four miles away, in the Muslim-majority area of Sheikhabad. Her husband is usually not home as he is a part-time sweeper who has to do double shifts in multiple hospitals to make ends meet. While women of the area usually depend on their male family members to fetch clean drinking water, as Christian women have faced repeated cases of harassment while fetching water from Sheikhabad, Nasreen is not as lucky as other mothers in the area, who have older sons to help them with outdoor chores. She has two more children, but they are not yet old enough to be allowed to venture out of Joseph Colony. Thus, Nasreen cannot manage to get clean drinking water every day alongside fulfilling the rest of her responsibilities, and her children are often forced to drink contaminated tap water. Drinking this water frequently causes diarrhoea, especially for Nasreen's baby, increasing the burden of her work and affecting her family's overall wellbeing.

Intersecting inequalities and clean drinking water

Lack of access to clean drinking water has aggravated the issue of marginalization for residents of Joseph Colony, and especially for women like Nasreen. The government has neglected the colony for decades, which many believe is discrimination on the basis of religion. The people of Joseph Colony, especially women, are not comfortable visiting the nearest water filtration plant in Sheikhabad for fear of discrimination and harassment. The memory of the brutal attack on Joseph Colony in 2013, in which more than 130 Christian houses were burnt to the ground by a Muslim mob, based on an accusation that residents were protecting a blasphemer, is still a source of tension for Christians and Muslims in the area. The implications of this situation for the lives of women in the colony are even worse given they are disadvantaged even within their own community, and the hostility of the Muslim community, combined with fears of harassment and catcalling, has seriously affected women's mobility. In this milieu, being a woman enhances experiences of marginalization for the minority community in Joseph Colony.

When Hive first reached out to the residents of Joseph Colony, their response was not very encouraging. Fear and mistrust have prevailed since the mob attack. Many NGOs have come into the colony offering assistance, but without accomplishing meaningful work. Initially, the community was hesitant, and engaging women was especially difficult due to cultural barriers and patriarchal norms. However, after sustained trust-building exercises over a period of three months, in the form of informal community dialogues, meetings and trainings, women's participation increased. Hive conducted surveys, in-depth interviews and focus group discussions to understand problems in the area. Rising unemployment, low literacy rates and lack of access to clean drinking water were identified as the most prevalent issues. Hive laid out the constraints it had due to limited budget, time and scope of the possible intervention and the community unanimously decided to address clean drinking water in the colony as the most pressing issue.

The community had been trying to get a water filtration plant installed in the area for over two decades, but had always faced disappointment when seeking support from NGOs and the government. Lack of clean drinking water has led to water-borne diseases in the area, and an intersection of issues emerged when it was learnt that the lack of clean drinking water was leading to the harassment of Christian women when fetching water from the nearby Muslim-populated area. Men also expressed their discomfort fetching water as they faced discrimination if passers-by learnt about their Christian background. This discrimination, which would take the form of name-calling and sometimes denying them water, stems from a false and radicalized notion that water becomes *najis* (impure) if a non-Muslim drinks from the same source, or uses the same premises or utensils.

Building a shared amenity and building shared trust

After gaining the community's endorsement, Hive started work on installing a water filtration plant inside the premises of Joseph Colony. The first step was to formalize a committee of the Colony's residents, who would not only help in setting up the plant, but also mobilize support for its maintenance and sustainability. Before kicking off construction work, Hive delivered a three-day needs-based training to potential committee members, addressing their apprehensions and equipping them with tools needed to meet the project's goals. This training took place inside a local church within Joseph Colony to ensure maximum participation. Consequently, a Ravadar Committee, a citizen-led committee comprising eight female and seven male members, was finalized. The name was inspired by the Persian word, *ravadar*, meaning tolerant. In addition to being gender inclusive, the committee represented all age groups of the local population. Some of its most active members were two young women, 22-year-old Cinderella and 26-year-old Maryam. It was decided that once the construction of the water filtration plant was completed, the committee would be responsible for the collection of the nominal fee from all households of the Colony for the plant's upkeep.

The Ravadar Committee worked with Hive to finalize the site for the water filtration plant, which had to be community-owned as privately owned land may have created problems in the future. A memorandum of understanding was signed between the Ravadar Committee and Hive, after which the technical side of the project, which included costing, scoping, purchasing, and construction, took place. In the process, the trust of the community also kept increasing as they saw actual work being done on the ground. Hive made sure to include community members in each step of implementation. Participation of younger women increased over time. Ensuring sustainability remained the prime concern before and during the construction of the plant. The plant was formally opened in August 2020 with a communal celebratory event and now provides clean drinking water to 400 households on a daily basis. It has become a source of relief for residents, especially women, of the area.

Project success and the way forward

The project has been providing clean drinking water to residents of Joseph Colony since its inception in August 2020. The citizen-led Ravadar Committee has not only ensured the sustainability of the water filtration plant by raising Rs. 15,000 (around $70) from the community on a monthly basis for technical maintenance but has also helped to address the Christian community's broader socio-political problems. The organization process that took place with the intervention has strengthened the community's resilience against religious marginalization by providing a forum for residents to discuss and mobilize for solutions. On one occasion, the committee wrote a letter to the District Administration to build a concrete road in the colony and successfully lobbied for its approval. Another example of the committee's proactive stance is its action to make sure Sawan Masih, a former resident accused of blasphemy in 2013, which led to the violent attack on the colony, does not return to Joseph Colony and imperil the safety of other residents. They asked the police to increase security around the colony upon hearing the news of Masih's acquittal from the blasphemy case and his possible return.

Lessons learnt in community organizing among marginalized religious groups

The project addressed a pressing sustainable development issue, access to clean drinking water, which intersected with the broader issue of religious discrimination that minority communities of Pakistan face on a daily basis. Hive's key learning with regard to similar interventions were five-fold:

1. *Why is there a lack of trust?* Understanding the unique circumstances in which a trust deficit has emerged between NGOs, governments and marginalized communities should inform community engagement methodologies.
2. *What solution would work better?* Priority-setting in the context of limited resources should be frequently employed to focus on practical and achievable tasks. This conversation should take place in a transparent manner with communities because they are the real beneficiaries.
3. *How to ensure women's participation?* Women's participation is critical to the sustainability of community development projects. Measures should be taken to ensure women's participation as a mandatory condition. Younger women should always be included as key stakeholders. Women's concerns and fears should be addressed throughout.
4. *How to drive community participation?* Citizen-led participatory action should be at the core of any project seeking lasting impact. NGOs should focus on addressing citizens' needs instead of asserting their own objectives and ensure financial transparency by involving citizens in project financials.
5. *How to understand the broader impact?* The broader impact of the project should be critically evaluated against the 'do no harm' principle. Programming with marginalized communities always has impact beyond its immediate scope, and this should be evaluated, understood and addressed.

16

Why Do Religious Minorities in Pakistan Receive Less Water?

Mary Gill and Asif Aqeel

Social inequalities for minority communities manifest in many ways, but in Pakistan, religious identity is an additional dimension that prevents decent living for non-Muslims, including the availability of clean drinking water. Religion plays an essential part in Pakistan at both political and societal levels, as Islam is the religion of the state. Non-Muslims comprise only 4 per cent of the population (Hassnain 2021). Most non-Muslims consist of Christians and Scheduled Caste (Dalit) Hindus, who live mainly in Punjab and Sindh. Both came from Hindu backgrounds and were so-called 'untouchables' because of their birth in 'inferior' castes. As a result, they are negatively perceived based on caste and religion.

Pakistan is among the most water scarcity-threatened countries in the world (Maqbool 2022; *The Economic Times* 2022). The groundwater level has steadily decreased in recent years (Mustafa 2018). In this situation, the marginalized have suffered the most (Reuters 2019). The development of water systems is often neglected or not undertaken in minority neighbourhoods, and water shortages or crises are most severe in minority neighbourhoods in Lahore (Aqeel 2018). Water pipelines in minority neighbourhoods are rusty, and water gets mixed up with sewage. The water from the tap cannot be used for washing, let alone drinking (End Water Poverty 2020). Among minority communities, it is often the case that some family members are busy all day bringing water for drinking and bathing from filtration plants installed in the areas of nearby Muslim-majority neighbourhoods. In an emergency, they use dirty water for washing purposes. Minority residents, especially children, suffer gastric and skin diseases on a regular basis. Because most sanitation workers in Pakistan are Christian, the irony of the situation is that the people who provide sanitation end up without it themselves. They are left behind due to their low social status.

Water inequality reflects political inequality

The inequalities in water access suffered by religious minority groups stem from religious inequalities built into Pakistan's political system. The distinction between minority and majority religious groups is a constitutional feature of Pakistan: Article 260(c)(b) of the Constitution of Pakistan defines 'Muslims' and 'Non-Muslims' and stipulates that non-Muslims cannot be the president (the head of the state) or the prime minister (head of the cabinet) of the country. Non-Muslims have little recourse with which to contest a general election at local, provincial or national levels.

Since Pakistan's creation, a trend has been that few Muslims would vote for a non-Muslim. In 1974, the Pakistani government introduced six seats for the representation of non-Muslims. The military dictator General Muhammad Zia-ul-Haq increased the seats to ten and then initiated a separate voting system for minorities in 1986. Hindus, Christians and Ahmadis voted for their coreligionists while remaining minorities were clubbed together. The electoral system was changed by another military dictator, Pervez Musharraf, in 2002, and since then, the old system has been restored. Now anyone can contest elections and vote for a person of any religion, except Ahmadis. The Fourth Constitutional Amendment declared Ahmadis to be non-Muslims. However, Ahmadis do not consider themselves non-Muslims but an offshoot of Islam. The political system identifies as they carry Islamic names, so they do not come into power. Despite the restoration of the political system, only three non-Muslims, all upper-caste Hindus, in Sindh Province got elected out of more than 1,000 parliamentarians in all assemblies. With this in view, the minority seats are not removed, and political parties elect minority parliamentarians based on the number of seats they secure in assemblies. Unfortunately, the minority representatives elected on these seats have no power, no participation in decision making and no say in the country's affairs (Aqeel 2018). At the time of independence, in 1947, about 44 per cent of the population living in the areas that now make up Pakistan were non-Muslim (Aqeel 2020). Religiously motivated partition uprooted millions of Hindus and Sikhs on the Pakistani side of the border and pushed them to migrate to India.

Similarly, millions of Muslims immigrated to Pakistan from India. This dramatically changed the religious composition in Pakistan (Aqeel 2020). Today, only 4 per cent of Pakistan's population is non-Muslim. Among them, Hindus and Christians are the largest groups. Hindus are mainly located in Sindh Province and Christians are in Punjab Province. Because of intergenerational exclusion, many of these disadvantaged minorities are extremely poor, live in irregular settlements and work in the lowest-paying occupations, which are considered the least desirable.

Societal and political segregation along religious lines has resulted in ghettoized neighbourhoods inhabited by religious minorities from Dalit backgrounds. Besides having second-class citizenship, certain minorities suffer social exclusion based on their downtrodden caste identities. For example, Christians predominantly come from the Dalit caste traditionally assigned to janitorial work. Today, an overwhelming number of sanitation workers in Pakistan are Christian. Lahore, the capital of the largest province, Punjab, has the largest Christian population in Pakistan. About 5 per cent of the people in Lahore are Christian. However, in this city of about 12 million people, almost 100 per cent of solid waste management workers are Christian. These workers, in most instances, live in segregated neighbourhoods that are deprived of basic amenities.

How water inequality and religious inequality reinforce each other

The practice of socially excluded places for outcastes thus continues. For example, data collected by the Center for Law and Justice (CLJ) in Lahore shows that there are 274 union councils, the smallest administrative unit in a district, and almost all have Christian neighbourhoods of varying size and population. Due to their social, political and cultural marginality, government water and sanitation provision bodies like the Water and Sanitation Agency (WASA) often ignore their complaints for years (Aqeel 2018). For example, about two years ago, WASA laid one new pipeline in Bahar Colony, Lahore, the second largest Christian neighbourhood in Lahore, but has since refused to grant connections to this new pipeline for most of the residents.

Inequality in water and sanitation access interlocks with religious inequality, producing a toxic mix of negative social outcomes. Low self-esteem because of internalization of caste-based shame, a sense of depravity of resources, the expenditure of extra hours in search of water, inadequate health outcomes, and various skin and stomach diseases are some of the long-term impacts on the residents of religious minority neighbourhoods. It is found that residents in the neighbouring areas inhabited mainly by Muslims did not lack clean water like the residents of Bahar Colony. A similar trend was found in Pakistan's largest Christian neighbourhood, Youhanabad, which has a population of nearly a hundred thousand but no water filtration plant. Therefore, its residents have no choice but to go to Nishtar Town, a neighbouring Muslim area, to bring clean water. This is primarily because non-Muslims, particularly those from Dalit backgrounds, have no connections to powerful actors, so they remain deprived of water.

The local government, responsible for providing basic amenities, and government-sponsored autonomous institutions like the Pakistan Poverty Alleviation Fund (PPAF), need to consider marginalized groups and pay special attention to bring them to par with the rest of society. The CLJ, with the support of the Institute of Development Studies (IDS), conducted a study in 2021 on the PPAF flagship programme implemented from 2009 to 2015 (Aqeel and Gill 2022). The programme was worth 250 million USD and was funded by the World Bank. Despite promises in the project proposal of reaching religious minorities in the distribution of poverty alleviation assistance, these marginalized sections were ignored during the implementation of the project. The same remains true for local government institutions. People at their helm usually do not consider minorities important and ignore their neighbourhoods. These practices of ignoring religious minorities in disrupting resources and support need to be changed. Otherwise, the marginality of minorities will continue, and they will be left behind in the Sustainable Development Goals (SDGs), demanded to be fulfilled by 2030.

The district authorities, like WASA, need to assess the unavailability of clean water in minority neighbourhoods. International organizations working on water need to see how marginalized communities in Pakistan suffer unavailability of water. Last, the government needs to survey minority neighbourhoods and assess where they lag in basic amenities compared to neighbouring areas.

References

Aqeel, A. (2018) Problems with the electoral representation of non-Muslims, *Herald*, 1 July.

Aqeel, A. (2020) *The Index of Religious Diversity and Inclusion in Pakistan*, Lahore: Center for Law and Justice.

Aqeel, A. and Gill, M. (2022) International assistance and impoverished religious minorities in Pakistan, in M. Tadros (ed) *What about Us? Global Perspectives on Redressing Religious Inequalities*, Brighton: Institute of Development Studies, 221–250.

End Water Poverty (2020) *End Water Poverty Progress Report: 2019–2020*, London: End Water Poverty.

Hassnain, K. (2021) Pakistan's population is 207.68m, shows 2017 Census result, *Dawn*, 19 May.

Maqbool, N. (2022) Water crisis in Pakistan: Manifestation, causes and the way forward, PIDE Knowledge Brief 60, Islamabad: Pakistan Institute of Development Economics.

Mustafa, W. (2018) As groundwater levels plunge, Lahore begins turning off taps, *Thomson Reuters Foundation*, 10 October.

Reuters (2019) World's poor pay more for water than the rich: UN, 19 March.

The Economic Times (2022) Pakistan among top ten countries facing severe water crisis, 17 April.

17

Drinking Water, Sanitation and the Religion Paradox in India

Nitya Jacob

Those who have less, value drinking water and sanitation more, and those who have more, value them less. I visited the areas mentioned in this chapter twice, the first time in the mid-2000s when an earlier sanitation programme was underway, and the second time in the late 2010s when the Swachh Bharat Mission was being executed. There have been many analyses of the access that people from different religions have to drinking water and sanitation in India. National programmes like the National Rural Water Drinking Mission, rechristened the Jal Jeevan Mission, and Swachh Mission, aim at providing universal access to drinking water and sanitation, respectively. The programmes do not take caste and religion into account and are ostensibly biased towards provisioning the poor.

But there is a paradox of poor access and high usage of facilities provided by these universal access programmes. A hypothesis based on limited available data and anecdotal evidence says that while Muslims have lower levels of sanitation access, they use toilets more than Hindus. The Indian situation regarding water and sanitation needs a somewhat nuanced understanding of access and usage. There are differences in the level of access that Hindus and Muslims have to these two basic services. There are greater differences in the way they use these services. This leads me to the hypothesis that there is a religion-blind paradox in the ways in which 'universal access' missions to provision the two are executed, and the facilities provided are used.

Ver Beek's seminal article 'Spirituality: A development taboo' demonstrated the ways in which 'people's spirituality is integrally interconnected with the decisions they make regarding their development and that development interventions often change people's spirituality and society without encouraging reflection upon or gaining consent to those changes' (Ver

Beek 2000: 41). Quoting this, Mariz Tadros (2022) says this interface between religion and culture complicates the nature of the phenomena that development policy makers and practices engage with on the ground.

Three anecdotes illustrate this paradox from recent first-hand experiences in rural India.

Toilets on hard rock

The first is from the north-western state of Rajasthan. In the dry Dholpur District, there is a panchayat (the smallest unit of local government in rural India) called Sarmathura. It is a large panchayat with about 22,500 people, spread over rocky hillocks and flatlands. The Muslims live in the hilly areas while Hindus occupy the lower slopes. The hilly areas are poorer, lacking in regular water supply, transport and drainage, even though the houses and streets are made of concrete and bricks. Many houses have dry toilets and the presence of excreta in the streetside drains is evidence of this.

There is little scope for open defecation, as the nearest open space is nearly two kilometres downhill. Houses are densely packed in this township. Rahmat, an entrepreneur who runs a cable TV business and lives in a large, well-made house, told me people have always had, and used, toilets made with their own money. Most were dry toilets, where the excreta goes directly into the streetside drain. A few had made septic tanks at huge expense (upwards of $1,000) and none were eligible for the subsidy the government provided for making toilets, amounting to about $150. Their problem was the cost, not the practice of using a toilet that was well ingrained.

As for household water, it came once in a few days and at low pressure. The supply pipes ran along the drains and leaks were common. The quantity and quality were both dubious. To cope, most households ordered delivery via tanker truck or depended on informal water vendors who provided 20 litre plastic bottles (for 20 rupees) exclusively for drinking.

Poor lives, poor water and sanitation

The next two examples are from the northern state of Uttar Pradesh (UP), India's most populous state, with a Muslim population of nearly 20 per cent. In Gujrain Village of Kanpur Dehat District, the headman is an upper-caste Hindu, Ram Trivedi. The poor received the government subsidy to make toilets through the panchayat to get rid of open defecation, but it was the Hindu settlements that got it first. Trivedi was cagey about admitting this.

The Hindu areas, most visible to visitors, had the usual cemented roads and houses. The village square is relatively clean. Most people had toilets, and water came from the many handpumps dotting the area that looked to be in good condition; piped water had not yet been introduced. The toilets, built inside the households, were for the women while most men preferred defecating outdoors. The average spend on a toilet was about INR 25,000 (GBP 200). But a short distance away, it was another story.

Rubaina is an elderly Muslim woman who took part in Trivedi's village sanitation mission. She was a member of the committee that patrolled the village morning and evening to ensure people in her village used their toilets. But she was old and tired, jobless and lived alone. In contrast to the Hindu part, the Muslim area was near the Ganga River. The lanes were muddy, and huts were made of mud with thatched roofs. Power lines dangled overhead and provided electricity only sometimes. She was blunt: the sanitation work only got done for the rich and upper-caste Hindus. The Muslims got their share much later. They were told to build toilets using their money and only then paid the subsidy. This contrasted with the Hindu area, where the subsidy was paid out in tranches as construction progressed.

They had to pledge jewellery, utensils or livestock to borrow the money and repaid this with interest to moneylenders when they got the subsidy. Same village, different standards. But they all used toilets, all the time. Clearly, they valued their possessions highly.

Drinking water came from handpumps here too. But their condition contrasted with the ones I saw earlier. The platforms were broken and the barrels were rusty. I tried one; the water seemed clear and tasted fine. But it had not been tested as far as anyone could remember. There were fewer handpumps in this shanty town than in the fancier part of the village and faults took longer to fix. They had their own ways to cope, relying on local Muslim men who were handpump mechanics. In the Hindu areas, there were more handpumps that appeared in a better condition. There too they relied on handpump mechanics, and the water tasted and looked fine.

Muslims provide quality service

The water and sanitation situation in Sarai Jiwan Village of Bijnor District was very different from Gujrain, even though they were both in the same state of UP. This was a completely Muslim village of about 2,000. Its headman Abdul Samad campaigned for toilets and made sure everyone built them in record time and used them regularly. They received the subsidy in tranches like the Hindus of Gujrain. The main difference between this village, and the Muslim areas of others, was that the headman of Sarai Jiwan was Muslim; the headmen of most others I had visited were Hindu.

The roads and houses were mostly of cement, and power lines did not dangle dangerously; they were taut on their poles. All the toilets were squat grey cement blocks and were used by both men and women. Samad was quick to point out that the water that came from handpumps was enough to meet the demands of the villagers and repairs were affected promptly.

Their condition was like those in the Hindu part of Gujrain. Even though the Muslims of Sarai Jiwan were not all well-off, 70 families returned the subsidy provided by the government saying toilets were a necessity and they would not take government money.

Putting a greater value on scarce resources

In all three cases – Sarmathura, Gujrain and Sarai Jiwan – Muslims had toilets and drinking water. But their access lagged behind the Hindus' and they had to find and fund their own means of getting these basic services as the government subsidies were delayed. The condition of their water supplies was also decidedly poorer than Hindus in the same village. The Muslim and Hindu areas were clearly demarcated in all cases.

The paradox comes when we look at larger-scale data on toilet usage by religion, even though this is somewhat dated. Muslims used toilets much more regularly than Hindus. They also took better care of their handpumps, though water testing was in the hands of the panchayat. The National Family Health Survey (NFHS) Round III released in 2005 showed 68 per cent of Hindu households defecated in the open. In comparison, only 43 per cent of the poorer Muslim households did so (Geruso and Spears 2015: 5).

For Hindus, a religious belief is that having a toilet near home would be ritually polluting. Emptying pits and septic tanks is another issue, as that is done mechanically; being a business proposition, upper-caste Hindus also operate pit-emptying machines. But Muslims had different ritual purity and pollution connotations and they were more likely to build and use simple, affordable latrines. While similar data was not available regarding drinking water, anecdotally it appeared Muslims had their own coping mechanisms to ensure at least minimal supply while Hindus depended more on the government system to install and maintain handpumps. The coping mechanisms were storage and an in-situ fault-fixing system.

The drinking water and sanitation missions with their emphasis on universal access serve the interests of the majority community in most places. Muslims, Dalits and Adivasis (tribal communities) are served only after the upper Hindu castes have been served, as in the cases outlined, and as newspaper reports over the years have drawn attention to (Geruso and Spears 2018).

There is discomfort with 'targeted programming' to remove this inherent bias in trickle-down development on the grounds that it could be seen to favour a particular religion or deny services to the other. In designing and executing a national programme, the government therefore does not mention any religion. Instead, it specifies that the programmes will reach vulnerable and excluded groups, such as tribals and Scheduled Castes (Hindus from lower castes), the differently abled, and so on. Providing drinking water and sanitation to people, regardless of ethnicity and religion, and ensuring excluded populations get the same services as others, should be the aim of 'universal access' water and sanitation programmes. What does emerge is the greater value that Muslims place on drinking water and sanitation when they get these services.

References

Geruso, M. and Spears, D. (2015) Neighbourhood sanitation and infant mortality, Working Paper 21184, Cambridge, MA: National Bureau of Economic Research.

Geruso, M. and Spears, D. (2018) Hindus are less likely to use a toilet than Muslims in India, *The Print*, 27 March, https://theprint.in/india/governa nce/hindus-are-less-likely-to-use-a-toilet-than-muslims-in-india/44959/ (accessed 9 December 2022).

Tadros, M. (2022) Religious equality and freedom of religion or belief: International development's blindspot, *The Review of Faith & International Affairs* 20.2: 96–108.

Ver Beek, K.A. (2000) Spirituality: A development taboo, *Development in Practice* 10.1: 31–43.

PART V

Infrastructure and the Economy

18

How Digital Discrimination Affects Sustainable Development for Religious and Ethnic Minorities

Kevin Hernandez and Becky Faith

As internet connectivity has expanded, it has become an integral part of all aspects of life; meaning that disconnection risks further excluding already-marginalized groups. Women's exclusion from access to and use of digital technologies is estimated to have cost the global economy over $1 trillion since 2011 (Alliance for Affordable Internet 2021). Internet shutdowns aimed at suppressing political dissent cost over $21 billion between 2019 and 2021 (Woodhams and Migliano 2022).

Although there is a significant body of work exploring uneven SDG gains resulting from digital inequalities experienced by marginalized groups, the implications for religious ethnic minorities have not been addressed. This chapter outlines five mechanisms which may result in religious ethnic minorities being less likely to benefit from digitalization: lack of internet access, increased likelihood to experience barriers once online, greater risk of online hate speech, internet shutdowns and automated discrimination.

It is important to note that these mechanisms apply to the large subset of ethnic and religious minorities who experience social, economic and political exclusion, especially those living in countries where they are actively oppressed. Multi-dimensional poverty within countries tends to be disproportionately concentrated among marginalized ethnic groups who also tend to experience poverty more intensely than other groups (UNDP and OPHI 2021). But not every minority group in every country experiences marginalization, and in some countries, religious ethnic minority groups might hold political power (for example, the Alawites in Syria (Qaddour

2013)) or control significant portions of a country's economy. There is significant variance in the likelihood of ethnic minorities experiencing exclusion or negative development outcomes across countries, with some countries showing very little difference in poverty levels between ethnic groups (UNDP and OPHI 2021). Some minority groups experience better development outcomes than the general population of a country (for example, the Quecha and Aymara indigenous groups in Peru) (UNDP and OPHI 2021).

Information and communications technologies and sustainable development

The links between information and communications technologies (ICTs) and sustainable development are recognized in three targets:

- SDG 9.C: universal and affordable internet access in least developed countries by 2020.
- SDG 5.B: increasing the proportion of women who have access to mobile phones and the internet.
- SDG 17.8: enhancing the use of enabling technology, in particular information and communications technology.

Digital technologies can be leveraged to enable progress towards all 17 SDGs, including telemedicine and e-learning improving access to health (SDG 3), education (SDG 4), and e-governance initiatives helping citizens to hold governments to account (SDG16) (ITU 2017).

Ethnic and religious minorities who have previously been excluded from employment opportunities, health services, education and governance processes can, in theory, benefit from using digitized services and platforms, yet links between digitalization and sustainable development are not automatic (Unwin 2017; Hernandez 2019). Technology tends to amplify both the effects of environments in which it is used and the capacity and intent of its users (Toyama 2011). In unequal societies, the dissemination of new technologies follows an unequal trajectory, leading to disproportionate gains for members of already dominant groups. Technology can only improve outcomes for marginalized groups with sufficient political will and capacity to implement solutions.

In contexts where state and non-state actors are promoting religiously homogenous societies (Tadros 2021), religious and ethnic minorities potentially have the most to gain from digitally enabled services and opportunities, but also tend to be the most likely to be left behind. International agencies have warned of the exacerbation of inequalities (SDG10) if marginalized groups are unable to access digital technologies on a par with the rest of society (Jahan 2015; UNDP 2019; World Bank 2016, 2019). Furthermore, dominant groups, governments and non-state actors may use technology in ways that further marginalize rather than empower religious and ethnic minorities.

Five mechanisms of digital discrimination

This section discusses five mechanisms by which inequalities experienced by religious and ethnic minorities can be amplified by digitalization: (a) unequal access; (b) further barriers once online; (c) victimization through hate speech and other digital harms; (d) internet shutdowns; and (e) prejudice in systems driven by artificial intelligence. These mechanisms are further amplified for women from religious ethnic minority backgrounds, who are the most likely to be negatively affected by all five issues. Globally, 62 per cent of men use the internet compared to 57 per cent of women. This divide is wider in least developed countries, where only 19 per cent of women use the internet (ITU 2021). There is also a geographical intersectional element, reflecting the global digital divide between high and low-income countries. A powerful example of this is the fact that, despite being warned about the platform's role in inciting religious ethnic violence in Myanmar as early as 2013, Facebook did not have a single employee in the country in 2018 and only a handful of Burmese speakers working in its monitoring operations (Stecklow 2018).

1. Less likely to have internet access.

Politically excluded minorities are less likely to be online than powerful ethnic groups (Weidmann et al 2016), meaning that they are less likely to benefit from digital economic opportunities. Marginalized religious and ethnic minorities typically have lower levels of digital access in both high and low-income countries (Grant 2020). In countries with state-controlled telecommunications infrastructure, dominant groups often practise 'ethnic favouritism' when allocating infrastructural investment (Weidmann et al 2016). In contexts with liberalized telecommunications markets, investment in profitable geographical areas is prioritized, leaving economically excluded minorities clustered in ghettoized regions (United Nations Secretary General 2020).

2. More likely to experience barriers once online.

Socially excluded religious and ethnic minorities often face additional barriers once they get online; economic marginalization makes the internet less affordable. Educational marginalization means religious minorities often lack the digital literacy skills needed to fully engage. Language barriers may exclude migrant and indigenous religious minorities from locally relevant content (Hernandez and Faith 2022). Ethnic and religious minorities without digital skills risk falling further behind in the job market (World Bank 2019).

In countries where powerful actors seek to further deprive religious minorities of their rights, governments often make it more difficult for religious minorities to remain online (Weidmann et al 2016). For example, both Burmese and Bangladeshi authorities have used various methods to keep Rohingya disconnected, including making it illegal to own SIM cards, requiring identification for SIM card registration and throttling mobile broadband speeds (Morshed et al 2021).

3. More likely to experience online hate speech.

Ethnic and religious minorities are disproportionately likely to experience online harassment, stalking and to be the victims of hateful digital content. Online religious hate speech refers to 'the use of inflammatory and sectarian language to promote hatred and violence against people on the basis of religious affiliation' online (Castaño-Pulgarín et al 2021: 2). This harassment includes derogatory language and daily abuse, and threats to life (Digital Rights Foundation 2021) as well as fake news and misinformation (Ridout et al 2019). Hate speech is amplified on social media (Ahmed 2020): messages can be spread anonymously, from a distance, and instantaneously (Evolvi 2018), automated with the use of bots (Albadi et al 2019).

A systematic review of online religious hate speech in Western countries found Muslims to be the most targeted group and online hate speech to be especially prevalent following high-profile incidents involving Muslim suspects (Castaño-Pulgarín et al 2021). Online religious hate is also pervasive in countries where state and non-state actors promote religiously homogenous societies, creating hostile digital environments that may shift offline, resulting in real-life discrimination, physical threats and violent events. In Egypt, Facebook was used to organize local Muslims to attack Coptic (Christian minority) homes in Kom al-Raheb, Samalut in 2018 (Grant 2020). In Myanmar, online hate spread via Facebook played a major role in the Rohingya genocide (Mozur 2018). In India, prominent radical Hindu priests have amplified the reach of videos calling for mass killings of Muslims via social media platforms (The Listening Post 2022).

4. More likely to experience internet shutdowns.

Internet shutdowns are 'intentional disruption of internet or electronic communications, rendering them inaccessible or effectively unusable, for a specific population or within a location, often to exert control over the flow of information' (Access Now 2022). They include blanket shutdowns where access is cut entirely, throttling access and blocking digital platforms and messaging applications. Analysis of secondary data (Access Now 2021) shows that religious minorities are more likely to be clustered in areas that are targeted with sub-national internet shutdowns: 105 of the 123 sub-national internet shutdowns (85 per cent) reported in 2020 occurred in regions predominately inhabited by religious minorities. Jammu and Kashmir in India alone accounted for 93 shutdowns.

In Myanmar, predominately Rohingya townships in Rakhine and Chin states experienced one of the longest internet shutdowns in history, lasting between June 2019 to February 2021. Civil society organizations (CSOs) reported that residents of some villages were unaware of the COVID-19 pandemic as late as June 2020, and that those who were aware were more susceptible to COVID-19 misinformation than people in other states (Human Rights Watch 2020a). Over 880,000 Rohingya refugees also faced internet shutdowns having fled Myanmar for Bangladesh (Reid 2021). The Bangladeshi government imposed shutdowns in refugee settlements between September 2019 and August 2020, throttling internet speeds to 2G, a speed often too slow to load most webpages (Karim 2020), and making it difficult for refugees to access education, humanitarian assistance and to keep in touch with families (Human Rights Watch 2020b).

5. More likely to encounter automated discrimination.

Artificial intelligence (AI) is increasingly used to automate decisions in many areas of life, from social protection to financial inclusion. While AI is presented as an impartial decision-making alternative to humans (Brayne et al 2015), these systems are unable to contextualize the historic data used to make predictions. Audits of job applicant screening algorithms have shown that they tend to suggest that women and racial and ethnic minorities are less desirable candidates for high-paying professional jobs (Bogen 2019). Similarly, audits of predictive policing algorithms have shown that they recommend police disproportionately track minorities and deploy police officers in marginalized neighbourhoods (Brayne et al 2015). These issues are especially problematic in contexts mired in historical inequalities between dominant and marginalized groups.

In some contexts, powerful actors are leveraging AI to deliberately disenfranchise marginalized groups. The Chinese government uses facial recognition software and CCTV cameras to control members of the Uyghur (Muslim) minority. One system in Sanmenxia was used on over 500,000 people in a month to determine whether a resident was Uyghur (Mozur 2019). Similar 'minority identification' systems have proliferated across China and some local start-ups are seeking to export the technology. One

Chinese start-up advertises its facial recognition software's ability to alert law enforcement officials if Uyghur or Tibetan numbers increase so 'police can carry out their goal of managing and controlling sensitive groups' (Mozur 2019). In India, a lawsuit was recently filed against Telangana State when a Muslim activist noticed the potential of a facial recognition system to target Muslims (Chandran 2022).

Conclusion

Digital technologies can enable progress on the SDGs for people who have been historically underserved by improving digital service delivery and increased access to information. However, these potential gains may go unrealized and progress against the SDGs may be derailed for religious minorities who experience intersecting inequalities on the basis of religion, and political and socio-economic exclusion unless the five mechanisms covered in this chapter are addressed. There is a need to get more religious minorities from marginalized backgrounds online and to help religious minorities overcome barriers they may encounter once online. The international community also needs to find ways to combat online religious hate while protecting freedom of expression, to discourage internet shutdowns, and to restrict applications of artificial intelligence that reinforce dominance over marginalized minorities. In addressing digital inequalities, women from religious minorities deserve particular attention. Reversing the mechanisms of digital discrimination will not be easy. But not doing so would mean religious and ethnic minorities fall further behind.

References

Access Now (2021) #KeepItOn: Fighting internet shutdowns around the world, www.accessnow.org/issue/internet-shutdowns/

Access Now (2022) #KeepItOn FAQ, www.accessnow.org/campaign/keepiton/keepiton-faq/

Ahmed, R.U. (2020) Turning on the hate, *Digital Rights Monitor*.

Albadi, N., Kurdi, M. and Mishra, S. (2019) Hateful people or hateful bots? Detection and characterization of bots spreading religious hatred in Arabic social media, *Proceedings of the ACM on Human-Computer Interaction* 3: 1–25.

Alliance for Affordable Internet (2021) The costs of exclusion: Economic consequences of the digital gender gap, Web Foundation, https://www.ictworks.org/wp-content/uploads/2021/11/Costs-of-Digital-Exclusion.pdf

Bogen, M. (2019) All the ways hiring algorithms can introduce bias, *Harvard Business Review*, 6 May.

Brayne, S., Rosenblat, A. and Boyd, D. (2015) Predictive policing, data & civil rights: A new era of policing and justice, *Data Civil Rights*, 27 October.

Castaño-Pulgarín, S.A., Suárez-Betancur, N., Vega, L.M.T. and López, H.M.H. (2021) Internet, social media and online hate speech, *Systematic Review, Aggression and Violent Behavior* 58.101608.

Chandran, R. (2022) In India's surveillance hotspot, facial recognition taken to court, *Reuters*, 20 January.

Digital Rights Foundation (2021) Religious minorities in online spaces: Research on their experiences in Pakistan, https://digitalrights foundation.pk/wp-content/uploads/2021/05/Religious-Minorities.pdf

Evolvi, G. (2018) Hate in a tweet: Exploring internet-based Islamophobic discourses, *Religions* 9: 307.

Grant, P. (ed) (2020) *Minority and Indigenous Trends 2020: Focus on Technology*, London: Minority Rights Group International.

Hernandez, K. (2019) Achieving complex development goals along China's Digital Silk Road, K4D Emerging Issues Report, Brighton: Institute of Development Studies.

Hernandez, K. and Faith, B. (2022) Measuring digital exclusion: Why what is counted is also what counts, *Digit Data Commentary* 1: 15.

Human Rights Watch (2020a) Myanmar: End world's longest internet shutdown, www.hrw.org/news/2020/07/27/myanmar-end-unlawful-internet-restrictions

Human Rights Watch (2020b) Bangladesh: Internet ban risks Rohingya lives.

ITU (2017) Fast-forward progress: Leveraging tech to achieve the global goals, Geneva: International Telecommunication Union.

ITU (2021) Measuring digital development: Facts and figures 2021, Geneva: International Telecommunication Union.

Jahan, S. (2015) *2015 Human Development Report*, New York: United Nations Development Programme.

Karim, N. (2020) Bangladesh to lift Rohingya internet ban as anniversary nears, *Reuters*, 24 August.

Morshed, K., Rahman, A., Hussain, F., Jahangir, Z. and Islam, T. (2021) *Exploring the Usage Trends and Impacts of Different Digital Platforms among FDMNs*, Dhaka: BRAC Centre.

Mozur, P. (2018) A genocide incited on Facebook, with posts from Myanmar's military, *The New York Times*, 15 October.

Mozur, P. (2019) One month, 500,000 face scans: How China is using A.I. to profile a minority, *The New York Times*, 14 April.

Qaddour, J. (2013) Unlocking the Alawite conundrum in Syria, *The Washington Quarterly* 36: 67–78.

Reid, K. (2021) Rohingya refugee crisis: Facts, FAQs, and how to help, *World Vision*, 25 March.

Ridout, B., McKay, M., Amon, K., Campbell, A., Wiskin, J., Seng Du, P.M. et al (2019) *Mobile Myanmar: The Impact of Social Media on Young People in Conflict-affected Regions of Myanmar*, Sydney: Save the Children and the University of Sydney.

Stecklow, S. (2018) Hatebook: Inside Facebook's Myanmar operation, *Reuters*, 15 August.

Tadros, M. (2021) Stop homogenising us: Mixing and matching faith and beliefs in India and beyond, *Coalition for Religious Equality and Inclusive Development*, 21 May.

The Listening Post (2022) Hate speech and online abuse: India's growing extremism problem, YouTube, 8 January.

Toyama, K. (2011) Technology as amplifier in international development. *Proceedings of the 2011 iConference*, New York: Association for Computing Machinery, 75–82.

UNDP (ed) (2019) *Human Development Report 2019: Beyond Income, beyond Averages, beyond Today: Inequalities in Human Development in the 21st Century*, New York: United Nations Development Programme.

UNDP and OPHI (2021) *Global Multidimensional Poverty Index 2021: Unmasking Disparities by Ethnicity, Caste and Gender*, Geneva: United Nations Development Programme and Oxford Poverty and Human Development Initiative.

United Nations Secretary General (2020) Socially just transition towards sustainable development: The role of digital technologies on social development and well-being of all, Geneva: United Nations Economic and Social Council.

Unwin, T. (2017) ICTs, Sustainability and development: Critical elements, in A.R. Sharafat and W. Lehr (eds) *ICT-Centric Economic Growth, Innovation and Job Creation*, Geneva: ITU.

Weidmann, N.B., Benitez-Baleato, S., Hunziker, P., Glatz, E. and Dimitropoulos, X. (2016) Digital discrimination: Political bias in Internet service provision across ethnic groups, *Science* 353: 1151–1155.

Woodhams, S. and Migliano, S. (2022) The global cost of internet shutdowns 2021 report, *Top 10 VPN*, 3 January.

World Bank (2016) *World Development Report 2016: Digital Dividends*, Washington, DC: World Bank.

World Bank (2019) *World Development Report 2019: The Changing Nature of Work*, Washington, DC: World Bank.

19

Poverty, Prejudice and Technology

Nighat Dad and Shmyla Khan

Pakistan: digital divisions along religious lines

It is safe to say that religious minorities are being left out of the economy and, by extension, mainstream society due to structural barriers, historic poverty and discrimination in occupations that religious minorities can take up. In this regard, many see technology as a tool in helping religious minorities access rights and opportunities that were otherwise denied to them. While predictions of technology being a great 'disruptor' that can parachute the disadvantaged out of poverty need to be taken with a massive pinch of salt, creating opportunities that account for technological changes and digital literacy can go a long way in ensuring religious minorities are in step with economic progress, and at the very least are not left behind. At present, economic progress in Pakistan is distributed unequally, with wealth being accumulated in the hands of a few. Technology can often provide platforms and economic opportunities otherwise denied to marginalized groups; however, it can also exacerbate these differences in some cases.

As the Pakistani government emphasizes technology-based education (*The News International* 2022) and development of the technology sector as being akin to a panacea to the economic woes of the country (*The Express Tribune* 2019), members of religious minorities are often stuck in poverty cycles, still confined to menial jobs (Korai 2021). In providing digital safety and literacy workshops to religious minority communities in the course of its work, Digital Rights Foundation (DRF) has found that there exists a yawning gap when it comes to technology access and literacy for religious minorities. In particular, women belonging to religious minorities suffer from a double-bind of gender and religious discrimination, finding themselves completely excluded from digital spaces and the tech economy (DRF 2021a). For women from religious minorities, the abuse and harassment that they face online is both on the basis of gender and religion, making them more vulnerable when they use technologies. Furthermore, women's access to technologies is often subject to gatekeeping by men within their communities.

Ensuring sustained, inclusive and sustainable economic growth within the tech economy, in concert with Pakistan's commitments under the Sustainable Development Goals, depends on digital literacy and skills being distributed equally across all the citizenry, regardless of religion, gender, class, disability and ethnic identity. In Pakistan, digital literacy is low across the board, with only 3 per cent of women able to copy or move a file or folder on a computer (Sey and Hafkin 2019), necessitating structural intervention into the school education curriculum at the governmental level.

Enabling digital safety for members of minority communities

As a civil society organization, DRF seeks to bridge the gap experienced by marginalized communities. Over the last few years, we have provided capacity-building workshops to religious minority groups on digital safety, tackling online misinformation and basic digital literacy. In these workshops, we have worked with interlocutors within communities to develop contextually relevant training modules responsive to their needs. Given the hate speech minorities face, a vital part of using technologies involves maintaining privacy to protect against retaliation and attacks on members of the community. Community leaders and human rights defenders within these communities also identified the need for training on laws and reporting mechanisms for digital hate speech and harassment. Feedback from these workshops has indicated that there is a greater need for such workshops, particularly among younger members of these communities, who are more likely to use digital platforms and thus are more vulnerable to hate speech.

To sustain the impact of its work, DRF has also formed a network with religious minorities to provide direct and timely support, such as through the Cyber Harassment Helpline (DRF 2021b). The helpline was born out of feedback from communities who identified the need for continued engagement, to keep up with the evolution of technologies. The network allows for long-term and responsive interventions which can evolve in concert with the evolving impacts of technologies, underscoring a more holistic conception of security that acknowledges that an individual's safety is tied to the security of the collective. Sharing resources and developments with the larger community can help create an enabling environment where safety becomes the baseline. Last, the network allows for the development of a support system for communities to share challenges and receive emotional and moral support from one another.

For women belonging to religious minority communities, DRF seeks to encourage the use of digital platforms and technologies to participate in the economy – by leveraging these platforms to grow home-based businesses and learn new skills. Given that Pakistan has one of the highest digital gender divides in the world (Carboni 2021), DRF has enabled this by conducting in-depth digital safety workshops for women, ensuring that their participation in online spaces does not lead to any additional insecurity due to their gender or religion. Furthermore, the digital safety workshops help the women negotiate using technologies within their home, given that familial attitudes often discourage women from using technologies or participating online.

DRF's interventions have been limited in scale, focusing on a set number of beneficiaries with whom the organization has developed long-term and mutually beneficial relationships. The focus has been to let religious minority communities define the terms of the relationship and co-create solutions, rather than following a top-down model, as is often common in development approaches. The economic and immediate impact of these interventions is often difficult to measure; however, there is a consensus within communities that creating capacity, in terms of skills and safety, result in an enabling environment for online and economic participation.

Working with the grain, listening and learning and sustaining efforts

Working with religious minorities has taught us a great deal about what these communities need and the nature of the exclusions they face. The foremost learning has been to practise humility when approaching marginalized groups. There is a tendency among tech-based experts to create new and expensive technological solutions for structural and societal problems. Often the solution does not lie in more technologies but rather in very basic interventions grounded in the modes of knowledge-sharing the community is familiar with. While solutions, such as workshops and capacity building, might appear to lack innovation, they are what the community might actually need.

Second, listening to the community is very important. No matter how much experience an organization has, nothing can substitute for lived experience. It is always better to start out with open-ended questions when designing activities. Working with activists and organizers from within religious minority communities and co-creating activities is always more meaningful and paves the way for long-lasting relationships. The process of co-creation for DRF has resulted in developing workshops and interventions that not only transfer knowledge from the organization to the community but rather make the transfer of knowledge two-way. Now all workshops that the organization conducts have a consultative element to develop recommendations and policy interventions based on experiences of the community. Community members see themselves as people who have a lot to teach stakeholders, such as social media companies, tech developers, civil society and policy makers. Viewing communities as co-partners rather than passive beneficiaries has been the key to DRF's success.

Last, organizations should ask themselves how they can make their work sustainable, not simply dependent on project-specific funding and activities. Sustainability is often predicated on prioritizing and investing in relationships of mutual trust, allowing for long-term change. While economic realities, especially a lack of resources and capital, have led to a dependency on externally funded projects, the next step of our work is geared towards exploring creative pathways towards sustained impact. The work can be difficult; however, one should remember that each activity, each intervention, chips away at the status quo, slowly but surely.

References

Carboni, I. (2021) Connected women: The mobile gender gap report 2021, GSMA, www.gsma.com/r/wp-content/uploads/2022/06/The-Mobile-Gender-Gap-Report-2022.pdf?utm_source=website&utm_med ium=download-button&utm_campaign=gender-gap-2022 (accessed 16 December 2022).

DRF (2021a) Religious minorities in online spaces, Digital Rights Foundation, https://digitalrightsfoundation.pk/wp-content/uploads/ 2023/02/CFLI-Policy-Brief-Final-Version_compressed.pdf (accessed 16 December 2022).

DRF (2021b) Helpline annual report 2021, Digital Rights Foundation, https://digitalrightsfoundation.pk/wp-content/uploads/2022/05/helpl ine-annual-report-2021-1.pdf (accessed 16 December 2022).

Korai, S. (2021) The never-ending plight of Dalits, *VoicePk*, 23 August, https://voicepk.net/2021/08/the-never-ending-plight-of-dalits/ (accessed 16 December 2022).

Sey, A. and Hafkin, N. (2019) *Taking Stock: Data and Evidence on Gender Equality in Digital Access, Skills, and Leadership*, Macau: United Nations University Institute on Computing and Society/International Telecommunications Union, www.itu.int/en/action/gender-equality/ Documents/EQUALS%20Research%20Report%202019.pdf (accessed 16 December 2022).

The Express Tribune (2019) PM Imran launches 'Digital Pakistan' initiative, 5 December, https://tribune.com.pk/story/2112360/digital-pakistan-pm-imran-addresses-launch-ceremony (accessed 16 December 2022).

The News International (2022) Academia, industry need to work together to uplift IT sector, 28 July, www.thenews.com.pk/print/977445-acade mia-industry-need-to-work-together-to-uplift-it-sector (accessed 11 November 2022).

20

Beyond the Rhetoric of Freedom: Religious Inequity in Nigeria

Chris Kwaja

Nigeria has an estimated population of around 200 million, thought to be evenly split between Christians and Muslims as the two dominant religious groups; however, as the last census in 2006 did not count ethnic or religious affiliation, there is no way to know this conclusively. Nigerians have unequal access to livelihoods at the state and community level based on their indigenous or settler status (Human Rights Watch 2006). This dichotomy overlaps with religious fault lines, becoming a major source of tension, with confrontations between adherents of the two dominant religions (Heneghan 2012). However, it is important to emphasize that the religious blocs are not homogenous. Intra-religious tensions also persist and have engendered sectarian demands for inclusion as a basis for addressing social injustice in the country.

As a 44-year-old Nigerian, I am a living witness to the impact of religious inequality on livelihoods and social cohesion. In the last three years, my work with communities across Kaduna and Kano in the north-west, and Plateau in the north-central region, also referred to as the Middle Belt, has focused on building and supporting a community of practice on the platform of Community Peace Advocates (CPAs).[1] The CPAs work with religious and

---

[1] Since 2018, the African Initiative on Peacebuilding, Advocacy and Advancement (AfriPeace) has been implementing a project on Strengthening Community Resilience and Building Social Cohesion in Kaduna, Kano and Plateau states, with support from the Open Society Initiative for West Africa (OSIWA).

other social networks to dismantle the structures of religious inequality by applying collaborative problem-solving approaches to religiously induced conflicts. The CPAs across Kaduna and Plateau states aim to strengthen the resilience of farmer and herder communities and to promote social cohesion.

Making economic growth more inclusive for faith communities represents a key pathway to ensuring better access to economic opportunities. Given that conflicts have impacted on religious communities disproportionately, a key strategy for the CPAs has been developing the skills and abilities of people drawn from the religious communities of the three states – Kaduna, Kano and Plateau – to cooperatively use market spaces, as well as share access to land and water resources, which have often been a basis for conflict between farmers and pastoralists.

Religion as a source of economic discrimination

Religion has become a major source of fear and resentment among communities in Nigeria. Kano and Plateau typify the phenomenon of religiously partitioned states in northern Nigeria. While the Christian residents in Sabon Gari community of Kano State complain of neglect by the Muslim-controlled government at the state level, the Muslims in the city of Jos have also accused the Christian-dominated government of Plateau of denying them access to basic services, such as roads, water, hospitals and education. "It took the intervention of the Deputy Speaker of the House of Representative, Hon Idris Maje[2] to rehabilitate the dilapidated roads within the Muslim communities in Jos North, due to the alleged refusal of the state government to discharge such responsibility" (Resident, Jos North Local Government Area (LGA), Plateau).

In the case of Sabon Gari, Kano, one resident complained: "the area is the only one with road and other social amenities that have been neglected by the state government, despite consistent appeals by the Christian community".

Segregated settlements within states have resulted in many communities losing their pluralism. "There is disruption of our social settings as a result of protracted religiously motivated conflicts. Because of this crisis, there is now segregation where the religious groups live separately, with little interaction" (Resident, Rigasa, Kaduna).

In Kaduna, the Southern Kaduna Peoples Union (SOKAPU) is one of the most visible voices that speaks on behalf of the many minority ethnic groups in Southern Kaduna (predominantly Christian), who are allegedly excluded by the Kaduna State Government (Admin III 2017). Due to their

---

[2]   Maje represents Wase in the House of Representatives. His constituency is over a hundred kilometres from these projects.

religious identity, Christians in Southern Kaduna have been deprived of jobs and other economic opportunities by the dominant Muslim elites that control power at the state level. On the other hand, the Southern Kaduna Muslim Ummah Development Association (SOKAMUDA) emerged as a voice representing the interests of Muslim minorities in Southern Kaduna, who also claim to be denied opportunities within the Southern Kaduna area by the Christian majority (Sociallogia Team 2020). So far, these two antagonistic entities have presented themselves as the mouthpieces and protectors of their respective groups.

Discrimination along the lines of religion is even more manifest in rural areas, where access to land is given more prominence, and access to opportunities is more closely linked to the notion of indigeneity. The enactment of the anti-open grazing law in Benue State was perceived by pastoralist communities (who are mostly Muslim) to be discriminatory in favour of Christians. There have been similar outcries by pastoralists against attempts to enact such laws in Plateau, Taraba, Ekiti and Ondo states, where the legislation is viewed as a direct attack against them and their livelihoods. "The cattle and sheep are the only source of livelihoods we have. If we are denied access to land for grazing, it means both we the pastoralists and our livestock will die" (Pastoralist, Bassa LGA, Plateau).

Communities are also polarized in Jos, Plateau. In the Tina Junction and Abattoir areas of the city, Muslims have been reportedly expelled from markets, according to a local Muslim trader interviewed. Similarly, according to a local Christian trader, Christians were also dislodged from the markets around the Gangare and Kwararafa communities. In the case of Borno State, it was reported that many of the Christian minorities that were abducted by members of Boko Haram were killed on account of their religious identities, while others were forcefully converted to Islam by the insurgents. Religious groups are further suspicious of policies of urbanization, which are seen as attempts to wipe out churches, according to the Christian Association of Nigeria (CAN) (PRNigeria 2021).

In the context of the predominantly Christian Sabon Gari community of Kano State, residents have consistently accused the Kano State Government of deliberately neglecting them on account of their religious identity. Residents defined such neglect in terms of dilapidated infrastructure, including poor roads and limited access to healthcare, water and schools. Abduction and forced conversion are also a phenomenon that has been reported by religious minorities in Kano, particularly targeting young Christian girls.

One major manifestation of the convergence between religious inequality and economic inequality lies in what the Christian Igbo population, a religious minority in Kano State, viewed as an attack on their livelihoods by the Muslim-dominated state government (Shuaibu 2013). In the aftermath of the introduction of Sharia law, despite the claim to secularity of the

Nigerian state, as provided in the constitution, the *Hisbah*, a religious police force, has consistently impounded beer in a bid to stop the consumption of alcohol (Mgboh 2021).

Religion and indigeneity

For several decades, Nigeria has attracted much attention due to the linkages between religion and indigeneity as key drivers of conflict (Kwaja 2011). Since 1994, Plateau has witnessed conflict in Jos North as a result of violent confrontations between the Hausa/Fulani, predominantly Muslims, and the Anaguta, Afizere and Berom, who are predominantly Christians. Though recognized throughout the country (Human Rights Watch 2006), practices of the certification of indigeneship are thought to reinforce discrimination against Nigerians outside their states of origin.

The determination of indigeneship, or nativity, is granted to citizens by the local government authority when someone is able to show their genealogical roots to a community within the LGA, which is also validated by the community traditional rulers. For persons that belong to religious minority groups, access to these certificates of indigeneship across the 774 LGAs of the country becomes difficult. In many instances, such persons are consequently denied opportunities for employments and jobs.

In Kaduna, Christians have complained of refusal by district heads to approve their indigene certificates. The same applies to Jos, where the Muslim communities also accuse the government of denying them certificates (Modibbo 2012), even though they've resided there for decades, with no other place to call home.[3] The implementation of Sharia in Kano, initially meant to apply only to Muslims, was expanded by the government to include non-Muslims. For instance, the Igbo community have accused the *Hisbah* of attacking their businesses and livelihoods through the impounding and destruction of alcoholic beverages.

'Since the Kano State Government is not interested in giving us jobs in the state because we are not indigenes, part of our legitimate business includes the sale of alcoholic products. By destroying our products under the pretext that they are prohibited under Sharia law,

---

[3] The issuance of certificate of indigeneship is a practice in Nigeria that is recognized by the constitution, reflecting the state of origin and cultural communities that people belong to. The issuance of such a certificate by the Chairperson of a Local Government Council is dependent on the approval of a district head, mostly a traditional ruler. The position and operations of a traditional ruler in the context of its practice in Nigeria is one that an individual is conferred with either by heredity or election/selection by a conclave of kingmakers.

as Nigerians, our rights under the constitution are violated. This means we are second class citizens in this country.' (Resident, Sabon Gari, Kano)

Working to overcome religious and economic inequality

In response to efforts towards addressing religious and economic inequality, local peace structures, such as the CPAs, are increasingly accepted as key agencies for conflict resolution and peacebuilding. The CPAs facilitate communication among protagonists to address potentially destructive mutual mistrust and strengthen social cohesion through dialogue (Odendaal 2010). The peacebuilding efforts between Fulani pastoralist and farming communities, divided along religious lines, strive to overcome the challenges of economic inequality through integrated rural market strategies that focus on conflict mitigation as a catalyst for the transformation of the rural economy. Beyond the activities of the CPAs, the establishment of the Light Microfinance Bank by the Church of Christ in Nations (COCIN), a denomination with a large following across Kaduna, Kano and Plateau, represents a deliberate attempt to provide members with credit facilities at very low interest rates, enabling the establishment of small-scale businesses (Ibrahim 2012).

In the aftermath of the conflict in Southern Kaduna, which affected most religious communities, institutions representing the two dominant religious groups – Christianity and Islam – played key roles in addressing some of the economic consequences of the conflict. The post-conflict environment is one in which religious institutions provided for the immediate needs of congregants as part of broader peacebuilding efforts (Shannahan and Payne 2016). For instance, the Christian Association of Nigeria, an umbrella organization of several Christian groups, set up a relief committee to address the economic shocks associated with the impact of the conflict on 13,000 Christians. On the part of the Muslim community, the Islamic Foundation of Nigeria and the Hudaibiyah Foundation of Nigeria provided humanitarian assistance and livelihood support to affected Muslims (Paul 2020: 61).

Conclusion

This chapter explores how religious and economic inequality are intertwined in Nigeria, through segregated settlement patterns, mutual suspicion, as well as unequal access to social services and basic amenities. The rights of religious communities have been violated, both through attacks perpetrated by insurgent groups such as Boko Haram (*Diplomat*

Magazine 2022), which have targeted minority Christian populations and other Muslim communities in Adamawa, Borno and Yobe states, and through legislative and political forms of discrimination. Not much has been done by the state to respond to such issues in a way that bolsters religious equity (USCIRF 2020). A common feature of state response is the initiation of dialogue processes and committees to look into the remote and immediate causes of such incidences, but there are minimal efforts towards providing access to justice for those affected by conflict in the form of compensation or reparations. In Nigeria, political, economic and social factors continue to converge as key catalysts for perpetuating state fragility (Usman and Bashir 2018), in a country where religion is both a unifying and divisive factor.

References

Admin III (2017) SOKAPU bitter over socio-political marginalization, *Forefront*, 16 December, https://forefrontng.com/sokapu-bitter-socio-politi cal-marginalization/ (accessed 19 December 2022).

Diplomat Magazine (2022) ICC prosecutor concludes first official visit to Nigeria, 24 April, www.icc-cpi.int/news/icc-prosecutor-mr-karim-aa-khan-qc-concludes-first-official-visit-nigeria (accessed 19 December 2022).

Heneghan, T. (2012) Poverty and injustice drive Nigeria's sectarian violence: Report, *Reuters*, 11 July, www.reuters.com/article/us-nige ria-violence-interfaith-idUSBRE86A0KP20120711 (accessed 19 December 2022).

Human Rights Watch (2006) They do not own this place: government discrimination against 'non Indigenes' in Nigeria, 25 April, www.hrw. org/report/2006/04/25/they-do-not-own-place/government-discriminat ion-against-non-indigenes-nigeria (accessed 19 December 2022).

Ibrahim, H. (2012) Nigeria: Jos COCIN commissions micro bank, *All Africa*, 10 December, https://allafrica.com/stories/201212101109.html (accessed 19 December 2022).

Kwaja, C. (2011) Nigeria's pernicious drivers of ethno-religious conflict, Africa Security Brief No. 14, Washington, DC: Africa Center for Strategic Studies, https://africacenter.org/publication/nigerias-pernicious-drivers-of-ethno-religious-conflict/ (accessed 19 December 2022).

Mgboh, D. (2021) Kano Hisbah impounds 5,760 cartons of beer, *The Sun*, 10 September, https://sunnewsonline.com/kano-hisbah-impounds-5760-cartons-of-beer/ (accessed 19 December 2022).

Modibbo, M.S.A. (2012) Survey of Muslim groups in plateau state of Nigeria, NRN Background Paper No. 4, Oxford: Nigeria Research Network, University of Oxford, www.qeh.ox.ac.uk/sites/www.odid.ox.ac.uk/files/BP4Modibbo.pdf (accessed 19 December 2022).

Odendaal, A. (2010) An architecture for building peace at the local level: A comparative study of local peace committees, Bureau for Crisis Prevention and Recovery Discussion Paper, New York: United Nations Development Program, www.un.org/en/land-natural-resources-conflict/pdfs/UNDP_Local%20Peace%20Committees_2011.pdf (accessed 19 December 2022).

Paul, S.T. (2020) The role of religion in peacebuilding processes in Southern Kaduna senatorial district of Kaduna state, Research report, Biu, Borno: Nigerian Army University.

PRNigeria (2021) FACT-CHECK: Is Borno government attempting to 'wipe out churches' in the state?, 11 August, https://prnigeria.com/2021/08/11/borno-wipe-churches-state/ (accessed 19 December 2022).

Shannahan, C. and Payne, L. (2016) *Faith-Based Interventions in Peace, Conflict and Violence: A Scoping Study*, Coventry: Coventry University, https://jliflc.com/wp-content/uploads/2016/05/JLI-Peace-Conflict-Scoping-Paper-May-2016.pdf (accessed 19 December 2022).

Shuaibu, I. (2013) Nigeria's Islamic police destroy 240,000 bottles of beer in Kano, *Reuters*, 28 November, www.reuters.com/article/us-nigeria-sharia-idINBRE9AR0P820131128 (accessed 19 December 2022).

Sociallogia Team (2020) RE: Southern Kaduna Christian leaders association: Right to reply: SOKAMUDA position, *Social Realities*, 14 September, https://sociallogia.wordpress.com/2020/09/14/re-southern-kaduna-christian-leaders-association-right-to-reply-sokamuda-position/ (accessed 19 December 2022).

USCIRF (2020) Nigeria 2020 international religious freedom report, Washington, DC: Office of International Religious Freedom, US Department of State, www.state.gov/wp-content/uploads/2021/05/240282-NIGERIA-2020-INTERNATIONAL-RELIGIOUS-FREEDOM-REPORT.pdf (accessed 19 December 2022).

Usman, A. and Bashir, S. (2018) Fragility of the Nigerian state and the challenge of Boko Haram violence, *Covenant University Journal of Politics and International Affairs* 6.1: 19–41.

21

Religious Identity–Based Inequality in the Labour Market: Policy Challenges in India

Surbhi Kesar and Rosa Abraham

The Indian economy has registered a sustained, almost four decades long, period of high economic growth. However, not only is this period marked by long spans of jobless and job-loss growth (Kannan and Raveendran 2019), but the economic gains of growth have remained unequally distributed along the lines of social and economic identities, especially gender, religion and caste. For example, Azam et al (2022) find that income mobility in India over the growth period has not been able to offset the existing caste and religion-based social hierarchies, and Asher et al (2018) find Muslims overall suffered downward occupational mobility.

Hindus, as per the official government labour force survey in 2017–2018, comprise about 82 per cent of the total population in the country, followed by Muslims, who comprise about 13 per cent. Other religious minorities in India include Christians, Sikhs, Jains, Buddhists and Zoroastrians, among others. In this chapter, we focus on religious differences between Hindus and Muslims because (a) the Muslim community is the largest religious minority in the country, and (b) the exclusion in economic and social spaces is particularly pronounced for Muslims. While the caste system has usually been associated with the Hindu religious group, for administrative purposes, the population is classified into Scheduled Castes (SCs), Scheduled Tribes (STs), and Other Backward Castes (OBCs). SCs and STs comprise 29 per cent of the Indian population, and OBCs comprise 43 per cent (as of 2017–2018). The caste groups classified as SCs and STs are seen to have faced the most social and economic marginalization, followed by OBCs. This administrative caste classification also forms the basis for caste-based affirmative action in India in the form of reservation policies. In this context, it should also be noted that while Hindu Dalits, that is, the 'ex-untouchable caste groups', are included in SCs, heavily ostracized Muslims have long been denied their pleas to be included in the SC administrative classifications (Deshpande 2011; Chandrachud 2023). Most marginalized Muslim groups have been classified as OBCs.[1]

Specifically in terms of labour market opportunities and outcomes, these differences are likely to manifest in the following ways: difference in opportunities and resources, such as access to education, prior to entry into the labour market (Mohanty 2006); persistent inequality in the access to employment and type of occupations in the labour market (Madheswaran and Attewell 2007); and unequal returns in wages, earnings, benefits and so on, when employed in the labour market (Madheswaran and Attewell 2007; Sengupta and Das 2014; Duraisamy and Duraisamy 2017). Notably, these differentials along the lines of caste and gender identity have been well documented in the economics literature, and policy interventions that centre these identities have played a key role in narrowing some group-based differentials, albeit at an excruciatingly slow pace (Mohammed 2019). However, the religion-based inequalities, and their intersection with other identity-based inequalities, have remained relatively underexplored in analysis and underemphasized in policy making.

Evolution of religious-based inequality in the Indian labour market

That the Indian growth experience has not produced commensurate levels of employment is evident in the consistently falling employment rate, even during the high growth phases of the economy – from 57 per cent in 1999–2000 to 45 per cent in 2018–2019.[2] Broadly, the proportionate fall in employment between 1999–2000 and 2018–2019 was similar among Hindus and Muslims (with employment for Hindus in 2018–2019 being 81 per cent that of 1999–2000 levels, and for Muslims 84 per cent). The fall was sharpest for marginalized SC and ST communities, with employment in 2018–2019 falling to nearly 75 per cent of 1999–2000 levels, whereas for the general category it was at 90 per cent. When we overlay religion and caste categories, we find that in terms of employment rates, between

---

[1] The survey data identifies a very small proportion of Muslims in the SC and ST categories, comprising 0.31 per cent of the population, which are typically those who converted from Hinduism.

[2] Employment rate is the share of employed individuals in the total working age (15 years or above) population.

Figure 21.1: Employment rate for different religion and caste groups between 1999–2000 and 2018–2019

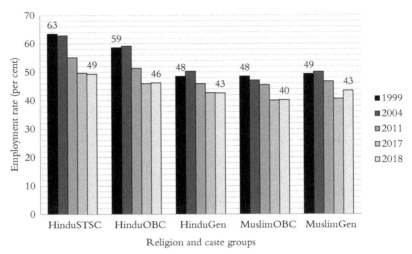

Source: Author's illustration based on UNU-WIDER (2021)

1999–2000 and 2018–2019, there has been a steady, and more or less similar, decline across each group (see Figure 21.1).[3,4]

While the employment rates provide a preliminary understanding of access to the labour market, the share of the groups in the working age population also needs to be considered. Indeed, the share of Hindus in the workforce has been similar to their share in the working age population between 1999 and 2019. For example, in 2019, Hindus accounted for 81 per cent of the working age population and about 83 per cent of the workforce, suggesting that Hindus were as represented in the workforce as they were in the population. However, for Muslims, their share in the workforce has been consistently lower than their share in the working age population and has been falling. For example, 85 per cent of the Muslim working age population were counted as in the workforce in 2018–2019, compared to 90 per cent in 1999–2000, suggesting a gradual, albeit small, exclusion of Muslims from the workforce.

Some stark results begin to appear when we extend this intersectional analysis of religion and caste to the nature of employment. There is

---

[3]   Prior to 2016, labour force surveys in India, known as the Employment-Unemployment surveys, were conducted every five years. Post 2016, labour force surveys have been conducted annually and are referred to as the Periodic Labour Force Surveys. This explains the frequency of data points.

[4]   The religious and caste affiliations are as reported by the household during the survey. We combine the information from the two to identify religion-caste sub-categories.

Table 21.1: Employment arrangements by caste and religious groups (1999–2000 and 2017–2018)

	HinduSTSC	HinduOBC	HinduGen	MuslimOBC	MuslimGen
1999–2000					
OAW	21.9	32.5	36.4	37.9	40.6
Employer	0.3	0.9	1.8	1.3	0.8
Unpaid	14.4	21.7	19.7	15.2	13.5
Salaried	9.5	12.1	25.8	13.6	14.9
Wage	53.9	32.8	16.3	32.1	30.2
2017–2018					
OAW	31.0	38.9	39.7	42.4	42.1
Employer	0.9	2.1	3.2	2.0	2.1
Unpaid	12.3	14.7	12.3	7.6	6.0
Salaried	17.3	22.0	33.5	19.8	23.7
Wage	38.6	22.5	11.2	28.2	26.2

Source: Authors' own calculations using Periodic Labour Force Survey (2017–2018)

evidence to suggest that employer-households typically earn higher than salaried worker households, followed by own-account worker (OAW) households and finally casual wage worker households (Kesar 2020). We find that, as of 2017–2018, general category Hindus were much more likely to be employers (3 per cent) and salaried workers (34 per cent) relative to other caste and religious identity groups (see Table 21.1). The proportion of casual wage workers, the most precarious of employment arrangements, is also much higher for general category Muslims (26 per cent) relative to general category Hindus (11 per cent), and also slightly higher for Muslim OBC (28 per cent) relative to Hindu OBC (23 per cent).

Notably, a gain in the proportion of salaried employment arrangements over 1999–2000 to 2017–2018 is seen across all groups. However, as of 2017–2018, the earnings of Muslim salaried workers and Muslim own-account workers, across general and OBC castes, were lower than their Hindu counterparts' (see Table 21.2).

Another significant change over this period has been the shift in India's occupational structure, with a reduction in the workforce dependent on agriculture, from about 60 per cent in 1999–2000 to 42 per cent in 2017–2018 (Table 21.3). This has, however, not been accompanied by the shift towards manufacturing – a sector usually associated with more secure and regular employment – that one might expect. Instead, there has been a

Table 21.2: Earnings in different employment arrangements by caste and religious groups (2017–2018)

	OAW	Employer	Salaried	Casual wage
HinduSTSC	7,236	14,038	12,751	5,181
HinduOBC	9,229	17,900	14,597	5,848
HinduGen	11,425	25,771	19,188	5,707
MuslimOBC	8,933	17,782	11,373	6,054
MuslimGen	9,683	16,900	12,363	5,991

Source: Authors' own calculations using Periodic Labour Force Survey (2017–2018)

Table 21.3: Distribution of industry within caste-religious category (1999–2000 and 2017–2018)

		Agriculture	Manufacturing	Construction	Services	Total
1999–2000	HinduSTSC	70.5	8.7	6.1	14.7	100
	HinduOBC	63.9	11.6	4.3	20.2	100
	HinduGen	51.4	11.9	2.8	33.9	100
	MuslimOBC	38.8	19.1	6.4	35.8	100
	MuslimGen	41.1	19.0	5.3	34.6	100
	Overall	*60.2*	*11.4*	*4.6*	*23.8*	*100*
2017–2018	HinduSTSC	50.7	9.8	16.9	22.6	100
	HinduOBC	45.0	13.4	10.3	31.3	100
	HinduGen	36.1	14.6	5.6	43.7	100
	MuslimOBC	25.3	22.3	13.7	38.7	100
	MuslimGen	28.5	20.9	13.4	37.2	100
	Overall	*42.4*	*13.5*	*11.5*	*32.6*	*100*

significant shift towards construction and services (see Table 21.3). The construction sector typically offers casual wage contracts and precarious working arrangements, while services are mostly associated with regular wage/salaried employment or self-employment with relatively better working conditions.

In general, the exodus from agriculture is seen across all caste-religious groups. But growth in the services sector has mostly favoured Hindus, while the construction sector has been more likely to absorb Muslims. Given that the dominant employment type in construction is casual wage work, while service sector employment tends to be in salaried jobs and self-employment, this points towards inequalities in the kinds of work that Hindus and Muslims have been able to access during this structural change process.

A challenging policy environment for tackling religion-based labour market inequalities

This brief snapshot of religion-based inequality and its intersection, to some extent, with caste-based inequality in the Indian labour market highlights the role of these identities in determining people's life chances and their likelihood of sharing in the economic growth and industrial development pursued under SDGs 8 and 9. Access to jobs by Muslims vis-à-vis their share in the working age population has followed a similar declining trajectory to that of their Hindu counterparts, and Muslims have become relatively underrepresented in the labour market. Further, Muslims have had less access to the better jobs that are available.

In India, caste-based reservation policies operational since independence have contributed to narrowing wage inequality and increasing occupational mobility across castes (Asher et al 2018; Hnatkovska et al 2021). However, religion-based affirmative action frameworks for minority communities who have faced economic and social marginalization are mostly very weak. The intersectional nature of these job-market inequities in India clearly begs greater attention to religion-based marginalization.

As Asher et al (2018) find, historically marginalized Scheduled Caste groups in India have experienced intergenerational upward mobility, but this has been almost completely offset by declining intergenerational mobility among Muslims. Moreover, the current period in India has been marked by higher (political) ostracization of Muslims through, for example, a significant increase in incidents of violence against Muslims, the amendment of the Citizenship Act to provide persecuted minorities from neighbouring countries a pathway to Indian citizenship (but with Muslims explicitly exempt from this) and ending the special status of the Muslim-majority state of Jammu and Kashmir, without consent from its citizens. In the face of ostracization, long-standing, religion-based economic inequities are likely to be exacerbated, making it even more important to foreground religious identity in analysing and addressing labour market inequities. At the same time, any policy that centres religion-based inequalities would need to carefully consider the negative impacts of identification of Muslims by the state in the current political climate.

References

Asher, S., Novosad, P. and Rafkin, C. (2018) Intergenerational mobility in India: Estimates from new methods and administrative data, Working Paper No. 560, Washington, DC: World Bank.

Azam, M. (2016) Household income mobility in India: 1993–2011, *IZA Discussion Paper No. 10308*, Bonn: Institute for the Study of Labor.

Chandrachud, A. (2023) *These Seats Are Reserved: Caste, Quotas and the Constitution of India*, Gurugram: Penguin Random House India.

Deshpande, A. (2011) *The Grammar of Caste: Economic Discrimination in Contemporary India*, Oxford: Oxford University Press.

Duraisamy, P. and Duraisamy, M. (2017) Social identity and wage discrimination in the Indian labour market, *Economic and Political Weekly* 52.4: 51–60.

Hnatkovska, V., Hou, C. and Lahiri, A. (2021) Convergence across castes, MPRA Paper No. 108980, Munich: Munich Personal RePEc Archive.

Kannan, K.P. and Raveendran, G. (2019) From jobless to job-loss growth, *Economic and Political Weekly* 54.44: 38–44.

Kesar, S. (2020) Economic transition, dualism, and informality in India, Centre for Sustainable Employment Working Paper 31, Bengaluru: Azim Premji University.

Madheswaran, S. and Attewell, P. (2007) Caste discrimination in the Indian urban labour market: Evidence from the National Sample Survey, *Economic and Political Weekly* 42.41: 4146–4153.

Mohammed, A.S. (2019) Does a good father now have to be rich? Intergenerational income mobility in rural India, *Labour Economics* 60: 99–114.

Mohanty, M. (2006) Social inequality, labour market dynamics and reservation, *Economic and Political Weekly* 41.35: 3777–3789.

Sengupta, A. and Das, P. (2014) Gender wage discrimination across social and religious groups in India: Estimates with unit level data, *Economic and Political Weekly* 49.21: 71–77.

PART VI

Inequalities

22

Religious Inequality and Economic Opportunity: Implications for SDG10

Simone Schotte

Reducing inequality: a persisting challenge

The issue of rising inequality and how to address it has become an important element of public debate all over the world. Its reduction is integral to the sustainable development agenda, and SDG10 commits the international community to lessening inequality within and among countries. Specifically, defining important milestones to achieving greater equality by 2030, the first four targets set out to (a) 'achieve and sustain income growth of the poorest 40 per cent of the population', (b) 'empower and promote the social, economic and political inclusion of all, irrespective of age, sex, disability, race, ethnicity, origin, religion or economic or other status', (c) 'ensure equal opportunity and reduce inequalities of outcome, including by eliminating discriminatory laws, policies and practices' and (d) 'adopt policies, especially fiscal, wage and social protection policies, and progressively achieve greater equality'.

After rising since the Industrial Revolution and stagnating at high levels for much of the post-war period (Qureshi 2018), global inequality – between people across countries – has been on decline for the last three decades. This reversal is good news, but in fact reflects the balance of two opposing trends: falling between-country inequality and rising within-country inequality. Figure 22.1 illustrates these patterns using the Gini index as a standard inequality measure.

On the one hand, inequality 'between' countries reversed course and has been narrowing, as economic growth picked up in several developing and emerging economies. Especially the rapid growth in bigger economies, such

Figure 22.1: Global inequality 1990–present

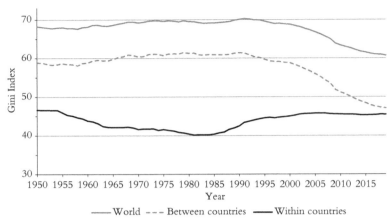

Source: Author's illustration based on UNU-WIDER (2021)

as China and, to a lesser extent, India, has greatly influenced this trend. As China's mean income converges toward the global average, the living conditions of hundreds of millions of people are improving (Gradín et al 2021). However, since between-country inequality captures the difference in average incomes, it tells little about how these incomes are distributed within countries, and whether poorer or richer parts of society benefitted the most from periods of economic growth.

Revealing a more complex picture, on the other hand, income inequality 'within' countries has been widening and its contribution to aggregate global inequality has increased. While inequality did not grow everywhere and trends are mixed over time, and across countries and regions, this aggregate rise is concerning and, if prolonged, may overturn the positive overall trend in global inequality. Despite the steady decline in extreme poverty for almost 25 years – which has been partly reversed by the COVID-19 pandemic – economic gaps continued to grow. Within countries, on average, the bottom 40 per cent of the population have a lower share in national income today than in the 1990s (UNU-WIDER 2021), and the richest people hold unprecedented levels of wealth. These within-country gaps are what 'ultimately frames people's lives and perceptions' and constitute the focus of most national policies that address inequality (Gradín et al 2021).

Religious inequality is one important, but often overlooked, dimension shaping within-country inequality. While no SDG is considered to be met unless it is met for everyone, SDG10 is the only one that explicitly recognizes religion as a potential ground for exclusion and discrimination (Tadros and

Sabates-Wheeler 2020). Around the world, people are being excluded from accessing economic opportunities, services and rights simply because of who they are, and what they do or do not believe in.

This chapter discusses how social exclusion on the grounds of religion translates into economic gaps. The second part explores this link from a conceptual perspective, while the third part takes a deeper dive into the processes that explain the relationship. The fourth part draws some lessons for research and policy.

Social exclusion and inequality of opportunity

Inequality has been conceptualized in various ways. The dominant approach in economics focuses on 'vertical' inequalities between individuals or households, based on ranking everyone in the population by their income or wealth. Common measures adapting this concept are the Gini index or the income share held by the bottom 40 per cent of the population. A second approach revolves around the analysis of identity-based social discrimination. These so-called 'horizontal' inequalities (HIs) between culturally defined groups 'cut across the distribution of income and wealth, and are the product of social hierarchies which define certain groups as inferior to others through the devaluation of their socially ascribed identities' (Kabeer 2016). Reflecting systematic differences based on attributes generally inherited at birth, HIs present a primary concern in many multicultural societies, in which certain ethnic or religious groups have been historically disadvantaged and discriminated (Kabeer 2016).

Religious and faith-based inequalities have long been a blind spot in development discourse. However, the ways in which these intersect with other 'horizontal' and 'vertical' inequalities, and their contribution to exclusions between and within groups, are increasingly being recognized (Bharadwaj et al 2021). 'Where inequalities overlap with each other, they give rise to an intersecting, rather than an additive, model of inequality, where each fuses with, and exacerbates, the effects of the other' (Kabeer 2016). This can explain why certain groups in society are systematically being left behind. Figure 22.2 illustrates this link. Religious and intersecting inequalities create a situation of social exclusion. This may manifest in public policies that constrain the political, civil, economic and cultural rights of marginalized groups, or be the result of social practice and prejudice, or both (Khan 2011). In consequence, those who are marginalized based on their identity face significant barriers to succeeding in many areas of life, independent of their talents and ability or willingness to use these talents. If not counteracted, this inequality of opportunity translates into inequality in outcomes, such as income, wealth, employment or learning achievements.

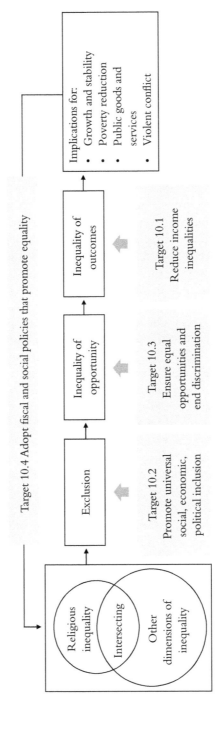

Figure 22.2: Link between religious inequality, exclusion and Sustainable Development Goal 10

Pronounced inequalities – particularly HIs reflecting persistent disadvantages for some groups in society who are denied income mobility and opportunity – are not only unjust. They also have negative implications for other dimensions of development, such as growth and macroeconomic stability (Dabla-Norris et al 2015), poverty reduction (Ncube et al 2014), provision of public goods and services (Uzochukwu et al 2020) and conflict risk (Stewart 2000; Mancini 2008; Hillesund et al 2018). The following section discusses these channels in more detail, illustrating how religious inequality and social exclusion can translate into economic inequality, and thereby produce a circular, reinforcing relationship that risks leaving the most vulnerable behind. As Figure 22.2 illustrates, the targets spelled out under SDG10 intend to address this circular relationship, by (a) reducing income inequalities, (b) promoting inclusion, (c) ensuring equal opportunities and (d) adopting fiscal and social policies that promote equality, among others. However, to credibly reduce inequalities and promote inclusion, understanding the channels and drivers of exclusion is key. Despite the overrepresentation of ethnic and religious minorities at the bottom of the income distribution (Mir et al 2020), the research and policy discussions of SDG10 have paid too little in-depth attention to ethnic and religious inequalities.

From religious to economic inequality

It is estimated that 891 million people worldwide experience discrimination on the basis of their ethnic, linguistic or religious identities (DFID 2005). While there is a considerable literature on the disadvantages experienced by marginalized ethnic groups and associated HIs, only some studies investigate the positive link between religious discrimination or polarization and inequality (see for example Dincer and Hotard 2011 for a cross-country study), and yet fewer assess the processes that explain this connection (Khan 2011). This section explores three core channels, which have been discussed in the literature.

Exclusion from labour market opportunities

The first concerns the exclusion of marginalized religious groups from economic opportunities on the labour market, which may be reflected in differential access to (good) jobs and pay gaps. While the accumulation of capital by a small group of very affluent people explains the increasing concentration of incomes among the richest 1 per cent, labour earnings remain the main source of income for most among the other 99 per cent of the population, and are therefore a key driver of income inequality. While statistics on the extent of religious inequality on the labour market are scarce because broad-based indicators such as the unemployment rate are rarely disaggregated by religious affiliation,[1] it has been shown that socially marginalized religious groups tend to be concentrated in low-paid and low-skilled jobs (see for example Mehta and Shree 2017 on India). Moreover, there is some evidence that disadvantage is reinforced where religious inequality intersects with other markers of exclusion, defined by caste, race, tribe, gender, disability or other socially constructed identities (Bharadwaj et al 2021).[2]

Labour market discrimination likely plays a key role in this regard. It may be reflected in the attitudes of hiring managers, or in the possibilities to raise capital to start a business. When people expect prejudice, this may also undermine their motivation to achieve, or parents may consider it less worthwhile to invest in their children's education. In practice, it is difficult if not impossible, however, to disentangle the impact of religious discrimination from other interrelated factors that frame exclusion. These may include the location of minority groups in remote areas with fewer education or employment opportunities, and a lack of social capital and networks to access opportunities (Khan 2011).

Constrained access to public services and redistribution

Second, religious inequality may constrain access to and limit the implementation of public policies that mediate income inequality – such as policies that regulate labour relations, favour the acquisition of skills or redistribute earnings via progressive tax-benefit systems. Institutional capacity, which plays a vital role in this regard, is often reduced in contexts characterized by pronounced religious inequalities. Both ethnic diversity and income inequality have been shown to negatively affect institutional quality (see for example Madni 2019 on Pakistan). Moreover, ethnic diversity tends to hamper redistributive policies, as individuals who belong to one ethnic group are generally less supportive of measures that redistribute scarce resources towards other ethnic groups (Dincer and Hotard 2011). This pattern may extend to groups defined based on religious identity. Another limiting factor is that many countries deny state benefits to non-citizens, which implies the exclusion of religious minorities

---

[1] This is partly because religion tends to be a fluid concept, which is not always captured in survey data. Exclusion in the public sector is relatively better documented, as a number of countries either provide very limited provisions, or even constitutionally exclude religious minorities from high-ranking positions (Khan 2011).

[2] For example, Heath and Martin (2013) show for the case of Britain that Muslim workers experience greater labour market penalties than those belonging to other (or no) religions, and Muslim women are most affected.

who experience discrimination in citizenship law and statelessness (UNHCR 2021).

Elevated risk of violent conflict and vulnerability to crises

In the worst-case scenario, the combination of HIs with political or economic grievances and perceptions of cultural exclusion increases the risk of crises and violent conflict (Besançon 2005; DFID 2005; United Nations and World Bank 2018; Carter 2021). These tend to hit the most vulnerable hardest, thereby leading to a perpetuation and intensification of inequality.[3] Violence and oppression can also directly target the economic base of religious minorities; for example, if their businesses are targets of violent attacks (as seen by Christians and Yazidis in Iraq), or they are being forcefully removed from their positions (as experienced by Shia professors in Bahrain in light of the events of the 'Arab Spring') (Khan 2011).

Conclusion

The drivers of religious inequality are deeply rooted in the social and political structure, and therefore present a complex challenge for development practitioners and policy makers to address (Bharadwaj et al 2021). An important step to give visibility to the issue is the collection of disaggregated socio-economic data by religious affiliation. While efforts will need to be respectful of the sensitivities related to gathering such information (Tadros and Sabates-Wheeler 2020), better data could aid the formulation and monitoring of targeted policies. Moreover, there is a need for measures which ensure that more incidences of discrimination are reported.[4] Affirmative Action policies – designed to provide special opportunities to historically marginalized social groups – can present an important step to address systemic HIs. However, a frequently raised concern is that these policies tend to mainly benefit the better off within target groups (Sowell 2008). To reach those at highest risk of being left behind, policies will need to be mindful of intersecting inequalities, use diverse designs to address different barriers and be embedded into a broader public policy agenda promoting non-discrimination, equal opportunities and social cohesion.

---

[3] Carter (2021) shows that people who experience social marginalization, discriminatory treatment and inequality prior to a humanitarian event are more vulnerable to the adverse effects of the crises.

[4] A survey of Muslims in the European Union showed that the majority did not report their experiences of discrimination to an organization or at the place where it occurred. Further, many were unaware about the prohibition of discrimination on the basis of ethnic origin in the labour market (Alidadi 2011).

References

Alidadi, K. (2011) Opening doors to Muslim minorities in the workplace: From India's employment quota to EU and Belgian anti-discrimination legislation, *Pace International Law Review* 23: 146.

Besançon, M.L. (2005) Relative resources: Inequality in ethnic wars, revolutions, and genocides, *Journal of Peace Research* 42.4: 393–415.

Bharadwaj, S., Howard, J. and Narayanan, P. (2021) Using participatory action research methodologies for engaging and researching with religious minorities in contexts of intersecting inequalities, CREID Working Paper 5, Brighton: Coalition for Religious Equality and Inclusive Development, Institute of Development Studies.

Carter, B. (2021) Impact of social inequalities and discrimination on vulnerability to crises, K4D Helpdesk Report, Brighton: Institute of Development Studies.

Dabla-Norris, M.E., Kochhar, M.K., Suphaphiphat, M.N., Ricka, M.F. and Tsounta, M.E. (2015) *Causes and Consequences of Income Inequality: A Global Perspective*, Washington, DC: International Monetary Fund.

DFID (2005) Reducing poverty by tackling social exclusion, DFID policy paper, London: Department for International Development.

Dincer, O.C. and Hotard, M.J. (2011) Ethnic and religious diversity and income inequality, *Eastern Economic Journal* 37.3: 417–430.

Gradín, C., Tarp, F. and Leibbrandt, M. (2021) Global inequality may be falling, but the gap between haves and have-nots is growing, *The Conversation*, 2 September.

Heath, A. and Martin, J. (2013) Can religious affiliation explain 'ethnic' inequalities in the labour market?, *Ethnic and Racial Studies* 36.6: 1005–1027.

Hillesund, S., Bahgat, K., Barrett, G., Dupuy, K., Gates, S., Nygård, H.M. et al (2018) Horizontal inequality and armed conflict: A comprehensive literature review, *Canadian Journal of Development Studies* 39.4: 463–480.

Kabeer, N. (2016) 'Leaving no one behind': The challenge of intersecting inequalities, World Social Science Report, Paris: UNESCO and the ISSC.

Khan, S. (2011) Religious identity and inequality in the MENA region, *Helpdesk Research Report*, Birmingham: University of Birmingham.

Madni, G.R. (2019) Probing institutional quality through ethnic diversity, income inequality and public spending, *Social Indicators Research* 142.2: 581–595.

Mancini, L. (2008) Horizontal inequality and communal violence: Evidence from Indonesian districts, in F. Stewart (ed) *Horizontal Inequalities and Conflict*, London: Palgrave Macmillan.

Mehta, B.S. and Shree, M. (2017) Inequality, gender, and socio-religious groups, *Economic and Political Weekly* 52.8: 56–60.

Mir, G., Karlsen, S., Mitullah, W., Bhojani, U., Uzochukwu, B., Mirzoev, T. et al (2020) Achieving SDG 10: A global review of public service inclusion strategies for ethnic and religious minorities, Occasional Paper 5, Geneva: United Nations Research Institute for Social Development.

Ncube, M., Anyanwu, J.C. and Hausken, K. (2014) Inequality, economic growth and poverty in the Middle East and North Africa (MENA), *African Development Review* 26.3: 435–453.

Qureshi, Z. (2018) Trends in income inequality: Global, inter-country and within countries, Brookings Institution Policy Brief, Washington, DC: Brookings Institution.

Sowell, T. (2008) *Affirmative Action around the World*, New Haven, CT: Yale University Press.

Stewart, F. (2000) Crisis prevention: Tackling horizontal inequalities, *Oxford Development Studies* 28.3: 245–262.

Tadros, M. and Sabates-Wheeler, R. (2020) Inclusive development: Beyond need, not creed, CREID Working Paper 1, Brighton: Coalition for Religious Equality and Inclusive Development, Institute of Development Studies.

UNHCR (2021) *Background Note on Discrimination in Nationality Laws and Statelessness*, Geneva: United Nations High Commissioner for Refugees.

United Nations and World Bank (2018) *Pathways for Peace: Inclusive Approaches to Preventing Violent Conflict*, Washington, DC: World Bank.

UNU-WIDER (2021) World Income Inequality Database (WIID), Version 31 May, Helsinki: United Nations University World Institute for Development Economics Research.

Uzochukwu, B.S., Okeke, C.C., Ogwezi, J., Emunemu, B., Onibon, F., Ebenso, B. et al (2020) Exploring the drivers of ethnic and religious exclusion from public services in Nigeria: Implications for Sustainable Development Goal 10, *International Journal of Sociology and Social Policy* 41.5/6: 561–583.

23

The Justice Gap: Religious Minorities, Discrimination and Accountability Challenges

Claire Thomas and Mary Gill

Mariam Bibi and her children were penniless and hungry. The children had stopped attending school since their father, Nadeem, died in a sewer in the small Pakistani town of Sargodha in October 2021. Nadeem's death was avoidable; he and a fellow worker, who also died, descended into a sewer after another colleague fell from a broken ladder. The emergency service crew attended but refused to go into the sewer, despite having protective gear and breathing apparatus. Eventually, another sewer worker (without any gear at all) descended and retrieved the bodies (who were reportedly alive when the rescue service arrived but subsequently died).

Nadeem, like many other poor Christians, worked in the sewers for 16 years but he was still a 'daily wager'. He had formally requested to become a permanent employee with more rights, but to no avail. His family was not automatically entitled to compensation. Nadeem got the emergency call at 10 pm that night and was reluctant to respond, but did so because he knew he could lose his job if he did not. Mariam Bibi initially took the brave decision to take on Nadeem's corporation, with the aim to force all such corporations to pay attention to the health and safety of their workers. "The union officials and others have contacted us offering 500,000 rupees to withdraw the case," Mariam said, "but we are fighting for justice, and it has a cost."

Sanitation workers in Pakistan

Christians form less than 2 per cent of Pakistan's population, but over 80 per cent of sanitation workers in major metropolitan districts. Job adverts regularly appear for sanitation workers stating that only non-Muslims need apply. Sanitation work is poorly paid, highly dangerous and, for many, extremely insecure. The fact that non-Muslims do this work seems to mean that the risks are ignored. At least 29 other workers have died in Pakistan unblocking sewers since 2017. In Lahore alone, 70 people reportedly died while carrying out sanitation work more broadly in 2019. This work is handed down within families and communities, essentially castes – ironic given caste's Hindu origin and Pakistan's Muslim authorities' opposition to that tradition. Sanitation workers are considered by many to be low class, uneducated and literally 'untouchable'. Little or no effort is made to ensure that they are safe at work; they regularly go down sewers known to contain noxious gases without any protective clothing, masks, gloves or breathing equipment.

No one has ever been held to account for the negligence which contributes to many workers' deaths and injuries each year. Families are threatened or paid off to not pursue complaints or to withdraw cases. Society at large does not seem to care that one, or two or 20 more sanitation workers have died.

Seeking accountability

The Centre for Legal Justice (CLJ) has been educating sanitation workers about their rights and campaigning for change for many years. Recently, with support from Minority Rights Group (MRG) as part of the Coalition for Religious Equality and Inclusive Development (CREID), CLJ lobbied successfully for sanitation workers working in COVID-19 quarantine centres and on hospital wards to receive personal protective equipment (PPE). While these campaigns have had some impact, ultimately corporations know that there are few consequences when people die due to their negligence, and the effort they are willing to put into change is limited. CLJ is working to secure a landmark judgement to find the responsible supervisors guilty of negligence. This has the potential to fundamentally shift three things that maintain this religious exclusion and its terrible impacts.

First, it will change the attitude of the supervisors who send workers down sewers with inadequate or no equipment, and with no regard for workers' safety. Knowing that they may be held responsible and have to personally answer in court for a sanitation worker's avoidable death will mean that they are less casual about other human beings' safety and wellbeing.

Second, it would send a signal to sanitation workers themselves, helping to convey increased agency to sanitation workers to demand adequate safety equipment. The people who do the work have gained experience as to the risks and know how to make the work safer, but they have no power, and are ignored.

Third, a landmark legal case would put pressure on corporations to provide protective equipment and expect safety rules to be followed. It may be possible to establish that the lack of attention to health and safety is at the level of the institution (leading to a judgement that the corporation must systematically ensure better protections for all their workers).

Steps for change

CLJ made contact with the families of the two dead sewer workers and the colleague that intervened to retrieve their bodies and identified a specialist, experienced and sympathetic lawyer willing to work pro bono. CLJ discussed Mariam's options carefully with her, including alternative means of support during the trial period, and the risk of her losing her litter-picking job. We interviewed Mariam, the family of the other victim, the sewer worker witness and many other witnesses. After considerable legal research, expert meetings and consultations, CLJ then made the decision to bring a case using the Islamic *diyat* law payment option (compensation payable under Islamic traditions where a death or injury has occurred) as Pakistan does not have an option to bring a case of corporate manslaughter. Locating the action squarely within the Muslim tradition is tactically strong as it relies on local traditions and not international norms.

No legal action has ever been taken in any of the 29 fatalities of sanitation workers, all of which raise similar issues. Mariam and her nephew were named as the complainant in the case, and tried hard to withstand the threats and pay out offers made by the management of the corporation and others. Eventually, however, they accepted an out of court settlement, compensation payout and a secure job for one relative in the corporation. Mariam was afraid to lose her job, which made taking a case against the corporation and their staff much more difficult. However, she now knows that she is equally as human as any other person in Pakistani society. She knows that her husband's and all the sanitation workers' lives are equally valuable, and the family's grief is the same, whether one is Christian, Muslim or Hindu. This may sound self-evident, but in Pakistan, many Christian and Hindu sanitation workers don't feel equally human. That Mariam felt able to take a stand, despite the tremendous pressure she faced, is a massive step forward.

It is important that at least part of the minority community in question is aware of their rights and willing to claim them; empowerment work is crucial. Second, carefully timed accompanying advocacy and media is necessary. A case that no one has heard of is more easily sidelined and can be repeatedly adjourned. However, there is a risk that more publicity may also attract hostility, and the courts also frown upon cases that have been 'tried in the media'. Wider advocacy and legal work are as important as a court win, which is never the end of the matter. Messages from the court case need to reach those who can change practices, behaviours and systems. In this case, this would mean ensuring the sanitation worker community know and celebrate the result and feel empowered by it, that the supervisors know that they may be held personally responsible and that corporations know that they may also end up in court if things don't change.

Key things to consider

1. Practically, you need a lawyer in your team, working for you, on a salary and based in your organization. If you can't have a paid experienced lawyer on your staff, you may need to team up with a legal rights organization to work together.
2. How independent are your courts? If there is a reasonable possibility that they will side with the party who is able to pay the largest bribe, this is not a route for you. Likewise, if a high-powered official can influence a judge.
3. Can you put in place the support that the complainant and witnesses will need? This can be financial, but also important is moral support and regular communication. This goes beyond just the complainant. If a legal challenge has real potential teeth to bring about change, those in favour of the status quo will surely fight it. They may seek to divide and rule the community by identifying someone who they can support to champion views that destabilize the campaign. They may even use third parties to threaten or attack the complainant or those close to them.
4. Are you in it for the long haul? Court processes are notoriously slow. And lawyers sensing a losing case may use every legal trick in the book to argue for a delay. Strategic litigation work does not fit neatly into 24–36 month project phases. You are at the mercy of the court, which can list a hearing or require a response with little notice. You can't plan ahead what evidence you might need to respond to other parties; if you are an organization that runs mostly on restricted fund projects, this kind of work is probably not for you.

24

Disability and Religious Inequality Intertwined: Double Discrimination against Deaf Jehovah's Witnesses in Uzbekistan

Dilmurad Yusupov

What is it like to face discrimination based on disability and religion? This chapter will explore how being a deaf person who chose to become a Jehovah's Witness (JW) in Uzbekistan results in double discrimination, based on disability and religious identity. People with hearing impairments in Uzbekistan are already one of the most underrepresented and marginalized groups in the country, due to negative attitudes and a prevailing lack of accessibility. In January 2021, a total of 25,022 people with hearing impairments were officially registered in the country.[1] However, this data is unreliable, and many deaf people are left behind in the Uzbek state statistics, lacking social support. Due to communication barriers and stigma, deaf people have been deprived of access to quality education and decent livelihood opportunities; being a member of a minority religious community in a Muslim-majority country has become a cause of further marginalization.

JWs are one of the disadvantaged minority religious communities in Uzbekistan and across post-Soviet countries in general. For instance, in Russia, JWs were officially labelled as extremist in 2017, and its members

---

[1] According to the data provided by the Society of the Deaf of Uzbekistan on the number of registered deaf and hard-of-hearing people with the organization. The total number 25,022 also includes students at special boarding schools, kindergartens and colleges – 5,505 children with hearing impairments across the country.

have been persecuted for their religious beliefs (Kravchenko 2019). There are about 4,000 JW adherents in Uzbekistan and only one registered JW organization. The Uzbek government is reluctant to register its other denominations across the country (Yusupov 2021). JW's religious activities are labelled as 'radically dangerous' (Atabaeva 2019) and are usually framed as 'missionary work', 'proselytism' and 'sects', which are considered, like terrorism, to pose a threat to majority Uzbek ethnic Muslims. Uzbek JWs are portrayed as having fallen victim to a 'dangerous sect'. Expectations of repentance and return to Islam become a precondition for their social inclusion, participation and access to financial and other kinds of support provided by Islamic charity institutions in Uzbekistan. Moreover, the minority of deaf people among JWs are also discriminated against by deaf Muslims within the already segregated deaf community, which may affect the unity of a nascent deaf rights movement in Uzbekistan.

In 2018, the Muslim Board of Uzbekistan (MBU), together with Tashkent city administration (*hokimiyat*), launched a project to make Islamic religious education accessible to deaf and blind communities across the country. MBU representatives organized weekly meetings at mosques and other public spaces separately for adults with visual and hearing impairments. Notably, more attention was given to deaf communities compared to blind people, as the former had less access to both religious and secular education. The intervention of the MBU happened in the context of a new president of Uzbekistan coming to power, Shavkat Mirziyoyev, who proposed the adoption of a new UN resolution on 'education and religious tolerance' (Mirziyoyev 2017). The joint MBU-Tashkent city project was presented as aiming to improve the accessibility of mosques for Uzbek deaf communities through providing Uzbek Sign Language (USL) interpretation of Friday sermons, Islamic preaching and religious literature.

However, arguably, one of the aims of the project was to raise spiritual awareness of the Uzbek deaf communities, at the expense of violating the rights of the minority Uzbek deaf JWs (Yusupov 2021). The problem here lies in the complex historical intertwining of ethnic and religious identification in post-Soviet Uzbekistan, which imposes an indisputable argument that Uzbeks must always be Muslims (Hilgers 2009). In this top-down paradigm of ethno-religious identification, Uzbek deaf people who become JWs or change their religion to one other than Islam, are considered by the Muslim majority as not capable of choosing their own religion independently. In other words, limited access to quality inclusive education, enshrined in SDG4, causes a cycle of marginalization of deaf people. They are treated not as equal citizens but as 'lost souls' (Yusupov 2021: 20) who have no legal or moral capacity to make free decisions when it comes to religion. Consequently, such paternalistic attitudes of the majority Muslim community constrain the freedom of religion of the minority deaf JWs. The progress on achieving

SDG10 is also impacted, as without the meaningful inclusion of all persons with disabilities it is not possible to reduce religious inequalities.

To break the cycle of marginalization of Uzbek deaf JWs, it is necessary to establish partnerships and dialogue between minority and majority religious communities, to nurture tolerance and respect towards each other. Ironically, it was the promotion of religious beliefs and practices of JWs among Uzbek deaf communities, through accessible means of communication and outreach, that served as an impetus for MBU to provide reasonable accommodation at local mosques. Provision of USL interpretation at religious institutions proved to be an important factor in enabling participation and inclusion of deaf people within faith communities. Promoting freedom of religion or belief (FoRB) within the Society of the Deaf of Uzbekistan and the wider deaf community would help to avert conflicts about religious identification among already-marginalized deaf people.

Article 12 of the Convention on the Rights of Persons with Disabilities (CRPD) stipulates 'equal recognition of all persons with disabilities before the law' (CRPD 2006). Uzbekistan finally ratified CRPD in June 2021 but, unfortunately, with the reservation that Article 12 would be substituted by national decision-making mechanisms (Government of Uzbekistan 2021). This means that the legal capacity of persons with disabilities in all aspects of life will not be equal to those of persons without disabilities, despite provisions about the right to freedom of thought, conscience and religion enshrined in the Constitution of Uzbekistan (Government of Uzbekistan 1992). Underrepresented and marginalized groups of people with hearing impairments in Uzbekistan have become objects of spiritual rivalry among the majority Muslim community in its struggle against Christian missionaries (Narzullaev 2018; Sobirov 2019). Although since 2018 many mosques across the country have become accessible for deaf men and women, intolerance towards deaf JWs both within the deaf society and Uzbek society in general resulted in double discrimination. Importantly, in the ongoing COVID-19 pandemic, Uzbek deaf JWs were often deprived of the social support given by Islamic charity organizations, which used religious affiliation as a certain criterion while allocating aid, thus putting Muslim persons with disabilities first and other minority religious groups second. MBU's intervention with the aim to make Uzbek deaf JWs repudiate and return to Islam has promoted intolerance and resulted in double stigma based on disability and religion.

Rather than promoting a human rights-based approach to disability following the CRPD (2006), MBU resorted to audism[2] by making deaf people vocalize to pray, thus treating hearing impairments as human defects

---

[2]   Social attitudes that put the hearing ability above the hearing impairment thus making deaf and hard-of-hearing people inferior to hearing people.

rather than as a part of human diversity (Yusupov 2021: 27). Treating deaf people as objects of their religious mission to bring back 'lost souls', representatives of the MBU perceived JWs as a threat to 'spiritual security', not realizing that their own activity can be framed as 'missionary work' or 'proselytism'. In this context, where the dominant religious group has disproportionate decision-making power, thanks to closely cooperating with the government, the existing legal framework becomes biased against minority religious groups. Thus, what is right and what is wrong, or what is 'missionary work' or what is not, is defined by the powerful religious group rather than the Law on Freedom of Conscience and Religious Organisations (Government of Uzbekistan 1998; Yusupov 2021: 9). In a predominantly Muslim society, it is important to control the majority religious group so that it does not abuse its power to discriminate minority religious groups.

Addressing FoRB for deaf and hard-of-hearing people in Uzbekistan matters for achieving progress on SDG10. Reducing inequalities based on disability and religion is important for addressing the general inequalities that matter for persons with disabilities. This is particularly relevant for the target SDG 10.2, which requires the state parties 'to empower and promote the social, economic and political inclusion of all, irrespective of age, sex, disability, race, ethnicity, origin, religion or economic or other status by 2030' (United Nations 2015). Three questions that any person should think about before implementing a project on redressing disability and religious inequalities are:

1. Who is most marginalized and underrepresented and what is causing such marginalization? Identify the cycle of marginalization.
2. What are the needs and priorities of such underrepresented groups to enable their participation and social inclusion?
3. Where is the fine line between individual FoRB and the group understanding of this concept? What safeguards should be in place to respect individual will, preference and choice of religion and/or belief?

References

Atabaeva, L. (2019) 'Stay neutral': Life of Jehovah's Witnesses in Uzbekistan, Central Asian Bureau for Analytical Reporting, 6 May, https://cabar.asia/en/stay-neutral-life-of-jehovah-s-witnesses-in-uzbekistan (accessed 14 March 2021).

CRPD (2006) *Convention on the Rights of Persons with Disabilities*, New York: United Nations, www.un.org/development/desa/disabilities/convention-on-the-rights-of-persons-with-disabilities/convention-on-the-rights-of-persons-with-disabilities-2.html (accessed 10 May 2023).

Government of Uzbekistan (1992) Constitution of the Republic of Uzbekistan, https://constitution.uz/en (accessed 20 May 2021).

Government of Uzbekistan (1998) Law on freedom of conscience and religious organisations, Pub. L. No. 618–I, https://lex.uz/docs/6117508 (accessed 20 May 2021).

Government of Uzbekistan (2021) Nogironlar huquqlari to'g'risidagi konvensiyani (Nyu-york, 2006-yil 13-dekabr) ratifikatsiya qilish haqida [Ratification of the Convention on the Rights of Persons with Disabilities], New York, 13 December, Pub. L. No. 695, https://lex.uz/docs/-5447413 (accessed 7 February 2022).

Hilgers, I. (2009) *Why Do Uzbeks Have to be Muslims? Exploring Religiosity in the Ferghana Valley*, Münster: LIT Verlag.

Kravchenko, M. (2019) Persecutions of Jehovah's Witnesses in Russia, in E. Clark and D. Vovk (eds) *Religion during the Russian-Ukrainian Conflict*, London: Routledge, pp 226–234.

Mirziyoyev, S. (2017) Address by H.E. Mr. Shavkat Mirziyoyev, the President of the Republic of Uzbekistan at the UNGA-72, presented at the 72nd Regular Session of the UN General Assembly, New York: United Nations, www.un.int/uzbekistan/statements_speeches/address-he-mr-shavkat-mirziyoyev-president-republic-uzbekistan-unga-72 (accessed 20 May 2021).

Narzullaev, O. (2018) Missionary work and proselytism are a threat to our spiritual security, *Muslim*, 3 December, http://old.muslim.uz/index.php/maqolalar/item/11926-missionerlik-va-prozelitizm-ma-navij-khavfsizligimizga-takhdid (accessed 24 July 2020).

Sobirov, I. (2019) Extremism and terrorism wreck development: Missionaryism and proselytism are a means of spiritual and ideological threat, *Muslim*, 22 November, http://old.muslim.uz/index.php/english/tarraiqiyot-kushandalari/item/17689-missionerlik-va-prozelitizm-ma-navij-mafkuravij-ta-did-vositasi (accessed 20 May 2021).

UN (2015) *Transforming Our World: The 2030 Agenda for Sustainable Development*, New York: United Nations Development Programme.

Yusupov, D. (2021) Deaf Uzbek Jehovah's Witnesses: The case of intersection of disability, ethnic and religious inequalities in Post-Soviet Uzbekistan, CREID Working Paper 8, Coalition for Religious Equality and Inclusive Development, Brighton: Institute of Development Studies, https://opendocs.ids.ac.uk/opendocs/handle/20.500.12413/16710 (accessed 25 January 2022).

25

What Is Distinctive about Religious Inequality? Challenges and Opportunities for Development Policy

Michael Woolcock

The three substantive papers in this section – two case studies (from Uzbekistan and Pakistan) and an analytical piece – remind us that inequalities can take different forms that may then compound their respective unwelcome effects on human welfare. In addition to economic inequalities, which may reduce access to material opportunities (for example, adequate nutrition and effective education) with enduring effects across one's lifetime, those who are from particular social groups can suffer all the more from sustained discrimination (World Bank 2005): they may be denied jobs for which they are well qualified, consigned only to the most menial or dangerous tasks; they may be refused basic services to which they are entitled by right; and they may be targeted for exclusion, harassment and physical violence (even genocide). What difference does it make, if any, both analytically and from a policy response perspective, when the basis for this type of social inequality is religious – that is, when one identifies with, or engages in the practices of, a particular faith-based community (or several, or none at all[1]) as opposed to a particular nationality, racial, occupational, caste, gender or

---

[1]   For example, atheists in Saudi Arabia, where it is normative for essentially everyone to have some form of religious identity. In this context, to overtly declare having no such identity – and to explicitly reject religious precepts of any kind – is more politically consequential than being a member of a recognized non-Islamic faith; indeed, taking such a stance is literally considered the equivalent of posing a 'terrorist threat'.

disability group? Why might it be especially difficult for *religious* inequality to be redressed by development 'policy'?

These questions could be answered in a number of ways, but for present purposes I seek to do so by engaging briefly with four development policy domains within which the distinctive salience of 'religion' as a basis for durable inequality (Tilly 1998) becomes apparent, presenting unique challenges but also potentially unique opportunities. First, 'religion' presents unique measurement issues. Prudent and effective 'policy' of course requires an empirical foundation on which resource allocation and accurate 'targeting' can rest. In modern life, our prevailing administrative systems take it as axiomatic that 'religion' is both a discrete demographic category and a discrete realm of life – we are Jewish, Catholic, Buddhist, Muslim or 'None', for example; more generally, secular modernity conspires most to regard their faith (or spirituality or lack thereof) as largely a private or personal matter that is kept separate from professional, political, economic and scientific life (Taylor 2007).

This is not always how today's modern lives were lived and not how our distinct social categories (and associated boundaries) were historically understood. Prior to modernity, there were few such boundaries between different realms of life, with (what we now call) 'religion' being instead an integrated realm of morality and behaviour, not – as it is so often regarded today – a prescribed set of creedal 'beliefs' to which one does or does not give intellectual assent (Harrison 2015). Many communities around the world, however, to this day, retain a vastly more holistic understanding of how life is lived, experienced and understood – something which most large-scale surveys (such as the census) cannot apprehend, requiring individuals, by design, to literally 'tick boxes' corresponding to their residence, gender, race, nationality, date and place of birth, occupation, marital status and religion.[2] Indeed, as Dirks (2001) has shown, the introduction by the British Raj of the first census in India, by virtue of requiring individuals to self-identify as a member of a specific caste, created (and subsequently reinforced) the notion of caste as a fixed rather than relatively more fluid category, thus rendering it both a basis for policy 'targeting' but also political mobilization.[3] In certain

---

[2]   On a related front, this tendency to collapse heterogenous articulations and meanings into singular categories can be seen in a recent high-profile study of 'folklore' (Michalopoulos and Xue 2021), in which the textual content of thousands of complex anthropological fables from around the world are assessed using machine learning techniques to discern their subsequent economic 'impact'.

[3]   See Hostetler (2021) for a related discussion of how, during the colonial period (and still today), the introduction of maps modernized space, the introduction of clocks and calendars modernized time, the introduction of money and contracts modernized exchange and knowledge, and so on. I stress, needless to say, that I am *not* making an argument for abandoning maps, clocks, calendars, money and formal legal procedures but rather noting

developing countries (and for certain communities in many places), the very act of trying to use 'policy' to redress religious inequality, in other words, requires rendering 'religion' in a distinctly modern way that itself may be a key part of the problem.

The second policy challenge of responding effectively to religious inequality is that governments, even or perhaps especially democracies, are structured to respond to the concerns of majorities – and those most likely to be affected by religious inequality are those who are members of religious minorities. Just as middle- and high-income democracies may struggle to focus on the concerns of their poorest citizens – since, to be re-elected, the ruling party will seek to articulate policies appealing to at least 51 per cent of the population – so too may those who are members of religious minorities, such as Christians in Pakistan, inherently struggle to forge a broad-enough constituency to support their cause. Here the appeal to upholding basic human rights for all (to which a country is a signatory) and principles of universal inclusion become vital, as does the role of domestic and international advocacy groups in stressing that the legitimacy of government actions stem not only from their legal authority but their demonstrated compliance with shared, perhaps even global, moral norms (Tyler 2006).[4] The current crisis in global democracy puts further strain on those seeking to engage domestic politics with (or on behalf of) religious minorities.[5]

A third 'policy' challenge accompanying efforts to redress religious inequality is that any policy that has already been somehow carefully specified (first challenge) and adequately supported politically (second challenge) is likely to be exceedingly complex to implement and evaluate. For example, the very act of declaring all religions and their members moral, legal and political equals is likely to immediately require formally defining what counts

---

that, as one of humanity's most ancient and widespread social practices, 'religion' is also modernized – thus ontologically changed – by the enactment of development policies, sometimes in ways far from being 'sociologically benign' (Bayly 2011: 50).

[4] Prevailing moral norms in a particular country may still be hostile to the interests of minority religious groups, but at least they can in principle be contrasted with broader (even regional or global) norms as a strategy for changing them. Such was the basis, for example, on which the long-standing practice of foot-binding of women in China came to a relatively rapid end in the early twentieth century (see Mackie 1996; on mechanisms that change honour codes more broadly, see Appiah 2011).

[5] The Swedish research group 'Varieties of Democracy' (V-Dem), having classified India as an 'electoral autocracy' in 2021, estimates that only 13 per cent of the current world population, across a mere 34 countries, lives in a fully democratic country, the lowest global average level since 1989 (Boese et al 2022). Today, more than twice as many countries are becoming more autocratic (33) than more democratic (15); around 70 per cent of the people in the world now live in an autocracy.

as a religion and religious behaviour. Are the views of cults, hate groups or militias 'protected' if they are framed as sacred expressions of their religion? Affirmative answers to such questions may then be invoked, paradoxically, to formally exclude or persecute those deemed to have a 'false' (but otherwise behaviourally benign) religion. The passage of such a policy may also have the unintended effect of eliciting strong pushback from those threatened by the invigorated 'empowerment' of minority religious groups, echoing ways in which, in certain contexts, those espousing established patriarchal views have sought to counter, sometimes violently, the political, vocational and social advancement of women.[6]

More generally, 'religion' and religious claims frequently operate in an epistemological space rather different from that invoked to determine optimal tax rates, minimum wages and import duties, where 'normal social science' can more readily inform public debate and identify where and how trade-offs might be made. Contending claims pertaining to the sacredness (or profanity) of particular places, texts, objects, clothing, people or behaviours, however, cannot be resolved empirically; any resolution is likely to require extensive dialogue and deliberation, and prior agreement on an overarching set of principles and procedures – forged by the participants themselves – by which it might be sought. In short, public policy is generally formed and formally assessed in one epistemological space, but its realization in the case of religion is likely implemented and experienced in another. Put differently, in the interaction between 'policy' and 'religion', the forms and underlying sources of legitimacy informing what counts as a question and what counts as an answer can be fundamentally different.

A fourth (and concluding) challenge is that identification with a particular religion may or may not be one of choice. For certain religions and in certain countries, entry into and exit from a particular religious group or social identity may be relatively costless (administratively, legally, socially, politically), with such actions widely regarded as a matter of personal discretion. In others, however, the opposite may be true: ethnic, national and religious identities may be inseparable; 'exit' may be legally impossible (for example, if one's birth certificate explicitly states one's religion); and one's very name itself may clearly convey not only one's religion but one's status within that religion. Indeed, in extreme cases, apostasy (changing one's religion) may be a criminal offence. Even so, the quintessentially 'social' nature of religious identity and practice means that policies enacted to promote religious inclusion at a particular point in time may not apply to the same (or the same number of) people at a subsequent point in time. Moreover, the policies themselves, by their very existence as public statements

---

[6]   On this phenomenon, see Berry (2015) on the plight of women in Rwanda.

of political intent, may provide a shifting set of incentives and imperatives for people to join, remain in or leave a particular religious community – or if these identities or affiliations can't be changed, may create corresponding conditions that subject them to deeply consequential forms of heightened discrimination or retribution.

Conclusion

If development is understood as a four-fold transformation of the economy (enhanced productivity), polity (rule by consent), public administration (professional independence and merit) and society (inclusion and shared national identity),[7] then it is the deep challenges associated with attaining 'progress' on this latter aspect that are at once the least appreciated but perhaps the most complex and consequential. And within the 'social' realm itself, the effects of modernity – instantiated via today's development projects and policies – on the nature and salience of religious identity, 'belief' and practice are especially vexing; in their own right (as discussed before) and because they interact and intersect with the other three realms to generate effects playing out across spaces ranging from individual experience and employment opportunities to Supreme Court decisions and the dynamics of international relations. Tensions between the quest for redressing religious inequality and the sites of developmental engagement manifest themselves in everyday matters (clothing, purity norms), in complicated social practices (education, health, debt), fundamental rights (livelihoods, security, voting) and the jurisdictional 'separation' (or fusion) of state and religious authority.[8] There are few, if any, technical fixes for resolving these conundrums – only what participants themselves, and their leaders, negotiate.

Affirming social equality and inclusion irrespective of one's religion or beliefs (or lack thereof) is at once an ancient and modern challenge – and thus will likely remain so long into the future. Efforts to redress these concerns through 'policy' run the constant risk of compounding rather than resolving underlying problems, but inaction is itself a policy response. Either way, these risks can be lowered if policy initiatives emerge from sources of authority and antecedent processes – that is, the administrative procedures by which and the specific groups by whom consensus is forged and enacted (Rao 2019) – that are broadly regarded as equitable and legitimate. As important as the technical aspects of the policy process surely are, equal attention must

---

[7]   See Pritchett et al (2013).
[8]   See Tadros (2020) for specific examples as they pertain to women from minority religious communities.

be given to creating and protecting the deliberative space within which this type of dialogue takes place (Gibson and Woolcock 2008; Woolcock 2023).

References

Appiah, K.A. (2011) *The Honor Code: How Moral Revolutions Happen*, New York: W.W. Norton & Company.

Bayly, C.A. (2011) Indigenous and colonial origins of comparative economic development: The case of colonial India and Africa, in C.A. Bayly, V. Rao, S. Szreter and M. Woolcock (eds) *History, Historians, and Development Policy: A Necessary Dialogue*, Manchester: Manchester University Press, 39–64.

Berry, M.E. (2015) When 'bright futures' fade: Paradoxes of women's empowerment in Rwanda, *Signs: Journal of Women in Culture and Society* 41.1: 1–27.

Boese, V.A., Alizada, N., Lundstedt, M., Morrison, K., Natsika, N., Sato, Y. et al (2022) Autocratization changing nature? Democracy report 2022, Guttenburg: Varieties of Democracy Institute.

Dirks, N. (2001) *Castes of Mind: Colonialism and the Making of Modern India*, Princeton, NJ: Princeton University Press.

Gibson, C. and Woolcock, M. (2008) Empowerment, deliberative development, and local-level politics in Indonesia: Participatory projects as a source of countervailing power, *Studies in Comparative International Development* 43.2: 151–180.

Harrison, P. (2015) *The Territories of Science and Religion*, Chicago, IL: University of Chicago Press.

Hostetler, L. (2021) Mapping, registering, and ordering: Time, space and knowledge, in P. Fibiger Bang, C.A. Bayly and W. Scheidel (eds) *The Oxford World History of Empire: Volume One: The Imperial Experience*, New York: Oxford University Press, 288–317.

Mackie, G. (1996) Ending footbinding and infibulation: A convention account, *American Sociological Review* 61: 999–1017.

Michalopoulos, S. and Meng Xue, M. (2021) Folklore, *The Quarterly Journal of Economics* 136.4: 1993–2046.

Pritchett, L., Woolcock, M. and Andrews, M. (2013) Looking like a state: Techniques of persistent failure in state capability for implementation, *Journal of Development Studies* 49.1: 1–18.

Rao, V. (2019) Process-policy and outcome-policy: Rethinking how to address poverty and inequality, *Daedalus* 148.3: 181–190.

Tadros, M. (2020) Invisible targets of hatred: Socioeconomically excluded women from religious minority backgrounds, CREID Working Paper 2, Brighton: Coalition for Religious Equality and Inclusive Development, Institute for Development Studies.

Taylor, C. (2007) *A Secular Age*, Cambridge, MA: Harvard University Press.

Tilly, C. (1998) *Durable Inequality*, Berkeley, CA: University of California Press.

Tyler, T. (2006) Psychological perspectives on legitimacy and legitimation, *Annual Review of Psychology* 57: 375–400.

Woolcock, M. (2023) *International Development: Navigating Humanity's Greatest Challenge*, Cambridge: Polity Press.

World Bank (2005) *World Development Report 2006: Equity and Development*, New York: Oxford University Press.

PART VII

Cities and Communities

26

Religious Inequalities, Inclusive Cities and Sustainable Development

Francesca Giliberto

Introduction

The crucial role of cities and communities in achieving sustainable development has been recognized in global development agendas. These include the 2030 Agenda for Sustainable Development adopted by the United Nations in 2015 and the Quito Declaration on Sustainable Cities and Human Settlements for All, also known as the New Urban Agenda, adopted during the UN Conference on Housing and Sustainable Urban Development in 2016. However, current research and approaches to sustainable urban development overlook societal issues related to the persistence of inequalities and exclusionary practices in urban contexts, particularly in the Global South.

   This chapter sheds light on the correlation between religious inequalities and the achievement of sustainable urban development. It discusses how reducing religious inequalities and fostering diverse and meaningful participation can contribute to more inclusive and sustainable cities – a largely unexplored topic. The chapter is divided into two main sections. The first introduces contemporary urban challenges and the measures proposed by the most relevant developmental agendas. The second examines how progress towards inclusive urban development is affected by the persistence of religious inequalities. Finally, it discusses the potential role of heritage, mentioned only once in the 2030 Agenda as part of Sustainable Development Goal (SDG) 11, to promote human-rights-based and people-centred urban development.

Towards inclusive and sustainable cities in the twenty-first century

Current challenges for sustainable urban development

For the first time in history, more than half of the global population live in cities. Urban environments, when well planned, are attractive centres for employment, business development, innovation, creativity, cultural interactions and greater societal freedoms (Florida 2011). This urban migration trend and its consequences for societies and places have been so considerable that some have called the twenty-first century 'the urban age' (Brenner and Schmid 2014: 1). It is estimated that urbanization will rise from 56.2 per cent to 60.4 per cent by 2030, with notable differences between geographical regions (UN-Habitat 2020: xvi). In fact, 96 per cent of urban growth is predicted to occur in East Asia, South Asia and Africa, and mainly in three countries (China, India and Nigeria).

Although urban transformations vary worldwide, cities have become central to global discussions around sustainable development, which have been mainly led by UN agencies. In this framework, intergovernmental organizations, national and local governments, policy makers, non-governmental organizations, academics and professionals, the private sector and representatives of indigenous and local communities have contributed to discussions tackling a wide range of global (urban) challenges. These include urbanization and migration trends, increasing demand for housing, infrastructure and services and unsustainable use of land and other resources (UN 2016b).

Affecting particularly the Global South, these urban changes have often resulted in the deterioration of urban quality, the proliferation of slums and informal settlements and the lack of essential services, like water supply and sanitation (Grubbauer and Mader 2021). They have also contributed to increasing multiple forms of poverty and inequalities, social exclusion, urban fragmentation and spatial segregation (Keivani 2010; Espino 2015). These challenges have been further exacerbated by the COVID-19 pandemic, humanitarian crises and rising climate change. In this context, the most vulnerable communities and individuals have often been the most negatively affected (UN 2016a). As a result of the COVID-19 pandemic, religious minorities have been further marginalized, discriminated against and scapegoated (Morthorst 2020).

The way forward: the 2030 Agenda and the New Urban Agenda

The 2030 Agenda and the New Urban Agenda represent significant milestones in global efforts towards sustainable urban development. Among the 17 SDGs proposed in the 2030 Agenda, SDG 11 aims to 'make cities and human settlements inclusive, safe, resilient and sustainable'. It emphasizes the need to implement participatory and integrated policies for urban planning and management, and for national and regional development. It also sets other development targets to improve the built environment (including housing and slums) and infrastructure and transportation systems to make them more accessible, safe, affordable, resource efficient and climate resilient. All this pays special attention to 'leave no one behind', including the poorest, and to empower women, girls and the most vulnerable people, including children and youth, persons with disabilities, people living with HIV/AIDS, older persons, indigenous peoples, migrants, refugees and internally displaced persons (UN 2015: Art. 6, 23).

The 2030 Agenda also recognizes, for the first time in a global development agenda, the important role that heritage can play in fostering urban sustainability (Hosagrahar et al 2016). Goal 11 explicitly mentions the relevance of heritage for development, stating how efforts are required 'to strengthen the protection and safeguarding of the world's cultural and natural heritage' (Target 11.4). The New Urban Agenda reaffirmed the global commitment to sustainable urban development as a critical step for the implementation and localization of the 2030 Agenda, and SDG 11 in particular, in an inclusive, integrated and coordinated manner (UN, 2016b: Art. 9). It aims to 'achieve cities and human settlements where all persons are able to enjoy equal rights and opportunities, as well as their fundamental freedoms' without discrimination of any kind (UN, 2016b: Art. 11–12).

Religious inequalities, heritage and sustainable (urban) development

Reflections on progress towards the achievement of SDG11

The degree to which global agendas towards urban sustainability take into consideration and promote social inclusion is still not prioritized compared to other (mainly environmental) considerations (Reeves 2005; Mirzoev et al 2022). The majority of publications on contemporary challenges for sustainable urban development focus on ecological and technical aspects and/or on issues related to spatial planning and urban mobility, although concepts of people-centred development (or sustainable human development) have achieved more prominence in the last 20 years (Zavratnik et al 2020; Carley et al 2001; Mahadevia 2001). These concepts are not only important for social considerations but also for other economic and environmental dimensions of sustainable urban development (Jenks and Jones 2010).

According to the Quito Declaration, urban development, in order to be sustainable, must enable full and meaningful participation of all population groups, without discrimination based on race, religion, ethnicity or socio-economic status, and the improvement of their quality of life (UN 2016b: Art. 11, 26, 42). Moreover, the 2030 Agenda specifies how it should support the creation of a society based on respect for all human rights and fundamental freedoms, and the promotion of pluralism and respect for diversity and equality (UN 2015: Art. 11, 19, 26, 40). Nevertheless, these two agendas pay insufficient attention to religious inequalities and religious minorities, who are often neglected in sustainable development discourses and are particularly vulnerable to discrimination (Mir et al 2020: 1–3; Tadros and Sabates-Wheeler 2020: 19). Neglecting religion, and religious inequalities, in urban discourses can undermine the development of place-sensitive (or community-sensitive) urban policies and strategies, and the achievement of sustainability objectives, particularly in terms of inclusion, equality, diversity and social justice (Narayanan 2015: 7).

A growing field of literature has recently explored the relationship between religious inequalities, Freedom of Religion or Belief (FoRB) and development, particularly through the work of the Coalition for Religious Equality and Inclusive Development (CREID) at the Institute of Development Studies. However, the interconnection between religious inequalities, FoRB and inclusive and sustainable cities is largely unexplored, with notable exceptions. Some scholars have explained how religion and beliefs support the physical construction and transformation of cities and are fundamental components of people's sense of place and cultural and urban identity, contributing to community cohesion, sense of ownership and belonging (Reeves 2005: 13; Greed 2016; Narayanan 2016). Others have explained how the presence of more powerful religious expressions and dominant religious identities can lead to the ghettoization of minorities and urban degradation, the proliferation of slums and informal settlements and the systematic marginalization, if not oppression, of minorities (Narayanan 2015: 4). Ongoing processes of discrimination and exclusion of certain individuals and communities based on their religion or belief – often intersecting with other aspects like gender, ethnicity, economic status and/or disability – can undermine their 'right to the city', which, according to UN-Habitat (2020: 147), means that 'all people ... should have equal opportunities and access to urban resources, services and goods'.

Religious heritage as a catalyst for sustainable cities?

Religion, spirituality and beliefs also influence how cities are used and shaped through various forms of urban heritage (Narayanan 2016; Singh et al 2020). Multifaceted heritage manifestations need to be adequately interpreted, preserved, managed and enhanced by policy makers, academics, practitioners and communities to make cities more sustainable. Particular attention needs to be paid to different forms of (religious) heritage and the plurality of associated values (Giliberto 2021a). Heritage does not refer only to historic buildings, monuments, archaeological sites and other tangible assets. It also includes urban spaces, entire historic cities and urban landscapes, and many intangible manifestations, including social practices, rituals and festive events, community knowledge and practices, performing arts and oral traditions and expressions (UNESCO 2003, 2011). Nevertheless, the definition and implementation of heritage policies and practices is often a selective and contested process, excluding voices diverging from official narratives and belonging to religious minorities and marginalized stakeholders that are often ignored or even silenced (Singh 2008; Silverman 2011; Monier 2021).

In this context, heritage – tangible and intangible, cultural and natural – can be effectively mobilized to achieve SDG11, and improve the quality of life of religious minorities. Several publications have shown the opportunities of harnessing heritage for sustainable urban development, highlighting its crucial role for social inclusion and cohesion, urban liveability, sense of identity and belonging, people's wellbeing and community resilience (Bandarin et al 2011; Labadi and Logan 2016). For instance, the shared use of urban areas, streets and open spaces can stimulate interaction, social exchange and integration between different communities (Labadi et al 2021: 76).

Other scholars have highlighted the potential of heritage practices to develop people-centred and human-rights based approaches (Silverman and Ruggles 2007; Wijesuriya et al 2017; Rosetti et al 2022). In fact, a participatory process for the interpretation, conservation, management and enhancement of the plurality of (religious) heritage values can be a catalyst for minorities' inclusion in decision making, and the implementation of more inclusive urban policies and practices (Giliberto 2021b: 46–49). A research project led by Newcastle University (UK) in Istanbul, for example, demonstrated how giving a central role to diverse urban communities in heritage interpretation can support the recognition of heritage assets excluded from official narratives (Giliberto 2021a: 4). This process allows the concept of heritage itself to be rethought more inclusively, while also opening new ways for local authorities and managers to engage with urban communities.

Heritage's contribution to fostering more inclusive and sustainable cities was recognized in the New Urban Agenda, which highlights its role in 'rehabilitating and revitalizing urban areas and in strengthening social participation and the exercise of citizenship' (UN 2016b: Art. 38, 125). However, the 2030 Agenda fails to recognize the complexity of heritage's contribution to inclusive cities and communities and sustainable development in general, by focusing solely on its protection and reflecting a rather limited approach to heritage for development (Labadi et al 2021: 12). Moreover, progress towards SDG 11 is measured only through per capita expenditure on cultural and natural heritage. While evaluation indicators are often narrowly based in economics because they can be more easily measured, this focus on the economic dimension does not capture the most relevant impacts, mainly related to cultural and social dimensions (Giliberto 2022).

Conclusion

There can be no sustainable cities where individuals and communities are left behind or marginalized because of their religion, faith, belief or spirituality. However, despite global efforts for promoting more inclusive and sustainable cities in the last 20 years, the implications of religious inequalities have been overlooked and not yet fully understood. Consequently, exclusionary practices, inequalities and marginalization persist in urban policies and practices. It is crucial to foster meaningful and inclusive participation and take concrete action, involving all stakeholders, and understand and respond to their needs, particularly those of the most vulnerable and marginalized. Much still needs to be done to develop meaningful, diverse, inclusive and sustainable ways for urban governance, planning and development. In this context, this chapter showed how religious heritage can be a catalyst to promote people-centred and human rights-based approaches in urban conservation, planning and governance, and make cities more inclusive and sustainable. However, further research is needed on how to implement this approach locally.

References

Bandarin, F., Hosagrahar, J. and Albernaz, F.S. (2011) Why development needs culture, *Journal of Cultural Heritage Management and Sustainable Development* 1.1: 15–25.

Brenner, N. and Schmid, C. (2014). The 'Urban Age' in question, *International Journal of Urban and Regional Research* 38.3: 1–25.

Carley, M., Jenkins, P. and Smith, H. (2001) *Urban Development and Civil Society: The Role of Communities in Sustainable Cities*, Abingdon: Routledge.

Espino, N.A. (2015) *Building the Inclusive City: Theory and Practice for Confronting Urban Segregation*, London: Routledge.

Florida, R. (2011) *The Rise of the Creative Class, Revisited*, New York: Basic Books.

Giliberto, F. (2021a) *Inclusive Development for Sustainable Cities*, Leeds: University of Leeds and UK National Commission for UNESCO.

Giliberto, F. (2021b) *Heritage for Global Challenges. A Research Report by PRAXIS: Arts and Humanities for Global Development,* Leeds: University of Leeds.

Giliberto, F. (2022) *Evaluating the Impacts of Cultural Heritage for Sustainable Development,* Leeds: University of Leeds and UK National Commission for UNESCO.

Greed, C. (2016) Religion and sustainable urban planning: 'If you can't count it, or won't count it, it doesn't count', *Sustainable Development* 24: 154–162.

Grubbauer, M. and Mader, P. (2021) Housing microfinance and housing financialisation in a global perspective, *International Journal of Housing Policy* 21.4: 465–483.

Hosagrahar, J., Soule, J., Girard, L.F. and Potts, A. (2016) Cultural heritage, the UN Sustainable Development Goals, and the new urban agenda, *BDC – Bollettino del Centro Calza Bini* 16.1: 37–54.

Jenks, M. and Jones, C. (eds) (2010) *Dimensions of the Sustainable City 2,* London: Springer.

Keivani, R. (2010) A review of the main challenges to urban sustainability, *International Journal of Urban Sustainable Development* 1.1–2: 5–16.

Labadi, S. and Logan, W. (eds) (2016) *Urban Heritage, Development and Sustainability: International Frameworks, National and Local Governance,* Abingdon: Routledge.

Labadi, S., Giliberto, F., Rosetti, I., Shetabi, L. and Yildirim, E. (2021) *Heritage and the Sustainable Development Goals: Policy Guidance for Heritage and Development Actors,* Paris: ICOMOS.

Mahadevia, D. (2001) Sustainable urban development in India: An inclusive perspective, *Development in Practice* 11.2–3: 242–259.

Mir, G., Karlsen, S., Mitullah, W., Bhojani, U., Uzochukwu, B., Okeke, C. et al (2020) *Achieving SDG 10: A Global Review of Public Service Inclusion Strategies for Ethnic and Religious Minorities,* Report, Geneva: The United Nations Research Institute for Social Development.

Mirzoev, T., Tull, K.I., Winn, N., Mir, G., King, N.V., Wright, J.M. et al (2022) Systematic review of the role of social inclusion within sustainable urban developments, *International Journal of Sustainable Development & World Ecology* 29.1: 3–17.

Monier, E. (2021) Whose heritage counts? Narratives of coptic people's heritage, CREID Working Paper 11, Brighton: Coalition for Religious Equality and Inclusive Development, Institute of Development Studies.

Morthorst, L. (2020) Scapegoating of religious minorities during COVID-19: Is history repeating itself?, *Coalition for Religious Equality and Inclusive Development,* 29 June.

Narayanan, Y. (2015) *Religion, Heritage and the Sustainable City: Hinduism and Urbanisation in Jaipur*, Abingdon: Routledge.

Narayanan, Y. (2016) Religion, urbanism, and sustainable cities in South Asia, in Y. Narayanan (ed) *Religion and Urbanism: Reconceptualising Sustainable Cities for South Asia*, Abingdon: Routledge: 1–24.

Reeves, D. (2005) *Planning for Diversity: Policy and Planning in a World of Difference*, London: Routledge.

Rosetti, I., Bertrand Cabral, C., Pereira Roders, A., Jacobs, M. and Albuquerque, R. (2022) Heritage and sustainability: Regulating participation, *Sustainability* 14: 1674.

Silverman, H. (ed) (2011) *Contested Cultural Heritage. Religion, Nationalism, Erasure, and Exclusion in a Global World*, New York: Springer Science + Business Media, LLC.

Silverman, H and Ruggles, D.F. (eds) (2007) *Cultural Heritage and Human Rights*, New York: Springer Science + Business Media, LLC.

Singh, R.P.B. (2008) The contestation of heritage: The enduring importance of religion, in B. Graham and P. Howard (eds) *The Routledge Research Companion to Heritage and Identity*, London: Routledge.

Singh, R.P.B., Kumar, S. and Rana, P.S. (2020) UN SDGs and context of holy-heritage cities in India: A study of Ayodhya and Varanasi, in S. Sahdev, R. Singh and M. Kumar (eds) *Geoecology of Landscape Dynamics: Advances in Geographical and Environmental Sciences*, Singapore: Springer.

Tadros, M. and Sabates-Wheeler, R. (2020) Inclusive development: Beyond need, not creed, CREID Working Paper 1, Brighton: Coalition for Religious Equality and Inclusive Development, Institute of Development Studies.

UN (2015) *Transforming our World: The 2030 Agenda for Sustainable Development*, New York: United Nations.

UN (2016a) *Leaving No One Behind: The Imperative of Inclusive Development. Report on the World Social Situation 2016*, New York: United Nations.

UN (2016b) *New Urban Agenda. Quito Declaration on Sustainable Cities and Human Settlements for All*, Adopted during the United Nations Conference on Housing and Sustainable Urban Development (HABITAT III) in Quito, 17–20 October.

UNESCO (2003) *Convention for the Safeguarding of the Intangible Cultural Heritage*, Paris: UNESCO.

UNESCO (2011) *Recommendation on the Historic Urban Landscape*, Paris: UNESCO.

UN-Habitat (2020) *World Cities Report 2020: The Value of Sustainable Urbanization*, Nairobi: UN-Habitat.

Wijesuriya, G., Thompson, J. and Court, S. (2017) People-centred approaches: Engaging communities and developing capacities for managing heritage, in G. Chitty (ed) *Heritage, Conservation and Communities. Engagement, Participation and Capacity Building*, Abingdon: Routledge: 34–49.

Zavratnik, V., Podjed, D., Trilar, J., Hlebec, N., Kos, A. and Stojmenova Duh, E. (2020) Sustainable and community-centred development of smart cities and villages, *Sustainability* 12.10: 3961.

27

ISIS Attack on the Divinely Protected City of Mosul: A Terrorist Attack on Diversity and Peace

Omar Mohammed

A city of history and coexistence

For centuries, the city of Mosul created and maintained a unique cultural identity. It has endured periods of bloodshed and extreme change in its structure, rule and architecture. Mosul has experienced almost 300 invasions by various foreign nations and empires since its founding almost 4,000 years ago. Nevertheless, it has always protected its cultural heritage and identity through language, literature or visual memory. Since its destruction by the so-called Islamic State of Iraq and Syria (ISIS), much research has focused on its tangible heritage without considering the local Mosuli identity. Space is the context through which we can examine the formation of time and ideas. Arguably, history functions as a means of communication when people can engage daily with their inherited surroundings. The recent invasion by ISIS and its subsequent defeat have left the city with staggering losses of both tangible and intangible heritage. Furthermore, since this destruction, hundreds of articles have treated and discussed culture as a material object disconnected from its main function of producing the city's identity.

Mosul and the ancient city of Nineveh have long lived with a collective memory based on the biblical story of Jonah, the prophet. Mosul became known, like Nineveh, as the city of Jonah, Madinat Younis. Jonah is said to have arrived in Nineveh and called on its people to accept his message. The city took a few days to respond, doing so just in time before God declared punishment against them. When the people accepted the message, they were granted divine protection. This is the story parents and grandparents traditionally tell children. The significance of the story and the role it played in shaping the social character of Mosul is of high importance in understanding the city. Jonah's historical site (or as it is locally known, Mazar Al Nabi Younis) is also one of the few places that represents the city's entire history, and according to several historical narratives, the place where Jews, Christians and Muslims lived together. It is also constructed over the royal palace of Esarhaddon, the Assyrian King (681–669 BC). It is a site visited by all the people of Mosul, regardless of their faith, ethnicity or background. You can rarely find a person in Mosul who does not have a story to tell about Jonah: the city prides itself on its divine protection. Whether Christian, Muslim, Yazidi or Jew, they all have this in common; even during economic crisis, people responded: '[there is] no need to panic or to worry, this is the city of Jonah, we will survive, and this too shall pass'. This sentiment has been kept alive in the city for centuries.

Brutality, history and scholarship

When ISIS occupied Mosul in June 2014 (and up to its defeat in 2017), Mosuli people used these exact words – no one could harm the city, for it has its guardian, Jonah. The city and its people hoped that the brutal attack of ISIS would end, but the unexpected happened. ISIS began systematically targeting the roots of confidence in the city. Their first target was the site of Jonah. When the people saw ISIS destroying the site, they realized the brutality of the intentions of the group to uproot Mosul's history. At this moment, Mosulis realized that if ISIS were capable of destroying this divinely protected place, they were capable of doing anything. The attack explained the doctrine of horror ISIS brought to the city. The attack did not only destroy a physical building, but the history, memory and social code of the city.

How does an ethnographer and historian write about violence against the history of his own city? How can he make sense of violent acts, for himself and for his readers, without compromising its sheer excess and its meaning-defying core? How can he remain a scholarly observer when the country of his birth is engulfed by terror? These were the questions raised by Errol Valentine Daniel (1996) in his book *Charred Lullabies*. His words seemed meaningful to me while I was writing this chapter. It is almost impossible to make sense of the events that have occurred in Mosul in recent years. The conceptual formation of the social fabric and heritage of any old city, and specifically of Mosul, with its hundreds of visible sites representing different historical periods, can be understood through various factors: the urban structure of its space; the connection between urban structure and the historical narratives on how the space was created (Khoury 1997; Tabbaa

2002); the interaction among its inhabitants, their daily lives and the visual memory they have established through various factors and activities that have shaped – on several bases – the narrative of their past and present; and the language, which significantly influences the formation of the historical story regarding space, time and people. Language becomes the main factor for understanding heritage development and its place in people's visual memory and historical narrative. Major historical works may not give us a clear understanding of Mosul's cultural heritage; everyday proverbs tell us how people engage with their heritage. Since this chapter does not address the role of the linguistic heritage of Mosul, the author will only use that indicator to explain the connection between space and people in relation to cultural heritage.

The history of the city, home to more than 600 mosques, tens of ancient churches, and dozens of synagogues, is deeply rooted in the narrative that ISIS aimed to destroy. Once it had occupied the city in 2014, ISIS began to carry out the systematic destruction of Mosul's identity. First, its leaders forced the city's non-Muslim inhabitants to flee, destroying their monuments to remove their heritage from the city's history. Then came the destruction of its ancient Assyrian monuments and cultural sites. After this brutality against Mosul's non-Islamic past, the invaders turned to the Muslim community; they began systematically destroying Islamic archaeological sites, as well as museums, libraries and manuscripts. They also took aim at Mosul's linguistic heritage. Where the city once had a rich, peaceful vocabulary of everyday words and phrases, the group implemented a vocabulary of violence and social division. We began to hear *diwan* instead of *wizara* (ministry), *hisba* instead of *shurta* (police), *Bayt al-mal* (house of money) instead of *al-Bank al-Markazi* (central bank). New labels were applied to the social classes: *ansar* (helpers) were the 'local' ISIS members and fighters; *muhajirun* (immigrants) were the ISIS foreign fighters; and *munasirun* (allies) were those non-members who supported and welcomed ISIS. Opponents of ISIS who were jihadists were called *mukhalifun* (transgressors). Finally, *āmma* (commoners) were the lower classes who opposed ISIS.

Mosul's markets had been established and divided by profession. Each market was named after the primary profession practised there. Some markets also took their names from the historical sites that make up the heart of the *suq*, such as *Suq Al Nuri*, which refers to the Al-Nuri Mosque. Other markets were connected to *waqfiyyat* (endowments) or *kuttabs* (elementary schools), or to a particular family that owned the land (Chalabi 1931; Al-Ali Beg 2005). Mosul's old markets' rise and growth contributed to a complex identity for the city and its people. Around the markets were the centres of the successive governments of the city. They also served as the political heart where the old and notable families of the city resided. This is also where the oldest churches of the various Christian sects were found and the heart of the Islamic cultural heritage. The markets of Old Mosul served as the heart of the city's unique coexistence and diversity. However, this diversity depended on economic collaboration based on the presence of each group's historical sites. All were merged in the markets to serve their cultural and economic interests, as the markets proved to be an important example where people could collaborate and work together. When the common interest was achieved, the markets became a space of manifestation, to call upon the people to return home and to demonstrate their ability to recover from a brutal war.

Conclusion

Societies and cities work in a very complicated and sensitive yet fragile system. It might seem strong, but it could also collapse at any moment if it is not continuously maintained. Unlike technical machines, where an error can be immediately flagged if it stops working, social structures take a very long time to realize errors, often when it is too late. In Mosul, most of the damage to the social structure and systems was caused by ISIS and the dysfunctional political system over decades. Nevertheless, we must acknowledge the Mosuli's fair share of responsibility that led to the collapse of the old system of trust. Over the decades, Mosul went through several devastating events that changed its systems of meaning, and the people stopped asking questions and became incapable of discussing sensitive topics. No question was raised when the city lost one of its important communities, the Jews, in 1948. This inability to reconcile with the past and to raise critical questions had heavily damaged the capability of the city to generate and modify its cultural space and the roots of its philosophical coherence, which is why, when ISIS arrived, the space was ready to collapse.

In order for Mosul to restore its system of meaning and trust, huge efforts need to be made, using all available methods to reconstruct its social code through culture, music, art and most importantly, visual art. Theatre and cinema can be two of the most needed elements in the city to help the people develop their imagination of the past but also to make it functional in the present and future. The city will have a chance to rebuild its spirit without missing the opportunity to develop a comprehensive social mechanism that helps the city and its people safely reach the future. Protecting and promoting this heritage in contemporary culture will create safe communication spaces between diverse groups of people. When you feel your identity is protected, you will act in a responsible way before the entire community. The cultural recovery of Mosul can be an essential step towards a full-scale reconciliation, to building trust for the Christians and Yazidis to be able to return to Mosul, and to ensuring a safe and peaceful future.

References

Al-Ali Beg, M. (2005) *History of Endowment Services in Mosul (1249–1337 AH 1834–1918 AD)*, Mosul: University of Mosul University.

Chalabi, D. (1931) *Makhutat Al Mawsil*, Mosul: Al Furat Publications.

Daniel, E.V. (1996) *Charred Lullabies*, Princeton, NJ: Princeton University Press.

Khoury, D.R. (1997) *State and Provincial Society in the Ottoman Empire: Mosul, 1540–1834*, Cambridge: Cambridge Studies in Islamic Civilization, Cambridge University Press.

Tabbaa, Y. (2002) The Mosque of Nur al-Din in Mosul, 1170–1172, *Annales Islamologiques* 36: 339–360.

28

Renaming Places in India: Conjuring the Present by Exorcising a Past

Rachna Mehra

On 29 August 2015, the Indian Express carried an article with the title 'Delhi exits "cruel" Aurangzeb road for "kind" Abdul Kalam' (Vatsa 2015). For the uninitiated, Aurangzeb (1658–1707) was a medieval period Mughal ruler in India who was decried for his policies, especially towards his Hindu subjects. Since he was considered to be a bigot by many scholars, the question arises as to why a street was named after an emperor with a controversial past? Before we come to the rechristening of the street, we need to explore the purpose behind urbanonym, or the process through which proper names are assigned to urban elements in settlements, including streets, squares, markets and so on. A concomitant idea is whether designating a street with the name of a ruler or an important figure is an attempt to denote a political past, or in case of the renaming, a deliberate effort to counter the historical narrative and influence the course of culture and religious fervour in days to come.

In the case just mentioned, Abdul Kalam's name not only replaces that of Aurangzeb but also indicates an anthropomorphization of a road which personifies the shift from a ruthless erstwhile ruler to the benign personality of a modern–day scientist. Dr Abdul Kalam (1931–2015), popularly known as the 'missile man of India', was involved in India's civilian space programme and also served as the eleventh President of India. Both figures belonged to the same minority community, but replacing Emperor Aurangzeb with Dr Kalam's name indicates the kind of loyalty expected from a citizen, who in today's day and age needs to prove his credentials by contributing to the welfare of the country.

Urbanonym, history and politics

Street names and historical figures share an unusual relationship, especially since many are named after rulers who may or may not have visited that city. Yet the names become embedded in collective consciousness, perception and memory for those who inhabit that place. The practice of naming or renaming places is not new, nor is it an exercise devoid of political implications, yet the pace at which it has happened in Indian cities in the last few years becomes questionable. Some recent examples are shown in Table 28.1.

These few examples are representative of a larger politics of erasure of the association of places with Muslim identity, linguistic origin and culture, which is treated as an aberration within an otherwise pristine Hindu past.

Name at stake

The city as a place signifies a physical or territorial boundary which is demarcated administratively. But as a space, it transcends that jurisdiction and represents a milieu of the cultural processes associated with its dwellers (Jayaram 2010). The practice of naming or rechristening a place, city, state, monument, railway station or street is not exclusive to Indian cities, but the recent trend in India indicates a specific purpose and strategy.

The Indian legislature gives broad guidelines for renaming a state or a city. It is a complex task involving administrative permission and infrastructural cost. In the case of renaming a state, the president, parliament and state legislative assembly are involved, whereas if a city has to be renamed, the state assembly takes the decision after due deliberation. In the case of a railway station, the state government sends a request to the Ministry of Home Affairs (MHA), and once a name is changed, a new station code is released and fed into the ticketing system. In all cases, public funds are spent on updating the road signage system, maps, and official and public addresses. Even though changing a name is not a simple process, political will is instrumental in ensuring a swift and smooth transition, since it is a project employing a certain iconography.

Dynastic era and cityscape

Urbanonyms serve a dual purpose; one relates to orientation (utilitarian), and the other is symbolic (commemorative) in nature (Azaryahu 1990). When the British planned the city of New Delhi from 1911–1931, they were under no obligation to honour the legacy of the Mughal dynasty they had replaced. They neither had a will to please them or strike any opportunistic alliance, yet they named the roads and parks after them. They wanted New Delhi to reflect the history of the city by naming roads

Table 28.1: Recent examples of renamed places

Old name	Place/ typology	Meaning	New name	Meaning/ implication	Year of change
Mustafabad	Town	Not available	Saraswati Nagar	Based on a river in Hindu mythology	March 2016
Allahabad	City	The Abode of God	Prayagaraj	Prayaga means a place of sacrifice or a confluence of rivers (sangam of Ganges and Yamuna)	October 2018
Mughal Sarai	Railway Junction	Sarai means inn or tavern	Dr Deen Dayal Upadhyaya	Popular ideologue founder of Bhartiya Jan Sangh who was found murdered near the station in 1968	August 2018
Faizabad	City	Not available; a city of former Muslim Chieftains in the eighteenth century	Ayodhya	Birthplace of Hindu Deity Lord Rama	November 2018
Hoshangabad	City	Hoshang Shah, (ruler) of Malwa Sultanate	Narmadapuram	A place on the banks of river Narmada	March 2021
Habibganj	Station	Habib is an Arabic word means beloved and it could imply here lovely city	Rani Kamlapati	Last Hindu Queen of Bhopal belonging the Gond community	November 2021

(continued)

Table 28.1: Recent examples of renamed places (continued)

Old name	Place/ typology	Meaning	New name	Meaning/ implication	Year of change
Muhammadpur	Village in Delhi	Pur indicates land given to a beneficiary	Madhavpuram	Madhav is another name for Hindu Deity Krishna. Puram is a suffix for places of dwelling	April 2022

Source: Created by author from different published sources and news reports

after rulers belonging to different dynasties irrespective of their religious, regional and political affiliation. This explains how the name of the Mughal Emperor Aurangzeb found its way into the naming of a particular Delhi lane, since the naming exercise was inspired by 'history and not politics or bigotry' (Sharma 2016).

In the post-Independence era, there were conscious efforts made to dissociate from symbols of the colonial era and the leaders of the newly formed nation named the streets after the freedom fighters of the country. Kingsway was named after Emperor George V, who visited India in 1911, and though the name was later changed to Rajpath (ruler's path) it didn't make much difference as it was a Hindi translation of the English word. Queen's way became Janpath (people's path). Many changed names of places succeeded in gaining currency in day-to-day parlance, whereas some failed to capture popular imagination. Connaught Place (CP), a business commercial hub in Delhi from the twentieth century, was officially renamed as Rajiv Chowk (the chowk was named after Rajiv Gandhi, the Prime Minister of India who belonged to the Indian National Congress party) (Brijanath 1995), but it did not strike a chord with the local population, whose sentiments still resonate with the earlier one (Sen 2021). This political party began the trend of naming the streets, schemes and policies after their leaders. From 2014 onwards, there has been a 'resurgence of cultural nationalism and populism – a manifestation of the Hindutva ideology' espoused by the ruling Bhartiya Janta Party (BJP) after it defeated the Congress party, which had ruled India for over five decades (Rubdy 2021). While the Congress left no stone unturned in naming places, stations, chowks, roads and institutions after their family members, the BJP is competing to outdo the dynastic politics by inserting its own version of the past in different places.

Cultural nationalism at the crossroads in the national capital

Many leaders belonging to BJP have begun to rally for changing the name of places belonging to medieval rulers, citing them to be 'barbarous' and 'outsiders'. Moreover, names with Arabic roots need to be sanitized or replaced with those representing Sanskritic or Hindu traditions. For instance, the appeal to rename 40 Mughal-era villages was justified on the basis that Delhi was no longer 'Mughlon ka Sarai' and hence the symbol of 'slavery in the city' should be removed (Pandey 2022). While names like Shajahanabad and Tughlaqabad in Delhi do reflect dynastic rules of the medieval era, their rulers were instrumental in building those parts of the city and bequeathed a rich socio-cultural and architectural heritage.

Narayani Gupta, an eminent historian, explains that settlements called 'pur' indicate land given by rulers and named after the recipient. In a way Humanyupur, Timarpur, and so on would refer to the beneficiaries and not the emperors. Earlier the *patha/sadak* (street) were sometimes referred to by their function or destination point and *galis/kuchas/mohallas/pols/paras* (lanes, bylanes, neighbourbood) by the name of a *haveli* (mansion) owner or of the occupation/ethnic identity of the inhabitants. By contrast, streets/avenues in the three British Presidency cities, roads in civil lines and cantonments were named after senior officials and army officers (Gupta 2016). It is true that streets were named after affluent and powerful people, which merits critical review, but nowadays this has turned into a contest where one ruler's name is being superseded by another belonging to a different generation.

Change the rules of the game, not the name

Returning to the example where we began, it goes without saying that A.P.J. Abdul Kalam is a revered figure and remembered for his immense contribution to science, whereas the policies of the medieval ruler Aurangzeb have been denounced by many scholars. But condemning an emperor's policies should be distinguished from vilifying his personhood as it tends to create a stereotype for minorities in a country. It is undeniable that most rulers are associated with bloody wars and Machiavellianism, whether they win or lose in politics. Moreover, languages like Urdu, Persian and Arabic have come to be associated with Muslim rulers and efforts are being made to purge them from associated place names, but to think of imposing one language in a nation which is linguistically and ethnically diverse will prove counterproductive.

The urge to defy a historical past and assert the linguistic supremacy of one language over the other may suit the project of cultural nationalism in the short run, but it disregards the rich ethnolinguistic diversity of India.

The dynamics of assimilation and the synthesis of Hinduism and Islam or for that matter evolution of other religious practices and linguistic influences defies the idea of a presumed purity of one culture or language that claims to represent the historical past of a region. The inter-cultural community interaction, behavioural conventions and local beliefs of people living in places outlives political regimes and jingoism. After all, attempts can be made to rewrite historical memory in a partisan manner, but the past cannot be changed summarily or absolutely.

References

Azaryahu, M. (1990) Renaming the past: Changes in 'city-text' in Germany and Austria 1945–1947, *History and Memory* 2.2: 32–53.

Brijanath, R. (1995) Govt comes under fire over renaming of Connaught Place, *India Today*, 15 September, www.indiatoday.in/magazine/indiasc ope/story/19950915-govt-comes-under-fire-over-renaming-of-connau ght-place-807756-1995-09-14 (accessed 19 December 2022).

Gupta, N. (2016) Name games, *Indian Express*, 28 May, https://indianexpr ess.com/article/opinion/columns/akbar-road-renamed-history-is-victim-2822492/ (accessed 19 December 2022).

Jayaram, N. (2010) Revisiting the city: The relevance of urban sociology today, *EPW*, 35: 50–57.

Pandey, N. (2022) End Mughal era slavery, rename Tughlaq Akbar road and other lanes: Delhi BJP chief to NDMC, *The Print*, 10 May, https://thepr int.in/politics/end-mughal-era-slavery-rename-tughlaq-akbar-road-and-other-lanes-delhi-bjp-chief-to-ndmc/950078/ (accessed on 5 May 2023).

Rubdy, R. (2021) Patterns of commemorative street and place renaming in India's two mega-cities: Mumbai and New Delhi, *Linguistic Vanguard* 7.5.

Sen, R. (2021) The politics of naming and renaming public spaces in India, *Hindustan Times*, 1 March, www.hindustantimes.com/opinion/the-polit ics-of-naming-and-renaming-public-spaces-in-india-101614520459026. html (accessed 19 December 2022).

Sharma, S. (2016) Renaming Aurangazeb Road after Kalam isn't right: Delhi was inspired by history, not bigotry, *Firstpost*, 2 September, www.firstp ost.com/india/renaming-aurangzeb-road-after-apj-abdul-kalam-new-delhi-was-inspired-by-history-not-bigotry-2416606.html (accessed 19 December 2022).

Vatsa, A. (2015) Delhi exits 'cruel' Aurangazeb Road for 'kind' Abdul Kalam, *The Indian Express*, 29 August, https://indianexpress.com/article/cities/ delhi/delhis-aurangzeb-road-to-be-renamed-abdul-kalam-road/ (accessed 19 December 2022).

29

Urban Development for Religious Equality: The Case of Youhanabad in Pakistan

Amen Jaffer

Lahore, the second largest metropolitan centre of Pakistan, has an estimated population of 13.5 million, which is overwhelmingly Muslim (95.4 per cent, according to the 2017 census). According to the same census, Christians are the largest religious minority of the city and comprise around 4.4 per cent of its population. Christians in Lahore (and elsewhere in Pakistan) have historically faced systematic marginalization on three different fronts.[1] First, they are a religious minority with a precarious citizenship status in a state that discriminates between its citizens on the basis of religion. Second, they occupy one of the lowest positions in the caste structures of Lahore, which results in occupational discrimination, as well as untouchability. Relatedly, they are also one of the poorest communities in the city, with limited access to social mobility and public services. On top of these historic exclusions, since the 1980s, there has been a rising trend of blasphemy allegations[2] and

---

[1] Ryan Brasher (2020) organizes the social science scholarship on Christians in Pakistan along two different lines. One approach emphasizes their status as a religious minority (Gabriel 2007; Ispahani 2017; Malik 2002; Pio and Syed 2016), while the other strand focuses primarily on their position in the caste structure (McClintock 1992; Walbridge 2003; O'Brien 2012; Singha 2018). See also Fuchs and Fuchs (2020) for an overview of the literature on religious minorities in Pakistan.

[2] Christians have been disproportionately impacted by Pakistan's blasphemy laws. Of all known blasphemy cases from 1947 to 2021 in Pakistan, almost 17 per cent of the accused and killed were Christians, while they comprise only 1.27 per cent of the country's population, according to the 2017 Census (Nafees 2021).

incidents of physical violence targeting the city's Christian community (Jabbar and Ali 2021).[3]

In these circumstances, the rise of Christian-only enclaves in Lahore can be viewed as an urban intervention to deal with some of the exclusions and threats faced by the community as a religious minority. Beginning in the 1950s, several such settlements were constructed in the south of the city. The largest of these was Youhanabad, which was established in the 1960s by a Catholic mission, and currently has an estimated population of around 200,000. This chapter makes sense of Youhanabad as a model urban development that was planned for addressing the challenges faced by Christians in Pakistan. Drawing on interviews with residents, business owners and others connected to the locality, this chapter examines the various ways in which lives are shaped by living and working in Youhanabad, exploring wider issues of religious inequality in Pakistan, and reflecting on the policy implications of such minority enclaves for urban development.

Youhanabad: a brief history

Father Henry, a Belgian Catholic priest, popularly known as the 'engineer priest', is widely acknowledged as the visionary and moving force behind the foundation of Youhanabad in 1960. Posted in Pakistan as part of a Catholic mission in the 1950s, he had already established a number of smaller colonies in the south of Lahore before laying the foundations for Youhanabad. His work of developing Youhanabad as a planned housing society was later taken over by Caritas, the social arm of the Catholic Church in Pakistan. Father Henry envisioned these real estate developments as links in a chain of Christian enclaves that would offer better lives to Christians in Punjab. However, the immediate need addressed by Youhanabad was one of providing access to affordable housing given the poverty of Christians in Lahore and other parts of Punjab, where home ownership levels were (and continue to be) extremely low. By offering land at low prices, which were to be repaid in easy and flexible instalments and providing subsidized building materials, Youhanabad offered an opportunity for home ownership to Christians. Initially, however, it was mostly rural migrants that took up this opportunity, since those already resident in Lahore considered it to be too far from the city.[4] It was only in the 1990s when Lahore's Christians began to move to Youhanabad in large numbers. By this time, Ferozepur Road, on which the settlement was located, had become a main thoroughfare of Lahore and the

---

[3] These include suicide bombings and mob attacks on Christian communities.
[4] The closest bus stop to Youhanabad even until the 1970s was some 2 km away and residents had to travel long distances to get to work and access urban services.

city had engulfed the locality. Today, Youhanabad is a sought-after locality where low-income families live side by side with middle-class Christians. While Muslims make up less than 2 per cent of its residents, they own around half of the almost 1,000 shops and businesses in its thriving markets.

Being Christian in Lahore

The lives of Youhanabad's residents can only be understood if placed in the larger context of Christian experience in Lahore. Nadeem Gill, who owns a small jewellery business in Youhanabad, describes the affective state of being a Christian in Lahore as one of constant 'pressure'. He elaborates that he is always on the edge and feels vulnerable because he does not know when someone will insult him. For example, if someone notices that he has a cross hanging from the rearview mirror of his car, they can simply walk up and hurl insults at him and there is absolutely nothing he can do about it. "We are treated like insects in this country. People here use the name of our caste as an expletive." Zakariya, a dance teacher who lives and runs a small dance studio in Youhanabad, echoed similar sentiments describing the care he has to exercise in his dealings with Muslims in Lahore. He lives in fear that something he has said or done may be misconstrued as offensive to their sensibilities.

According to Saleem, whose family purchased a 4,500 square feet plot of residential land in Youhanabad in 1961, these feelings of vulnerability and suspicion among Christians can be traced back to the 1980s when the military dictator, Zia-ul-Haq, unleashed a programme of Islamization of state and society. Growing up in Lahore before this era, Rafiq describes a social milieu in which he was hardly aware of his Christian identity. He lived in a mixed religious neighbourhood and his closest friends were Muslims. He even participated in Islamic rituals and festivals. Zia's regime, however, promoted the politicization of religion and division of society. On the one hand, it introduced a number of laws in the name of protecting Islam that specifically targeted religious minorities (Rahman 2012) while on the other, it encouraged religious identity as a primary modality of belonging. While earlier Christians had been moving to Youhanabad in search of affordable housing, the desire to live with other Christians and seek safety in numbers had now also become a major motivation.

Raja's experience of relocating to Youhanabad in 2000 is instructive: "I was born and raised in a village near Gujranwala and also lived and worked in Karachi for many years. However, it was only when I moved here that I felt like I truly belonged, that this was home." He went on to explain that he felt that his dignity was protected in Youhanabad, and no one could vilify him for being Christian. Nadeem added that Youhanabad also provided him with economic opportunities that were not available in other parts of Lahore. This is because Christians are systematically denied entry into several occupations and businesses due to caste barriers in many of Lahore's economic sectors that limit them to low-paying, menial jobs. Giving the example of his own occupation, Nadeem shared that Christians are not taught the goldsmith trade or allowed to run a jewellery business in the city. They can only learn such profitable trades by hiding their religious identity or practising them in Christian enclaves.

Youhanabad under siege

The experiences shared here suggest that Youhanabad serves as an important refuge for a marginalized religious group. However, its ability to provide safety to Christians in Lahore was dramatically compromised on 15 March 2015, when Youhanbad was rocked by planned suicide bombings that targeted two of its largest churches (Aslam et al 2022). The bombing and subsequent riots, in which two Muslim men were set ablaze, unleashed a wave of terror in the settlement (Sanam 2015).[5] A mob comprising around 300 men from a neighbouring locality attacked Youhanabad and the Pakistan Rangers, a paramilitary federal law enforcement organization, was called in to control the situation. According to Roger, who had grown up in Youhanabad, these events led to a mass exodus of residents who feared that their lives were in danger if they remained in the settlement, and many sought asylum in other countries. For Parvez, who has lived in Youhanabad since the 1970s, things have not been the same since. He chose an interesting analogy to describe this disruption, claiming that Youhanabad was becoming Israel and emerging as a major threat to the powers that controlled the city. Niamat, a relative of Parvez, elaborated that a lot of foreign funding was pouring into businesses and non-profit organizations of the locality and the government feared that the 'lowly' Christians were becoming too powerful and had to be cut to size. However, the bombings and their aftermath laid waste to these developments. The sense of security and opportunity that Youhanabad offered to Christians was shattered. According to Saleem, many people in Youhanabad have still not overcome the trauma unleashed by those events.

Conclusion

Youhanabad was planned and envisioned as an urban project that would not only offer housing to Christians but also work for their social, economic and

---

[5]   Instead of offering sympathy to the Christians of Youhanabad, the public reaction to these events focused on the lynching of these men and turned into a backlash against the Christian community (Sanam 2015).

political uplift. As a project for the development of Christians in Lahore, it has met with mixed results. It has offered a few avenues for socio-economic mobility for residents who were able to avail the limited educational and economic opportunities on offer. However, this is by no means a widespread phenomenon and a large number of residents continue to languish in poverty. As a refuge for a minority group, it should be stressed that Youhanabad was not founded to perform this particular social function for Lahore's Christians, since they were already well integrated into their various neighbourhoods at the time. It is religious polarization and the targeting of religious minorities, since the 1980s, that increased its importance as an enclave where Christians could feel secure in the city. However, Youhanabad's very renown as a Christian settlement has paradoxically now made it a target for extremist violence.

Youhanabad is a case of missed opportunities. Divisions along sectarian and party lines among Christians have continued to plague the community, and Youhanabad is not considered a powerful force in the city of Lahore's politics. Saleem and Roger lay the blame for this on the shoulders of the self-serving alliance between the local leadership and religious clergy. Instead of developing democratic institutions and practices, these leaders have promoted their own self-interests and indulged in politics of patronage, with the result that Youhanabad's Christians are unable to exert any serious pressure on the state to respond to its many needs. On the contrary, the state's policies and political structures have strengthened an unrepresentative leadership that has repeatedly failed to address the development needs of residents. It is consequently critical to foster conditions that promote internal democratization of marginalized religious communities, dismantling political structures of patronage and promoting alternative forums for thought and dialogue that are not under the control of established political leaders or religious institutions.

References

Aslam, M.A., Aslam, T. and Zubair, M. (2022) Religious violence towards minorities: The case of Youhanabad Church attack in Pakistan, *Liberal Arts and Social Sciences International Journal* 6.1: 1–16.

Brasher, R. (2020) Pride and abstention: National identity, uncritical patriotism and political engagement among Christian students in Pakistan, *South Asia: Journal of South Asian Studies* 43:1: 84–100.

Fuchs, M. and Fuchs, S.W. (2020) Religious minorities in Pakistan: Identities, citizenship and social belonging, *South Asia: Journal of South Asian Studies* 43.1: 52–67.

Gabriel, T. (2007) *Christian Citizens in an Islamic State: The Pakistan Experience*, Aldershot: Ashgate.

Ispahani, F. (2017) *Purifying the Land of the Pure: A History of Pakistan's Religious Minorities*, New York: Oxford University Press.

Jabbar, N. and Ali, U. (2021) 'Like a hair drawn from flour': Everyday militarization and female recruitment for church security teams in Pakistan, *Global Studies Quarterly* 1: 1–11.

Malik, I. (2002) *Religious Minorities in Pakistan*, London: Minority Rights Group International.

McClintock, W. (1992) A sociological profile of the Christian minority in Pakistan, *Missiology* 20.3: 343–353.

Nafees, M. (2021) Blasphemy cases in Pakistan: 1947–2021, Center for Research & Security Studies, https://crss.pk/blasphemy-cases-in-pakistan-1947-2021/ (accessed 30 November 2022).

O'Brien, J. (2012) *The Unconquered People: The Liberation Journey of an Oppressed Caste*, Karachi: Oxford University Press.

Pio, E. and Syed, J. (2016) Marked by the cross: The persecution of Christians in Pakistan, in J. Syed, E. Pio, T. Kamran and A. Zaidi (eds) *Faith-Based Violence and Deobandi Militancy in Pakistan*, London: Palgrave Macmillan: 187–207.

Rahman, T. (2012) Pakistan's policies and practices towards the religious minorities, *South Asian History and Culture* 3.2: 302–315.

Sanam (2015) Have the Lahore church bombings and the lynchings that followed revealed rifts within pakistan's Christian community? *The Caravan: A Journal of Politics & Culture*, https://caravanmagazine.in/vantage/lahore-church-bombings-lynchings-rift-pakistan-christian-community (accessed 10 March 2023).

Singha, S. (2018) Christians in Pakistan and Afghanistan: Responses to marginalization from the peripheries, in D. Philpott and T.S. Shah (eds) *Under Caesar's Sword: How Christians Respond to Persecution*, Cambridge: Cambridge University Press: 226–259.

Walbridge, L. (2003) *The Christians of Pakistan: The Passion of Bishop John Joseph*, London: Routledge Curzon.

PART VIII

Climate and Nature

30

Religious Inequality and Environmental Change

Shilpi Srivastava and Vinitha Bachina

The rapid pace of environmental change in the form of biodiversity loss, environmental degradation, pollution and climate change is threatening the wellbeing of human and non-human systems across the globe. Unfortunately, the enormity of this challenge is rarely matched by the 'solutions' that are advanced by global and national policy makers, who continue to promote simplistic, top-down and techno-centric 'fixes' (Srivastava et al 2022) often overlooking the social and cultural dimensions of these changes and their impacts, especially for those who are on the frontline of climate change, including minorities. This chapter focuses on the intersection of religion and religious inequality with SDGs 12 (sustainable production and consumption), 13 (combat climate change), 14 (life below water) and 15 (life on land). Since these SDGs are directly linked to challenges related to the environment and ecosystems, we explicitly focus on the intersection of religion and religious inequality with what we broadly understand as environmental change.

These four SDGs are unified by certain common principles. These are: (a) sustainable management and use of resources, including marine and terrestrial resources based on principles of fairness, equity and avoidance of harm to environmental and human systems; (b) building adaptive capacity, awareness and strengthening overall resilience to combat various forms of environmental change (desertification, climate change, biodiversity) with a special emphasis on building local capacity; and (c) effective planning and integration of policies at local, national and global levels (UN 2016). Drawing on these principles as the key hooks for advancing these SDGs, we analyse how religious inequality intersects with these principles and what the broader implications are for sustainable development.

Our approach in this short review is as follows: we tease out the key themes emerging from these SDGs and locate them within the broader scholarship of environmental change. We observe that there are two important ways in which religion and religious inequality are framed within this scholarship: first, as an axis of marginality whereby systemic and structural vulnerabilities and discrimination exacerbate exposure to impacts and limit or reduce adaptive capacity to further shocks and stressors; second, as an enabler for collective action and solidarity whereby religious language and practices are used as a resource for mobilizing and/or helping people deal with the uncertainties of environmental change (Hulme 2017; Oxley 2020).

We explore these two dimensions in the subsequent sections drawing on diverse examples, ranging from climate change to biodiversity conservation. We underline that although religious inequality may not be an explicit focus within this literature, it forms an important axis within the broad category of social differentiation, especially within local communities. By contrast, religious inequality rarely appears as a key factor within the planning and policy literature (Tadros 2021). Furthermore, while attempts have been made to disaggregate environmental impacts by social and political dimensions of inequality, attention to religious heterogeneity and inequality remains limited in international policy debates (Baird 2008).

Freedom of religion or belief, religious inequality and environmental change

For the majority of scholarship, the core focus is on the unique experiences of various communities and their relationship with the environment (Nyong et al 2007; Salick and Ross 2009; Leonard et al 2013). However, the adverse impacts of climate change, by virtue of belonging to minority groups, remain 'hidden' under other axes of inequality or the broad category of 'vulnerability' and are rarely made explicit. For example, categories such as 'urban poor' or 'rural poor' can often mask the impacts felt by the minority communities. Hence, although the rapid rise of global warming affects everybody, the impacts of climate change are accentuated by existing inequalities which directly affect the adaptive capacity of individuals and vulnerable communities (see Mehta et al 2021), including – among others – religious and non-faith minorities and indigenous people across the world (Petersen 2019). This is due to diverse forms of procedural, distributive, recognitional and cognitive injustices that these communities may be subjected to because of their minority status and ensuing policy bias and blindness to which we now turn.

The intersection of religious inequality with environmental change

Religious marginality can broadly be differentiated into the impacts of environmental change due to discrimination and marginalization (Baird 2008) and the extent, or lack thereof, of recognition of such groups in climate action policies and interventions (Mihlar 2008; Honig et al 2021). In many cases, these minority groups reside in marginal environments, often living in disaster-prone areas (such as low-lying areas prone to flooding or other environmental hazards) and are directly dependent on natural resources for their livelihoods (Muhumuza, this volume). This not only puts them on the frontline but also amplifies the cascading impacts of climate change in relation to other basic services, such as food, water and sanitation and health access (Petersen 2019; Mehta et al 2021). For example, access to emergency aid and relief measures can also be hindered by a community's religious identity, as marginalized groups reside in remote, disaster-prone areas, where the quality of housing is poor. This makes them the most affected and yet the last to receive emergency relief measures. When they do receive aid, powerful or dominant groups can dictate its distribution (Baird 2008).

Access to relief and resources to build adaptive capacity is also tied to their social, political and economic status which reproduce these diverse forms of inequality (Tadros 2022). For example, the devasting floods in Assam, India in June 2022 have caused widespread destruction and loss of life so far. However, its disastrous impact was felt more acutely by the Bengali-speaking Muslims who were living in makeshift homes that got submerged or washed away. These floods occurred nine months after these groups were forced out of their villages and into temporary settlements by the majoritarian Hindutva-leaning government, under suspicion of being 'illegal' immigrants from Bangladesh (Hoque 2022).

Environmental change has also created manifold uncertainties for local communities as their livelihoods are often dependent on natural resources (such as pastoralism, subsistence agriculture and artisanal fishing). For instance, Mihlar (2008) and Baird (2008) argue that environmental change is contributing to the fading away of community structures and religious practices. Among those with faith in African traditional religions, there have been changes in their beliefs about rain making, soil fertility, farming practices, religious festivals/ceremonies and so on due to changes in historically established weather patterns (Christian 2014). This has led to the loss of traditional identity and cultural heritage. A similar trend is observed among the Fakirani Jat herders, a Muslim community following Sufi practices, settled along the north-west coast of India. As climatic uncertainties (such as droughts, floods and salinity intrusion) intersect with the wider political economy of aggressive industrialization, these herders find themselves at the margins of state policy, which has historically denigrated pastoralism and also their indigenous practices around sustainable grazing (Ohte et al 2021). Many young herders have now migrated out of the region to take up insecure contractual employment in nearby industries (Srivastava and Mehta 2021; Srivastava et al 2022). In many instances, the loss and damage faced by these communities through the loss of cultural heritage coupled with the loss of access leads to distributive and recognitional injustice (see Tifloen, this volume).

Inherent policy biases and prejudices against indigenous and traditional knowledge also lead to diverse forms of recognitional and cognitive injustices (Newell et al 2021). This is demonstrated in a broad range of scholarship where indigenous communities have been dispossessed of their land and environmental resources in the name of biodiversity conservation (Vidal 2016). This is further exacerbated by the fact that these minority groups also witness diverse forms of procedural injustice since they have little to no voice in decision making (Newell et al 2021). Due to systemic biases and prejudices, religious minorities are often unable to demand a response or influence climate action as they are often ignored and excluded by policy makers, and this adversely affects their political engagement with the state. For example, Honig et al (2021) in their work in Kenya show how leaders of Muslim community groups have faced difficulties eliciting responses from their local politicians, thus severely limiting their agency to highlight the specific problems faced by the community.

This policy blindness can also be reproduced in global climate action where context-specific manifestations and the underlying 'secular' assumptions around climate solutions can overlook differentiated impacts on particular communities. For example, calls to push for plant-based diets as a mitigation strategy need to be situated in specific social and cultural contexts. While, on the one hand, these solutions can marginalize livestock-based livelihoods (such as pastoralism, see Scoones 2022), they can also get deeply enmeshed in charged political contexts. For example, in India, the deliberate push for vegetarian diets can also 'weaponize' discriminatory attitudes towards religious minorities and caste groups, providing more fodder for the deliberate targeting of meat-eating minority communities, such as Muslims, Christians, Adivasis and Dalits (Parikh 2016; Karpagam et al 2019). Similar trends are witnessed in the push for renewables, whereby indigenous communities are being dispossessed in the name of climate action and mitigation (Torres-Contreras 2020; Srivastava et al 2022; Muhumuza, this volume). Hence the intersection of religious inequality with other forms of inequality (economic, spatial, political) can substantially limit the adaptive capacity of vulnerable groups, who bear the brunt of environmental change, are the least responsible for creating these changes, and have little to no voice in decision making on climate action.

Leveraging religious heterogeneity to address environmental change

A rich body of work explores the relationship between religion and environmental change underlining the critical role that religion plays within human-environment relationships (Veldman et al 2013; Hulme 2017). For example, in his comprehensive review on the role of religion and climate change, Haluza-DeLay (2014) argues that religion serves a cosmological role (helping people to understand and associate meaning to the world) and provides social and collective functions (norms, beliefs and practices that shape resource sharing or social capital). Through deep ethnographic engagement, scholars have unpacked how religion acts as both a barrier as well as an enabler to adaptation (Veldman et al 2013; Haluza-DeLay 2014).

There is a strong push to integrate religion in addressing climate change with the academic and policy literature (see Veldman et al 2013; Dasgupta and Ramanathan 2014; Hulme 2017) to harness the social and collective function of religion (Haluza-DeLay 2014) although most scholars acknowledge that there is variation in understanding what 'religion' means in a particular context and also its diverse social roles. Here, religion is seen as a 'moral force' for unifying collective action through tapping into 'the deeply held values and motives if cultural innovation and change are to be lasting and effective' (Hulme 2017: 15).

However, religion and environmental change do not always share an 'enabling' relationship. Several studies have highlighted how religious beliefs can also limit climate action, exacerbate vulnerabilities and/or produce counterproductive results (see Veldman et al 2013). Hence, it is important to engage with religious heterogeneity (recognizing differences among religious traditions, practices and beliefs) in particular contexts through which environmental change is experienced and politicized (Hulme 2017). This also requires taking into account indigenous knowledge and wisdoms that are held sacred by people on the margins and reversing the recognitional injustice that these communities have been subjected to and are targeted for.

Conclusion

Impacts of climate change are not felt equally by all, and intersecting inequalities further intensify difficulties to respond, cope, recover or adapt to unprecedented environmental changes (Bharadwaj et al 2021). Religious inequality is often experienced in combination with other forms of inequality and its role in the production of vulnerability should neither be underestimated nor overestimated (Petersen 2019; Tifloen, this volume). Vulnerable groups, whose dimensions of marginality could be a combination of factors, such as race, caste, sexuality, age and religion, do not experience development challenges equally and hence must not be treated homogeneously in policy action. Framing environmental problems to include people's religious repertoires is important for bringing to the fore the moral, social and cultural dimensions of climate change debates. This in turn can help in challenging the top-down solutions that are often framed either as a 'techno-centric fix' or in terms of market-based solutions (Oxley 2020). To reach a 'dignified' level of sustainable human development concerning the climate SDGs (Kartha and Baer 2010), it would be catastrophic to overlook the differentiated impacts, capacities and systemic vulnerabilities faced by diverse religious minorities experiencing intersecting inequalities and indigenous people who assume sacred norms and beliefs if we are indeed serious about leaving no one behind.

References

Baird, R. (2008) The impact of climate change on minorities and indigenous peoples, Briefing, London: Minority Rights Group International.

Bharadwaj, S., Howard, J. and Narayanan, P. (2021) Using participatory action research methodologies for engaging and researching with religious minorities in contexts of intersecting inequalities, CREID Working Paper 5, Coalition for Religious Equality and Inclusive Development, Brighton: Institute of Development Studies.

Christian, N.G. (2014) The impact of climate change on African traditional religious practices, *Journal of Earth Science & Climatic Change* 5.7: 209.

Dasgupta, P. and Ramanathan, V. (2014) Pursuit of the common good, *Science* 345.6203: 1457–1458.

Haluza-DeLay, R. (2014) Religion and climate change: Varieties in viewpoints and practices, *Wiley Interdisciplinary Reviews: Climate Change* 5.2: 261–279.

Honig, L., Smith, A.E. and Bleck, J. (2021) What stymies action on climate change? Religious institutions, marginalization, and efficacy in Kenya, *Perspectives on Politics*, doi:10.1017/S153759272000479X

Hoque, M. (2022) As millions devastated by Assam floods, double tragedy for evicted Bengali-speaking Muslims, *Article 14*, 27 June.

Hulme, M. (2017) Climate change and the significance of religion, *Economic & Political Weekly* 52.28: 14–17.

Karpagam, S., Leroy, F. and Cohen, M. (2019) India is not a 'vegetarian country' like the EAT-Lancet Report would have us believe, *The Wire*, 16 November.

Kartha, S. and Baer, P. (2010) The right to development in a climate constrained world: The Greenhouse Development Rights framework, in M. Voss (ed) *Der Klimawandel*, Wiesbaden: Springer VS.

Leonard, S., Parsons, M., Olawsky, K. and Kofod, F. (2013) The role of culture and traditional knowledge in climate change adaptation: Insights from East Kimberley, Australia, *Global Environmental Change* 23.3: 623–632.

Mehta, L., Adam, H.N. and Srivastava, S. (2021) *The Politics of Climate Change and Uncertainty in India*, London: Routledge.

Mihlar, F. (2008) Voices that must be heard: Minorities and indigenous people combating climate change, Briefing, London: Minority Rights Group.

Newell, P., Srivastava, S., Naess, L.O., Torres Contreras, G.A., and Price, R. (2021) Toward transformative climate justice: An emerging research agenda, *Wiley Interdisciplinary Reviews: Climate Change* 12.6: e733.

Nyong, A., Adesina, F. and Osman Elasha, B. (2007) The value of indigenous knowledge in climate change mitigation and adaptation strategies in the African Sahel, *Mitigation and Adaptation Strategies for Global Change* 12.5: 787–797.

Ohte, N., Yamamoto, K., Chatterjee, R., Joshi, P., Srivastava, S. and Mehta, L. (2021) Mangrove ecosystems in the coastal zone of Kutch, western India, used for traditional pastoralism: Effects of climate change and social conditions on long-term biomass variability, presented at AGU Fall Meeting, 13–17 December: SY45D-0807.

Oxley, N. (2020) Unsettling the apocalypse: Uncertainty in spirituality and religion, in I. Scoones and A. Stirling (eds) *The Politics of Uncertainty: Challenges of Transformation*, London: Routledge.

Parikh, T. (2016) Beef, biryani, and Indian politics, *The Diplomat*, 16 September.

Petersen, M.J. (2019) Freedom of religion or belief and climate change, FoRB Leadership Network Briefing Paper 5, Copenhagen: Danish Institute for Human Rights.

Salick, J. and Ross, N. (2009) Traditional peoples and climate change, *Global Environmental Change* 19.2: 137–139.

Scoones, I. (2022). Livestock, methane, and climate change: The politics of global assessments, *WIREs Climate Change*: e790.

Srivastava, S. and Mehta, L. (2021) The social life of mangroves: Neoliberal development and mangrove conservation in the changing landscape of Kutch, *Environment and Planning E: Nature and Space*.

Srivastava, S., Bose, S., Parthasarathy, P. and Mehta, L. (2022) Climate justice for whom? Understanding the vernaculars of climate, *IDS Bulletin* 53.4: 101–124.

Tadros, M. (2021) Stop homogenising us: Mixing and matching faith and beliefs in India and beyond, *Coalition for Religious Equality and Inclusive Development*, 21 May.

Tadros, M. (2022) Religious equality and freedom of religion or belief: International development's blindspot, *The Review of Faith & International Affairs* 20:2: 96–108.

Torres Contreras, G.A. (2020) The politics of wind energy in the Isthmus of Tehuantepec: wind, land and social difference, PhD thesis, Brighton: University of Sussex.

United Nations (2016) *Annex IV: Final List of Proposed Sustainable Development Goal indicators, Report of the Inter-Agency and Expert Group on Sustainable Development Goal Indicators* (E/CN.3/2016/2/Rev.1), New York: United Nations.

Veldman, R.G., Szasz, A. and Haluza-DeLay, R. (2013) *How the World's Religions Are Responding to Climate Change*, London: Taylor & Francis.

Vidal, J. (2016) The tribes paying the brutal price of conservation, *The Guardian*, 28 August.

31

Discrimination against Minorities and Its Detrimental Effect on Biodiversity Conservation: Lessons from the Batwa 'Pygmies' around Semuliki National Park, Western Uganda

Moses Muhumuza

Religion and eviction

In 2014, I guided a team of Tanzanians that were visiting Uganda on an exposure visit to learn about how local communities in Uganda participated in the conservation of national parks. We visited Semuliki National Park (SNP), where we were informed about how the Uganda Wildlife Authority (UWA) was in conflict with the Batwa, who had been evicted and resettled in a camp in 1994, and were prohibited from accessing the park. The Batwa are forest people, often referred to as 'pygmies'. They live spread over the Great Lakes region and parts of Central Africa. The cultural leader, or king, of the Batwa in Semuliki, Nzito, narrated how their presence in SNP had enhanced biodiversity conservation through their cultural and religious beliefs. Nzito argued that the Batwa believe in the presence of forest gods who grant (or deny) permission to harvest certain resources. Since their eviction, the park has become severely degraded due to illegal and unsustainable activities, such as deforestation by neighbouring communities. We learned from the Warden in Charge of SNP that the Batwa's eviction was effected through a combination of coercion and enticement by UWA and the Adventist Development and Relief Agency (ADRA), an organization under the Seventh Day Adventist Church, one of the dominant religious groups in the villages neighbouring the SNP. While UWA's objective was to implement a law that prohibited humans from living in the national park, ADRA aimed at converting the Batwa to Adventism by enticing them with incentives, such as educational materials and food.

The eviction of indigenous people from their lands and disregard for their beliefs while creating national parks is a common phenomenon in Africa (Brockington and Schmidt-Soltau 2004). Apart from the Batwa in Semuliki, other Batwa populations have been evicted from the Bwindi and Mgahinga National Parks in south-western Uganda (Bularda 2017; Bitariho 2013) and other national parks in East Africa (Lewis 2000). Studies show that indigenous people who inhabited areas now gazetted as national parks were not ecologically 'noble savages' (Hames 2007), but had a number of active and conscious natural resource conservation strategies (Saikia 2008). Eviction of local indigenous communities from their traditional lands and disfranchisement from the practice of their beliefs is responsible for the high incidence of human-wildlife conflicts. For example, 16 fires occurred in or around the Bwindi Impenetrable National Park[1] during a drought in 1992 following the park's establishment, and it was later learned that a third of these fires had been started by local residents with the deliberate intent of destroying the park to protest new restrictions limiting their access (Blomley 2002). In March 2021, six lions were poisoned in Queen Elizabeth National Park by local communities in protest of UWA's efforts to limit their access to park resources (Muhumuza 2021). The State of Biodiversity in Africa report (UNEP-WCMC 2016) shows that biodiversity degradation is escalating as a result of these conflicts across Africa's protected areas.

Reconnecting religion to conservation

There are various social service programmes implemented by UWA and non-governmental organizations (NGOs) who work in communities neighbouring SNP, targeting the Batwa to enable them to adapt to living separately from the park, but they generally neither enhance the welfare of the Batwa nor the conservation of the SNP (CCFU 2017). Focusing on the plight of the Batwa, I led a research team comprising UWA and Fauna and Flora International (FFI) project staff, convening a programme to reconnect the Batwa to the forest and enhance their welfare. The focus was on enabling the Batwa to derive their survival and livelihood from the SNP, despite living

---

[1]   The name derives from the word 'Bwindi' from the Runyakitara word 'Mubwindi' which means 'a place full of darkness'. This name comes from the extensive strands of bamboo interspersed among the larger forest hardwoods which makes the area 'impenetrable'.

outside the park. Where previous approaches had detached the Batwa from their beliefs and coerced them to engage in activities such as agriculture, that were foreign to their hunter-gatherer way of life, the project was designed on the view that conservation is a behaviour which is influenced by the beliefs of the Batwa. Drawing on the theory of Planned Behaviour (Azjen and Madden 1986) and the model of responsible environment behaviour (Chao 2012), the project emphasis was on how behaviours are determined by intentions, which are shaped by individuals' beliefs.

First, we documented the beliefs, knowledge, cultural rituals, traditional rules and leadership system of the Batwa. Acknowledging that traditional cultures have some practices that are similar to modern biodiversity conservation strategies but which have not been recognized (Colding and Folke 2001), we interrogated how the Batwa conserved biodiversity in the SNP. It was found that the Batwa cultural system comprises beliefs in gods and spirits, taboos, totems, traditional knowledge, cultural rituals, and traditional rules and regulations (see Figure 31.1).

Figure 31.1: How the beliefs, knowledge and practices of the Batwa conserved biodiversity in Semuliki National Park

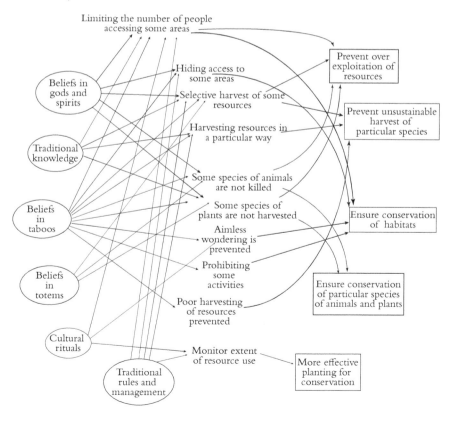

Second, based on the understanding that Batwa beliefs, knowledge and practices could enhance the conservation of biodiversity in Semuliki National Park, we implemented a Cultural Values and Conservation Project funded by FFI in partnership with UWA. The Bamaga trail was established exclusively for the Batwa to exhibit their cultural beliefs, knowledge, norms and practices to tourists who paid for the experience. The Batwa were also granted access to some resources in the park by SNP authorities, such as medicine, materials for crafts and firewood for subsistence use.

Partial successes and remaining tensions

The project led to the recognition that the Batwa are not only stakeholders in the conservation of SNP, but they can also contribute to the conservation of SNP through their beliefs, knowledge and practices. The project enabled the Batwa to revitalize their traditional beliefs, knowledge and practices along the Bamaga trail and enhance their income. This led to the appreciation by the Batwa that they can to some extent survive in the forest despite their enduring resettlement.

However, from a conservation perspective, this approach did not halt biodiversity degradation in SNP. There is still biodiversity loss in SNP due to forest depletion (Biswande 2019): "The Batwa are the main suppliers of fuel wood illegally collected from the park to all the neighbouring trading centres," an SNP Warden explained.[2] The local communities rely on the Batwa to extract resources for commercial purposes because of their knowledge and experience of the forest. The presence of the Batwa in the park had even partly deterred poachers and illegal resource use by the neighbouring community: "Actually, the eviction of the Batwa from the park has caused more biodiversity conservation challenges than when they were there" (Warden, SNP).

The limited success at preventing degradation in SNP are multifaceted. The restrictions within UWA policies prevented us from fully implementing the project based on our documented findings about Batwa beliefs, knowledge and practices. UWA also restricted Batwa access to the park to conduct activities that were considered illegal but not necessarily unsustainable. However, the most significant limiting factor was that the project focused on the effects of resource use for the Batwa's survival and livelihoods, rather than the conservation of biodiversity in SNP. The project should have used a holistic strategy for education, negotiated access, alternative livelihoods and decentralized co-management (ENAD). In this strategy, a conservation education package based on Batwa traditional knowledge, beliefs and

---

[2] Personal observations, interview, February 2022.

practices should have been designed and implemented, enabling the Batwa to negotiate with the UWA to have access to resources that could be sustainably utilized; emphasizing Batwa livelihood activities using protected area resources for eco-cultural tourism activities, rather than agriculture and trade, and working with the UWA to decentralize resource use monitoring, utilizing the Batwa's traditional leadership structure.

Lessons for conservation projects

When working with communities that have been evicted from protected areas, but still live in close proximity to them, it is important to ask what their traditional beliefs, knowledge and practices are to understand their relevance to biodiversity conservation. They do not only influence illegal access to resources in protected areas, but also sustainable utilization of them. Conservation Biology, a discipline that informs contemporary biodiversity conservation interventions, should incorporate local people's traditional beliefs, knowledge, norms and practices, given their influence over resource use. This strategy would contribute towards the attainment of SDG15. Drawing on these insights from conservation work with the Batwa in SNP, conservation authorities and policy makers should ask: in what ways are conservation efforts likely to be affected by local people's beliefs, knowledge and practices? How can the beliefs, knowledge and practices of marginalized local people be harnessed to enhance their welfare in tandem with biodiversity conservation? And how can conservation efforts ensure that the rights of local communities to access protected area resources are protected?

References

Ajzen, I. and Madden, T. (1986) Prediction of goal-directed behaviour: Attitudes, intentions and perceived behavioural control, *Journal of Experimental Social Psychology* 22: 453–474.

Biswande, K.J. (2019) Bundibugyo residents question cutting trees in Semuliki National Park, *Uganda Radio Network*, 20 November, https://uga ndaradionetwork.net/story/bundibugyo-residents-question-cutting-trees-in-semuliki-national-park (accessed 2 September 2022).

Bitariho, R. (2013) Socio-economic and ecological implications of local people's use of Bwindi Forest in south western Uganda, PhD thesis, Mbarara: Mbarara University of Science and Technology.

Blomley, T. (2002) Natural resource conflict management: The case of Bwindi Impenetrable and Mgahinga Gorilla National Parks, southwestern Uganda, Care International, www.treesforlife.info/fao/Docs/P/y4503e/y4503e11.pdf (accessed 2 September 2022).

Brockington, D. and Schmidt-Soltau, K. (2004) The social and environmental impacts of wilderness and development, *Oryx* 38: 140–142.

Bularda, D. (2017) The story of the evicted Batwa tribe in Uganda, *Youth Time*, 25 July, https://youthtimemag.com/the-story-of-the-evicted-batwa-tribe-in-uganda/ (accessed 2 September 2022).

CCFU (2017) In the name of conservation: The eviction of the Batwa from Semuliki Forest, Bundibugyo, Cross Cultural Foundation of Uganda, https://crossculturalfoundation.or.ug/wp-content/uploads/2021/01/In-the-Name-of-Conservation-The-eviction-of-the-Batwa-from-Semul iki-Forest-Bundibugyo-@CCFU2017.pdf (accessed 2 September 2022).

Chao, Y. (2012) Predicting people's environmental behaviour: Theory of planned behavior and model of responsible environmental behaviour, *Environmental Education Research* 18.4: 437–461.

Colding, J. and Folke, C. (2001) Social taboos: 'Invisible' systems of local resource management and biological conservation. *Ecological Applications* 11(2): 584–600.

Hames, R. (2007) The ecologically noble savage debate, *The Annual Review of Anthropology* 36: 177–190.

Lewis, J. (2000) The Batwa Pygmies of the Great Lakes Region, Minority Rights Group International, https://minorityrights.org/wp-content/uplo ads/old-site-downloads/download-150-Batwa-Pygmies-of-the-Great-Lakes-Region.pdf (accessed 2 September 2022).

Muhumuza, M. (2021) Lions poisoned in QENP: An indicator that UWA's 20% revenue sharing arrangement does not work, *New Vision*, 25 March, www.newvision.co.ug/category/blogs/lions-poisoned-in-qenp-an-indica tor-that-uwas-95568 (accessed 2 September 2022).

Saikia, A. (2008) Folklore and environment, *A Quarterly Newsletter from National Folklore Support Centre, India* 20: 3–4.

UNEP-WCMC (2016) The state of biodiversity in Africa: A mid-term review of progress towards the Aichi biodiversity targets, United Nations Environment Programme World Conservation Monitoring Centre, www. unep.org/resources/report/state-biodiversity-africa-mid-term-review-progress-towards-aichi-biodiversity (accessed 2 September 2022).

32

A Wounded Landscape and the Right to Protest at the River Club Site

Rifqah Tifloen

In July 2021, developers Liesbeek Leisure Properties Trust (LLPT) began construction on land that is sacred to the Khoi-San[1] and Khoena,[2] indigenous descendants of Southern Africa. The Khoena are skilled hunter-gatherers and nomadic farmers, but they are not a homogenous group. They have a green cosmology towards the enhancement of harmony between all living beings. They live in close proximity to nature – the Creator is the giver of rain, health and abundance (Boesak 2017). The First Frontier War in 1659 and theft of land resulting in the first evictions (Jenkins 2021: 36) of the Khoena violently severed that sacred link.

LLPT's proposed R4.6 billion River Club Project in Cape Town, South Africa will house the Africa headquarters of Amazon. Opposition to the development in the form of protests (Mafolo 2021) has aimed to safeguard cultural heritage, biodiversity, and stop the capture and destruction of green space by private capital. However, despite the indigenous protest and an interim interdict of March 2022 to halt this development,

---

[1] The legal government term being used is 'Khoi-San', while some traditional structures use the term 'Khoisan' (Bam 2021: xxii).

[2] 'Khoena' is a gender-neutral term and the name by which the indigenous people nearest to the Cape of Good Hope preferred to call themselves (Moodie 1838; Wells 1998). With reference to the work of June Bam (2021), I want to add a disclaimer that terms are never fixed and are constantly revisited in both scholarship and politics. She outlines the debates around the terms 'indigenous', 'first nation' and the colonial backdrop around classifications in South Africa. The preferred term used in this chapter is Khoena.

construction has commenced at the sacred natural site. LLPT claims that the development will conserve the intangible heritage[3] of the broader Two Rivers Urban Park (TRUP); however, this chapter argues that placing a site of historical and spiritual significance under the control of a private company will deny the Khoena rights to exercise their freedom of religion or belief (FoRB).

Heritage legislation devoid of Indigenous Knowledge Systems

The Khoena people's perpetual struggles for recognition make accessing any of the Sustainable Development Goals (SDGs) that much harder. The influence of international definitions of heritage are evident in the South African National Heritage Resources Act (NHRA), owing to the fact that it is based on Roman and Roman-Dutch law (Du-Toit 2014), which has its basis in Christianity and prioritizes the preservation of tangible heritage such as buildings (Skosana 2017). Some scholars (Hahlo and Kahn 1968; Hosten 1983; Chanock 2001; Skosana 2017) have suggested that South Africa's current heritage legislation overlooks indigenous knowledge and belief systems and the natural world in which these are embedded. Consequently, the area affected by the proposed TRUP development remains ungraded and unprotected, despite its heritage significance.

Indigenous-inspired definitions of heritage acknowledge and protect intangible and tangible heritage, while making provision for the relationship that indigenous communities have with the dead.[4] In the case of the TRUP, an official heritage grading would prevent the land simply being sold to the highest bidder, allowing indigenous community-led conservation to take place with suitable funding to implement such a vision. "A fundamental problem in the Western Cape government is the absence of a traditional affairs[5] office," said Marco Morgan, an urbanist from Cape Town. One

---

[3]   The Two Rivers Urban Park landscape has high cultural values of historical, social, aesthetic, architectural, scientific and environmental significances. It possesses a strong sense of place (Baseline Heritage Impact Assessment for the River Club, February 2020).

[4]   Beliefs such as the treatment of remains (that are symbolic of ancestors) with respect, as well as performing traditional rituals and ceremonies to appease the ancestors (Skosana 2017).

[5]   Traditional authority refers to when a person receives their decision-making power through long-standing customs, cultural or religious beliefs or traditions. The mission of the Department of Traditional Affairs is to coordinate traditional affairs activities across government through the development of appropriate policies and a regulatory framework governing traditional affairs; provision of support to the traditional affairs institution; enhancement of information and knowledge management on traditional affairs; and promotion of culture, heritage and social cohesion.

cannot talk about heritage without land. Speaking from his experience as a City Planner, Morgan added, "the role of culture is absent in any planning legislation."

These experiences are important in situating the broader disjuncture between religion and development at the level of policy and practice in various disciplines, highlighting the need for a more deliberate vision for development so that integrating culture goes beyond 'add religion and stir'.

The role of civic associations in development

As stated on the Observatory Civic Association's (OCA) website (OCA 2022), it represents the interests of residents and businesses in the residential area and has partnered with over 60 Khoisan groups, environmental NGOs and civic associations in opposition to the River Club development to call for heritage grading of the entire TRUP. Currently one of the main arguments by the applicant in the court case is that the developer-led consultation process was flawed, with some communities left out entirely. Additionally, OCA has noted the grounds to appeal the environmental authorization which include flooding concerns, biodiversity risk and conflict with climate change policies.

Prior to the legal action, a number of community engagements included online campaigning, community mobilization, education processes to discuss the significance of the land, protests, cultural ceremonies at the site, press events and sit-ins. Heritage Western Cape has referred the TRUP to the South African Heritage Resources Agency for Grade I heritage status. At the time of writing, the application for heritage grading remains under review. The OCA has also petitioned against the water use licence for the site as another avenue of the campaign strategy, which temporarily delayed alteration of the TRUP. However, the suspension of the water licence was subsequently lifted.

An important contextualizing element to understand the persistence of these developments is the lack of sufficient support for communities to engage on how to activate the NHRA: "For example, knowing how to comment on developments, when and which platforms, and how much to engage to activate these pieces in the legislation, and how to appeal it if it is unheard," said Morgan.

Violence and intimidation against activists who try to defend their human rights is endemic in South Africa. The OCA chair, Leslie London, and Goringhaicona Khoi Khoin Indigenous Traditional Council (GKKITC) high commissioner, Tauriq Jenkins, have experienced several smear and lawfare attacks (London 2022). "Some of the biggest constraints we've encountered has been intimidation, it is easy to bully people without the same economic power," said Nadine Dirks, campaign manager of Liesbeek Action Campaign (LAC).

> 'The organisation itself is completely run by volunteers – we face major constraints related to funding and are constantly fundraising to keep our legal recourse going. Unfortunately, it costs money to fight capitalists. We also faced an incredible amount of pushback from local government and the City, as well as some politicians who are in favour of this development for political reasons.'

LAC's objection to the land being privately owned is that the development will threaten the investigation for national heritage grading, climate resilience and indigenous community-led conservation of the site. Furthermore, LAC claims that infilling the sacred natural site with concrete is a form of ongoing ethnocide through the erasure of Khoena and San peoples' cultural history and indigenous knowledge systems. With this background, particularly in the face of the converging economic, social, ecological and climate crises, any development that threatens climate resilience will undermine the efforts carried out at the international level (including at The Convention on Biological Diversity (CBD 2022) to preserve biodiversity and the sustainable use of its components.

Nothing about us, without us

For other groups who have faced similar development struggles, Dirks reflected on the slogan used by many social movements in South Africa – 'nothing about us, without us'; we have the right to consent. People's life experiences and narratives should be placed at the core of understanding constitutional rights. TRUP heritage protection could follow examples locally where this has ultimately been successful. For example, Morgan explained how in the case of the Cape Malay Quarter, a historic Malay Muslim neighbourhood which was threatened by gentrification and development, the community resistance and mobilization efforts resulted in the Cape Town City Council approving the inclusion of the Bo Kaap area in a Heritage Protection Overlay Zone (HPOZ). The HPOZ protects heritage places that the city considers to be conservation-worthy, in terms of its heritage strategies. In this, the tangible and intangible aspects of heritage places are acknowledged. Morgan shared his experience in placing heritage on the agenda at local civic associations (LCA) meetings. The coming together of engaged community members, including from heritage protection societies and civic groups, could reduce participation fatigue and build greater 'counter-power' which challenges inequality and generates solidarity. An intersectional grassroots approach could, with deeper connections between LCAs, embed in a social movement an alternative vision for development, making it harder for developers to co-opt one particular group.

References

Bam, J. (2021) *Ausi Told Me – Why Cape Herstoriographies Matter*, Cape Town: Fanele.

Boesak, W. (2017) The cultural heritage of South African's Khoisan, in A. Xanthaki, S. Valkonen, L. Heinämäki and P. Nuorgam (eds) *Indigenous Peoples' Cultural Heritage*, Leiden: Koninklijke Brill NV.

CBD (2022) Convention on biological diversity, www.cbd.int (accessed 9 December 2022).

Chanock, M. (2001) *The Making of South African Legal Culture 1902–1936*, Cambridge: Cambridge University Press.

Du Toit, F. (2014) *Roman-Dutch Law in Modern South African Succession Law*, Nijmegen: Ars Aequi Maandblad.

Hahlo, R. and Kahn, E. (1968) *The South African Legal System*, Cape Town: Juta.

Hosten, W.J. (1983) *Introduction to South African Law and Legal Theory*, Durban: Butterworths.

Jenkins, T. (2021) When it flows, it floods, *New Agenda: South African Journal of Social and Economic Policy* 79.

LLPT (2020) River club proposed development project, https://theriverclubct.co.za (accessed 3 June 2022).

London, L. (2022) A sustained and vicious attack on the Campaign – but we are not out, Change.org, 24 November.

Mafolo, K. (2021) Bo-Kaap's 'walk of resistance' against Amazon's River Club development, *Daily Maverick*, 17 June.

Moodie, D. (ed) (1838) *The Record or, A Series of Official Papers Relative to the Condition and Treatment of the Native Tribes of South Africa*, Cape Town: AS Robertson.

OCA (2022) Two Rivers Urban Park, https://obs.org.za/two-rivers-urban-park/ (accessed 1 February 2022).

Skosana, D. (2017) Protecting the dead: The South African National Heritage Resources Act in context, in M.C. Green, R.I.J. Hackett, L. Hansen and F. Venter (eds) *Religious Pluralism, Heritage and Social Development in Africa*, Stellenbosch: Conf-RAP.

Wells, J.C. (1998) Eva's men: Gender and power in the establishment of the Cape of Good Hope, 1652–74, *The Journal of African History* 39.3: 417.

33

Climate Justice for the
Religiously Marginalized

Lyla Mehta

Climate change is one of the most critical development challenges of our times. As acknowledged by the Intergovernmental Panel on Climate Change (IPCC 2022), human-induced climate change has led to more frequent and intense extreme events in the form of floods, droughts, heatwaves and cyclones, causing massive adverse impacts and losses and damage to nature and people. These events are becoming the new normal in both the Global North and South and reiterated at annual gatherings, such as the Conference of the Parties (COP), the United Nations Framework for Climate Change (UNFCC), and also UN and national summits. Climate change and other forms of environmental change, such as biodiversity loss, pollution and environmental degradation of life-giving resources such as water, have massive impacts on human wellbeing, as well as planetary health. While everybody is affected, it is now widely acknowledged that the most vulnerable people and systems are disproportionately so (IPCC 2021). These include indigenous peoples, marginalized groups and vulnerable communities.

While the science is now clear and largely undisputed, there remain deep differences in the ways in which climate change and other kinds of environmental change are dealt with in science, global development and the policy spheres, and how ordinary people (characterized as the 'below' by Mehta et al 2021) make sense of and experience climate change in their everyday lives. Indeed, ethnographic research on climate-induced calamities often documents how local communities evoke the wrath of God or the Gods to make sense of the impacts of these extreme events. For example, in recent research on climate change in the drought-prone drylands of Kutch in western India and the wetlands of the Sundarbans Delta in Bengal, we found local communities evoke the power of God/Gods to unleash so much destruction which they often attribute to too much sinning in the world (Mehta et al 2021). Here, it is belief that helps people make sense of rapid and extreme changes that cause such damage to their livelihoods, agricultural lands and livestock.

Relatedly, religion and also cosmological beliefs provide ethical and social norms that call for transformative change to lifestyles, consumption patterns and ways of living and being on Earth, and also co-existing with other non-human species and beings. They provide visions regarding how to deal with the challenges of a changing climate, both in the here and now and for the future. Examples include Pope Francis' encyclical *Laudato Si: On Care for Our Common Home* (Pope Francis 2015) that offers an ethical vision regarding 'human dignity, responsibility and purpose' (see Hulme 2017) or the Dalai Lama's call to global political decision-makers to fight against inaction and ignorance and work towards a more climate-friendly world, especially so that the youth can regain their future (The Dalai Lama 2020). And there are numerous examples from indigenous beliefs and systems that draw on equitable and caring human nature relations. For example, indigenous world-views of the Māori and other indigenous groups marginalized in policy 'are sophisticated repositories of the natural world and human nature relations' (Oxley 2020: 167). Thus, religion not only makes sense of the climate collapse that many vulnerable communities are already living with but also offers hope, visions and ways to transform human nature relations to be more synergistic rather than extractive. Thus, it is important that climate adaptation, as well as environmental and conservation programmes, build on the beliefs, knowledges and practices of local communities, indigenous peoples and minorities, rather than alienate them.

Religious inequalities and barriers to freedom of religion or belief (FoRB) exist in most societies. These can also affect a person's ability to both live with and adapt to human-induced climate change and also to respond when disaster strikes. There can often be a strong relationship between ethnicity, caste, religious belief and access to and exclusion from services (Shah and Shah 2022). Many vulnerable and marginalized people belong to religious minorities. As demonstrated by Srivastava and Bachina (this volume), they often reside in disaster-prone, marginalized environments (for example, low-lying coastal areas prone to flooding) and are often discriminated against and excluded from relief and benefits. Their livelihoods tend also to be more risky. The case of sanitation workers or manual scavengers is a good case in point. In South Asia, most of them belong to lower or discriminated caste groups (for example, Dalits in India and lower-caste Christians in Pakistan). They are not only exposed to risks from this work (see Thomas and Gill, this volume), but these risks are also amplified during extreme weather events such as flooding (Tadros 2022a). Thus, it is very important that policy makers and local officials ensure that the needs and rights of religiously marginalized groups are met and protected during extreme weather events. This could include providing protective gear to sanitation workers who often lack PPE while they do their work, or ensuring that excluded minorities are not by-passed in relief and rehabilitation programmes during floods and cyclones.

Muhumuza (this volume) has described how many indigenous peoples and minorities across Africa are evicted from their lands while national parks are created, often in the name of conservation. At the same time, their cosmological beliefs concerning the forests, waters and lands are ignored and belittled. In the case of the Batwa (so-called pygmies) in the Semuliki National Park in western Uganda, efforts were made to both convert them to the Seventh Day Adventist Church from their traditional animist beliefs, and to evict them from their natural environment. This resulted in both an increase in human–wildlife conflicts (for example, fires, death of lions) and loss of biodiversity. Instead, it would be more helpful to design conservation programmes that build on rather than alienate the world-views and lifestyles of indigenous groups such as the Batwa.

All over the world, indigenous peoples are subjected to dispossession because their lands, while 'remote', are usually resource rich and targeted by mining companies, national parks and so on. Tifloen (this volume) discusses how the Khoisan, the first peoples of South Africa, have land that is of historical and spiritual significance to them that is now targeted by the Liesbeek Leisure Properties Trust (LLPT) to build the River Club Project in Cape Town for Amazon (LLPT 2020). This alienation from their spiritual lands will not only affect their sense of place, livelihoods and wellbeing but also has negative impacts on the Khoisan's FoRB.

Tadros (2022b) argues that FoRB is a blindspot in development policy and practice, and this could also be said about climate and environmental policies too. This includes the SDGs where religious inequality is not highlighted upfront. Many minorities suffer due to their religious beliefs and practices, both in terms of not realizing their basic freedoms but also due to underlying power differentials (Tadros 2022b). SDG13 urges us to 'take urgent action to combat climate change and its impacts' (UNEP 2022), and Target 13.b explicitly calls for promoting 'mechanisms for raising capacity for effective climate change-related planning and management in least developed countries and small island developing states, including focusing on women, youth and local and marginalized communities'. Yet this SDG fails to mention religion or culture. This is despite the fact that, in 2021, eight out of ten people identified with religion in countries that are recipients of overseas aid (Tomalin et al 2019). The central tenet of the SDGs is 'to leave no-one behind'. This means an inclusive approach to development, and paying attention to marginalized people and their voices, needs and perspectives. The same can be said about climate and global environmental change impacts. Marginalized groups and minorities who are discriminated against on the basis of religion often experience multiple forms of exclusion, due to the intersections of religion, caste, gender and class. This is why their concerns need to be taken seriously and addressed via more inclusive environmental and adaptation policies, which embrace diversity and are explicit about processes of discrimination and injustices.

It is also important for national governments to recognize the importance of FoRB in terms of climate and environmental change. This is because promoting mainstream understandings of religion can undermine syncretic and plural beliefs and practices that often play a key role in both coping with environmental disasters and also conserving natural resources. All around the world, billions of people mix and match beliefs. In India, for example, Hindus often pray at Sufi shrines and Hindus and Muslims go to churches to get blessings (Shah and Shah 2022). Indigenous Adivasis may officially be Hindu or Christian but still maintain their indigenous beliefs and practices regarding nature and conservation (Mader 2022). People can be 'secular' but also be culturally rooted in a religious tradition (like myself as a Parsi Zoroastrian who grew up in Bombay, now Mumbai, India). Policy processes should thus avoid binary thinking in terms of secular vs religious, and instead consider that many people may have fluid relationships regarding their religious identity or identities. While those who are agnostic or secular may often disregard certain doctrinal matters, they may identify with or be proud of the religio-cultural heritage they were born into.

It is important that this syncretism is not undermined through national policies that tend to focus either on 'officially' recognized religions or, sadly, promote majoritarian views, as in the case of India (Shah and Shah 2022). For example, the Sundarbans delta is a so-called climate hotspot across India and Bangladesh and is home to over 5 million people. Belief in *Bonbibi* (the lady of the forest) shapes the way residents respond to the perils of life in the delta. Syncretic beliefs in *Bonbibi* unite Hindus, Muslims and Adivasis across political and religious divides (Jalais 2014). But the spread of Hindutva in India and more rigid forms of Islam in Bangladesh are undermining these syncretic beliefs and indigenous ways of living with and coping with radical environmental change and disasters.

Policies committed to sustainable development, both at the national and global levels, need to support cultural, syncretic and indigenous values and world-views (even around so-called 'sacred sites and groves'). SDG13 and future policies on sustainable development also need to take into account the loss and damage that has been encountered by marginalized and vulnerable people, largely due to colonialist and extractivist policies on the part of rich and privileged actors and countries. Ultimately pushing for a decolonial and intersectional perspective on climate and sustainability can lead to a greater appreciation of multiple ontologies (including of religious minorities and indigenous peoples) and open up debates and pluriversality. These will not only validate and lift the perspectives of marginalized groups but will also contribute to achieving climate justice and more sustainable and respectful human nature relations (Johnson et al 2022).

References

Hulme, M. (2017) Climate change and the significance of religion, *Economic and Political Weekly* 28: 14–17.

IPCC (2022) Climate change 2022: Impacts, adaptation and vulnerability, Working Group II Contribution to the IPCC Sixth Assessment Report, Cambridge: Cambridge University Press.

Jalais, A. (2014) *Forest of Tigers: People, Politics and Environment in the Sundarbans*, London: Routledge.

Johnson, D.E., Parsons, M. and Fisher, K. (2022) Indigenous climate change adaptation: New directions for emerging scholarship, *Environment and Planning E: Nature and Space* 5.3: 1541–1578.

Mader, P. (2022) 'We put God and drums in the front': Spirituality as strategy in an Adivasi self-empowerment movement, in M. Tadros (ed) *What about Us? Global Perspectives on Redressing Religious Inequalities*, Brighton: Institute of Development Studies.

Mehta, L., Adam, H.N. and Srivastava, S. (eds) (2021) *The Politics of Climate Change and Uncertainty in India*, London: Taylor & Francis.

Oxley, N. (2020) Unsettling the apocalypse: Uncertainty in spirituality and religion, in I. Scoones and A. Stirling (eds) *The Politics of Uncertainty: The Challenges of Transformation*, Oxford: Routledge: 164–174.

Pope Francis (2015) *Encyclical Letter: Laudato Si of the Holy Father Francis – On Care for our Common Home*, Rome: Vatican Press.

Shah, R. and Shah, T. (2022) The other invisible hand: How freedom of religion or belief fosters pro-social and pro-developmental outcomes for the poor, in M. Tadros (ed) *What about Us? Global Perspectives on Redressing Religious Inequalities*, Brighton: Institute of Development Studies.

Tadros, M. (2022a) COP27: Climate justice: Where do the religiously marginalised fit in?, *Global Issues*, 14 November.

Tadros, M. (2022b) Religious equality and freedom of religion or belief: International development's blindspot, *The Review of Faith and International Affairs* 20.2: 96–108.

The Dalai Lama with Franz Alt. (2020) *Our Only Home: A Climate Appeal to the World*, London: Bloomsbury.

Tomalin, E., Haustein, J. and Kidy, S. (2019) Religion and the Sustainable Development Goals, *The Review of Faith and International Affairs* 17.2: 102–118.

UNEP (2022) Goal 13: Climate action, United Nations Environment Programme.

PART IX

Peace and Justice

34

The Significance of Freedom of Religion or Belief for Peace, Justice and Strong Institutions

W. Cole Durham, Jr

The aim of this chapter is to focus on one specific dimension of the relationship between freedom of religion or belief (FoRB) and the Sustainable Development Goals (SDGs) – namely its relationship to SDG16, which calls for Peace, Justice and Strong Institutions. The aim of SDG16 is to 'promote peaceful and inclusive societies for sustainable development, provide access to justice for all and build effective, accountable and inclusive institutions at all levels'. SDG16 is integrally related to all the other SDGs, because it sets forth the foundational institutional conditions necessary to achieve all the others. In a similar way, FoRB is foundational to building the kinds of social conditions and institutions that SDG16 aspires to create.

This is not necessarily obvious from the explicit framing of SDG16 and its related targets and indicators. Most of the targets focus on issues seemingly unrelated to FoRB: reducing violence and death rates (Target 16.l); ending abuse, exploitation, trafficking and violence against children (Target 16.2) reducing illicit financial and arms flows and combatting organized crime (Target 16.4); substantially reducing bribery and corruption (Target 16.5) and so on. Even those targets that seem relevant don't directly address FoRB. Rather, they address more abstract issues, such as promoting the rule of law and equal access to justice (Target 16.3); protecting fundamental freedoms, in accordance with national legislation and international agreements (Target 16.10); and promoting and enforcing non–discriminatory laws and policies for sustainable development (Target 16.B).

The absence of explicit focus on FoRB in the official formulation of SDG16 and its tracking mechanisms is not altogether surprising. Measuring

FoRB is notoriously difficult, and the linkage of FoRB to establishing peace, promoting justice and helping to assure strong institutions is complex and sometimes indirect. Yet it is difficult to imagine that these objectives can be attained where FoRB is not protected.

Inattention to FoRB issues becomes even more apparent when one turns to efforts aimed at reversing slowed progress during the COVID-19 pandemic towards achieving the SDGs. Adjustments are articulated primarily in terms of new financial steps that are necessary (see, for example, Sachs et al 2022), with a focus on practical pathways for increasing SDG financing (Sachs et al 2022: 3). According to the 2022 Sustainable Development Report, '[a]chieving the SDGs is fundamentally an investment agenda … [focusing on] building physical infrastructure and key services'.

There is some recognition that 'bedrock principles of the SDGs of social inclusion, global cooperation, and universal access to public services are needed' (Sachs et al 2022: 3), but in a world with shrinking financial resources, priority is placed on 'six SDG Transformations' which, with the exception of quality education, relate primarily to physical resources. Significantly, SDG16 is not listed among these key priorities (Sachs et al 2022: 35, 40–46), and FoRB remains a forgotten priority.

With this in mind, the aim of this chapter is to demonstrate that FoRB provides the fundamental underlying social and political architecture vital for the achievement of SDG16, and by implication, for the other SDGs as well. The ideal of human dignity, which is integrally linked to freedom of thought, conscience and religion, is critical to stabilizing just social orders, and, as such, is critical to just peace at all levels – global, national, local, family and individual relations (Durham and Clark 2015).

In many ways, this is simply a restatement of a time-tested axiom of modern pluralist societies. But this axiom is paradoxical in key respects. It entails requiring members of society to respect the right of others to hold beliefs that may be deeply different from their own. This in turn means that social structures cannot be based on specific sets of commonly held values, except the reciprocally recognized right for different groups and individuals (subject to only strictly limited restrictions) to choose and act on their own values. For this reason, the canons of FoRB often seem counterintuitive at the level of ordinary politics, where differing values are often at the heart of incendiary conflicts.

The dark side of religion

It is important to address the common misperceptions that exaggerate the role that religion plays in social conflict, and to explicate the crucial role that FoRB plays in achieving, stabilizing and strengthening social peace, including its role in protecting dignity, anchoring the rule of law, making stable pluralism possible and identifying various practical ways that FoRB can contribute to the achievement of SDG16. During much of human history, religion has been viewed as a major source of social tensions and divisiveness. Because religious differences are deep and non-negotiable, they lead to intractable conflicts that have littered the pages of history. While there is some truth to this account, there are several reasons to think this picture overstates the dark side of religion. We are much less naïve about thinking that religion *per se* is a cause of conflict. Historically, the secularist historical account of the emergence of religious freedom, according to which the Westphalian achievement of religious peace was accomplished by relegating religion to the private sphere, has been subjected to rigorous academic challenge (Cavenaugh 2009).

Close analysis of conflicts that involve religious actors often demonstrate that it is not religion itself that causes conflicts but a variety of other factors (see Powers 2010: 319–320, Toft 2012: 138–142). Violence in the name of religion may reflect the instrumentalization of religion by other social actors. This is not to claim that religion is never responsible for violence and conflict but simply a reminder that great care should be taken in attributing blame.

The reciprocity of dignity

Dignity is an idea that has its roots in a variety of traditions – from antiquity, from theology, from Enlightenment philosophy and more (see McCrudden 2013). It is an idea that serves as a foundation for, an objective of and a criterion of, human rights thinking more generally. The ideal of dignity has a generative power in discourse with the potential to expand vision and raise sights. It has an inherent reciprocity, impelling those on one side of a moral argument to take the dignity of others into account.

Moreover, it is a discursive concept with an upward trajectory. It typically serves as a basis for generating agreement and building common understanding – building consensus on a higher plane than might have been reached without the appeal to dignity. Where conflicts arise, it can point to grounds for reconciliation. As the Punta del Este Declaration reminds us, the concept of dignity is not merely a static minimum condition for peace. It dynamically reinforces the core of pluralistic stability. Protecting dignity generates gratitude as a social by-product which translates into stability-reinforcing loyalty. This is the deep inner force sustaining peace, justice and strong institutions, as called for by SDG16.

The difficulty with the foregoing picture is that it can be overshadowed by the paradox at the centre of practical implementation of FoRB ideals. The challenge is that the deep stabilizing and centripetal forces elicited by dignity and FoRB can easily be overwhelmed by centrifugal forces of polarization emanating from deep differences. Such tendencies are all too often exacerbated in our sound-bite culture by media that highlights and compounds polarization, splitting us into rival tribes.

The way forward

Even in our polarized and polarizing times, however, dignity and its related legal shield, the right to FoRB, can be helpful. Consider the following ways that respect for dignity and FoRB can contribute to building and strengthening a stable and just peace:

1. Taking religious freedom seriously can help stabilize constitutional moments.

Constitutions are not drafted behind Rawlsian veils of ignorance. They are forged by people exerting courage at times of political crisis. In such pre-constitutional moments, constitutional norms which threaten religion or belief groups are unlikely to be stable. Candid recognition of legitimate FoRB concerns can defuse suspicions that can otherwise poison the constitution-making atmosphere.

2. It is important to remember some of the practical ways that religious actors can contribute to resolution of conflict and peacebuilding.

In times of conflict, religious freedom secures the ability of religious leaders to assume peacebuilding roles as trusted conflict mediators. Religious freedom helps cultivate an array of socially productive virtues, such as tolerance, reflective thinking, generosity, altruism, law-abidingness, honesty, helpfulness to others and social trust. It also helps nurture the mediating institutions between the individual and the megastructures of society that can otherwise contribute to alienation and anomie (Berger and Neuhaus 1977).

3. Religious institutions, if duly protected, can be helpful in opening channels of dialogue and negotiation.

They can build peace in practical ways by making key mediating personnel available to peace processes. FoRB can also contribute to strengthening the material foundations needed for just peace. If religious institutions and believers are protected in their core dignity, they can expend less energy on self-protection and the resulting peace dividend translates into increased social and material production (Durham and Clark 2015: 296–297).

4. Protecting dignity in general and protecting FoRB in particular create important filtering mechanisms in society, which help to optimize the

social goods generated by religion, while imposing restrictions on religious evils (Durham and Clark 2015: 294–295).

In this regard, it is helpful to think of religious freedom norms as finely honed tools which, if exercised properly, can restrict the dark side of religion, while protecting core values of pluralism, freedom, dignity and the countless other social goods with which religious freedom is empirically correlated.

Conclusion

FoRB constitutes a vital part of the foundational architecture of SDG16. It is critical for defusing conflict, creating the conditions from which peace can crystallize, and maintaining the dynamics that can stabilize and strengthen peace. It lies at the heart of what makes stable pluralism possible. FoRB is both a feature and a criterion of justice and just institutions. No society that violates FoRB qualifies as just. States that violate FoRB lack the neutrality and impartiality that are essential characteristics of the rule of law. Beyond such formal injustice, infringing FoRB violates the substantive requirements of human dignity. Societies that violate FoRB lack stable, sustainable strength. Unjust power may exert sway for a time, but it lacks the stabilizing dynamism that respect for deep difference provides. For all of these reasons, and many more, FoRB is foundational for SDG16 because it is foundational for the peace, justice and strong institutions which SDG16 aspires to achieve.

References

Berger, P.L. and Neuhaus, R.J. (1977) *To Empower People: The Role of Mediating Structures in Public Policy,* Washington, DC: American Enterprise Institute for Public Policy Research.

Cavenaugh, W.T. (2009) *The Myte of Religious Violence: Secular Ideology and the Roots of Modern Conflict*, Oxford: Oxford University Press.

Durham, Jr, W.C. and Clark, E.A. (2015) The place of religious freedom in the structure of peacebuilding, in A. Omer, R.S. Appleby and D. Little (eds) *The Oxford Handbook of Religion, Conflict, and Peacebuilding*, Oxford: Oxford University Press.

McCrudden, C. (ed) (2013) *Understanding Human Dignity*, Oxford: Oxford University Press.

Powers, G.F. (2010) Religion and peacebuilding, in D. Philpott and G.F. Powers (eds) *Strategies of Peace: Transforming Conflict in a Violent World,* Oxford: Oxford University Press.

Sachs, J., Lafortune, G., Kroll, C., Fuller, G. and Woelm, F. (2022) From crisis to sustainable development: the SDGs as roadmap to 2030 and beyond, Sustainable Development Report 2022, Cambridge: Cambridge University Press.

Toft, M.D. (2012) Religion, terrorism, and civil wars, in T.S. Shah, A. Stepan and M.D. Toft (eds) *Rethinking Religion and World Affairs*, Oxford: Oxford University Press.

35

Recovering from the Trauma of Insurgency in Northern Nigeria

Maji Peterx

In Nigeria, religion affects every sphere of public life, from politics to educational admission and employment. While a quota system is in place intending to make sure positions and appointments reflect representation from every region, its outcomes in practice are widely perceived to be unfair. Nigeria is a nation with an almost exactly even share of Muslims and Christians. The southern part of the country is predominantly Christian and the north predominantly Muslim, with a few states in the 'Middle Belt' having a predominantly Christian population. Borno State in the northeast (the operational base of the radical Islamist insurgency group, Boko Haram) is a predominantly Muslim state with a minority Christian population in its southern part. The minority Christian population suffer discrimination, unequal opportunities, marginalization and prejudice, all of which they experience as traumatizing. Additionally, the Boko Haram insurgency, with its attacks, killings and displacement, has subjected them to continuous, cumulative trauma with no focused support and nowhere to run for succour.

Despite Boko Haram being known to also attack Muslims and bomb their places of worship, non-Muslims usually suffer more severe attacks and are the group's primary targets. Furthermore, Christians are not given the same opportunities and privileges as others in the areas of employment, educational admission, political appointments and so on. It is almost impossible for Christians in Borno to contest for any political position beyond the local level (councillor, Local Government Chairman, State Assembly), such as national assembly positions (House of Representatives/Senate) or governor of the state. No Christian, no matter how popular, experienced or well placed, has ever stood for governorship, which would almost certainly be an impossible venture. Christians in Borno are not even offered the deputy governor position, like in other states with sizeable Christian and Muslim populations, such as Gombe, Kaduna and Adamawa.

There are also indigenous religions, whose open adherents number less than 1 per cent, that are even more marginalized compared to members of the two major religions in Nigeria, Christianity and Islam. As such, very few people openly proclaim they are adherents of indigenous religions, despite it being common knowledge that some members of the dominant religions patronize traditional spiritual leaders and priests privately and practise indigenous religious rites in secret, seeking protection amulets, spiritual powers or safety from enemies, evil plots and attacks.

Addressing divisions and healing communities' trauma

The Global Center on Cooperative Security, an international non-profit peace and security think tank, funded a project that seeks to create a community that is inclusive of all in Borno and Yobe states in northern Nigeria, especially in communities that have experienced mass atrocities and are traumagenic (where trauma is endemic). The Preventing and Transforming Violent Extremism (PTVE) project was based on the premise that the collective effort of community members is vital in creating a support structure that enables the building of resilience (see also Kwaja, this volume, for a more economic opportunity-focused approach on building communities' resilience in a different part of Nigeria). When people are confronted by loss, displacement and attacks by violent extremist groups, this is compounded by discrimination and marginalization on account of faith or belief.

To address the challenges in select communities of Maiduguri, Damaturu, Mubi and Michika, Carefronting Nigeria (the organization that implemented the PTVE project) carried out a context analysis to ascertain the communities' principal needs, and then trained a selection of youth, women and men, and religious and traditional leaders on Trauma Consciousness and Resilience (TCR). Participants were then organized into support groups, with first responders and psychosocial first aiders trained to support others who are traumatized within the community. This training functioned to reduce trauma triggers, anger and the desire for vengeance, promoting instead forgiveness and reconciliation. A woman whose niece was abducted by Boko Haram and later returned with her own child said: "I just felt the hate melting away, I won't live my life angry with others for ruining the life of my niece, we can't undo what has happened. Rather, I will support her to move on and pick up the pieces."

The project focused on teaching 'Shared Humanity' (an approach that emphasizes that we are humans first, before any other identity) and how endemic and transferable trauma is, emphasizing people's need to come together and to heal together; one person's trauma can affect a whole family, and one family's trauma can impact the whole community. To tackle insurgency, all hands must be on deck, and this necessary collectivism is hindered by discrimination and exclusion.

When people settle in a place and have lived there for a long time, they call it home, but when they start feeling like they are being treated unfairly and with prejudice, they begin to feel like strangers in their own home. This feeling may be worsened by the fact that, while Nigeria's constitution guarantees freedom of religious belief, people do not experience this in practice for they cannot practise their religion or beliefs freely without fear.

In Borno, Christians already feel marginalized and are easy targets for violent extremist groups like Boko Haram, the Islamic States of West African Province (ISWAP) and the Vanguard for the Protection of Muslims in Black Africa (Ansaru), who subscribe to extremist versions of Islam. In this circumstance, minority groups already often nurse grudges and anger and do not feel committed to the growth, development and cohesiveness of the community as a whole because of how they have been treated and how they expect future generations to be treated in Borno. Such feelings and emotions compound trauma and heighten fear and insecurity. This became evident during the basic training sessions in TCR, which allowed participants to express pain, anger and anguish through narrative exercises. Participants shared very personal experiences of atrocities they had either witnessed or experienced. A participant screamed and asked, "How can I heal? They killed my father and 90 days later they killed my husband. How can I heal, how can I ever stop grieving? I just want to die too."

Thankfully, this participant's story is different today – she has processed what happened to her, has been able to come to terms with it, to accept it and to start living again. The experiences shared during these sessions prompted the development and integration of training on forgiveness and reconciliation as an intermediate step before progressing to more advanced TCR Training.

The basic training aims for participants to deal with their personal trauma, while the aim of the more advanced training is for participants to support others that are traumatized. The intermediate forgiveness and reconciliation training helps participants deal with anger, grudges and revenge-seeking behaviours, promoting 'letting go' and 'moving forward'. For example, one participant who had lost family members (their father, brother, sister, nephews and nieces) and who had also taken in the orphans from the attack, openly expressed his desire for vengeance and to kill the perpetrators of the crime. The participant broke down in the workshop, and through this was ultimately able to let go. Today, he is an advocate of forgiveness and reconciliation, convening community forums to build trust and relationships across religious communities.

Collective problem solving and 'Hidden Processing'

This approach helps the communities to bond, based on an understanding that, if they need to heal as a community, they must heal together. Trauma affects everyone. If minorities' trauma is ignored, their trauma will impact the fabric of the whole society. Highlighting what is at stake and what everyone stands to gain redirects community members' focus and attention towards community growth, development and peaceful coexistence. When opposing groups find a solution to a collective challenge, it influences the group response. This is the focus of 'Hidden Processing', which emphasizes altering stereotypes and biases without explicitly naming them. With Boko Haram as a common enemy, limiting everyone's freedom and threatening their economy and livelihoods, people are at risk irrespective of religion, belief or tribe. Tackling a collective problem together is how a relationship of support and 'standing for one another' begins.

There is a well-known expression that 'an enemy is someone whose whole story you have not heard yet'. I remember listening to the confession of a perpetrator who revealed that they had been forced to use violence or they themselves would be killed. That these violent acts were born from an effort to save their own lives made me see the perpetrators of these acts differently. The impact of the PTVE project was to bring people with different experiences together, reflecting the importance of collective problem solving and the catharsis and necessity of facilitating spaces for the processing of trauma for marginalized communities in northern Nigeria. It is necessary to facilitate individual and collective recovery from painful experiences to enable the community to grow, rather than react.

36

Religion, Caste and Marginality: Reflections on the Indian Criminal Justice and Prison System

Devangana Kalita

Zeeshan Mallick, an 18-year-old Muslim man, was arrested by Delhi Police on 20 November 2021. Accused of stealing a packet of cigarettes, he was lodged in South Asia's largest prison, Tihar Jail in Delhi. Zeeshan never returned home. Three months later, on 17 February 2022, his dead body was given to his family, bearing bruises and broken bones; the police authorities claimed he died due to 'illness' (NH Web Desk 2022). The family found the police narrative dubious given Zeeshan had been perfectly healthy when they had recently visited him in prison, but their demand for a proper investigation into his death in custody went unheard.

Ugandan prisoner under trial, Jesca Sarah Kafeeco, whom I had met during the 13 months I spent in Tihar's Jail No. 6, met a similar fate. In August 2020, Jesca died while undergoing surgery for injuries that she had sustained during a brutal assault by jail authorities on African women prisoners, who had held a protest to demand that the interim bail to decongest prisons during the COVID-19 pandemic, which had been granted to certain categories of Indian prisoners, also be extended to foreign prisoners (*The Hindu* 2020a). Jesca had not even participated in the protest – she was attacked because she was a black woman. Zeeshan or Jesca's death are not 'exceptions'; they constitute a glaring reality in Indian prisons, where violence and torture have become institutionalized.

Who lives and dies in Indian prisons? An analysis of India's prison population

Between 2018–2021, nearly five people have died every day in India's prisons (*The Times of India* 2021). Yet state scrutiny into the rising deaths under judicial custody has been minimal, with even the basic legal procedures for reporting and investigating such deaths routinely violated. Based on an analysis of data from the annual reports of the National Human Rights Commission (NHRC) from 1996–1997 to 2017–2018, the National Campaign against Torture estimates that 71.58 per cent of the people who died in custody were from poor or marginalized sections of society (*The Hindu* 2020b). This is not surprising since the Indian prison population largely constitutes people from religious minorities and historically marginalized groups. People from these communities are criminalized and jailed in numbers that are much higher compared to their share in the population at large, as Table 36.1 shows (*Economic and Political Weekly* 2020). The latest Prison Statistics India Report from 2020 shows that 65.90 per cent of prison inmates, a total of 315,409 inmates, belonged to Scheduled Castes (SC), Scheduled Tribes (ST) and Other Backward Class (OBC) categories (Mint 2021; Gurmat 2022).

Table 36.1: Caste and religion of prison population in India

	Percentage of those under trial	Percentage of convicts	Percentage of population (as per 2011 census)
Scheduled castes	20.9	20.9	16.6
Scheduled tribes	10.5	13.9	8.6
OBC	34.3	37.2	41.0*
Religion of prisoners			
Hindus	67.0	75.7	79.8
Muslims	19.6	17.4	14.2
Sikhs	3.5	2.3	1.7
Christians	2.2	3.1	2.3
Others	0.6	1.5	2.0

Note: In the analysis of this data, it is to be noted that the state of Maharashtra has not provided caste and religion segregated data for undertrial prisoners. * This is as per National Sample Survey Organisation (NSSO) 2006, since census does not have data on OBC population.

Source: National Crime Records Bureau Ministry of Home Affairs (2020)

A study by National Law University, Delhi, about the socio-economic profiles of 373 of 385 prisoners currently on death row in India revealed the disparate impact of the death penalty on marginalized communities. Seventy-six per cent, or 279 prisoners, are from lower castes or religious minorities, 74.1 per cent are from economically vulnerable backgrounds, 23 per cent have never attended school, 62 per cent have not completed their secondary education (Sen 2016). In the state of Gujarat, where 9.67 per cent of the population are Muslim, 15 out of 19 prisoners sentenced to death were Muslims.

'Crime' and 'punishment': who gets jailed and who gets justice?

While Dalits, Adivasis and Muslims are overrepresented in prisons, survivors of crimes who belong to these communities find it extremely difficult to even register criminal cases or gain a fair investigation into incidents of attacks against them based on their caste, gender or religious identity. For instance, the conviction rate in the Scheduled Castes and Scheduled Tribes (Prevention of Atrocities) Act stood at just 7 per cent in 2020 (Express News Service 2022). Under the current Hindutva regime, the distinct identities and socio-cultural practices of religious minorities, such as their rituals of prayer, food habits or choice of clothes, has been proscribed to such an extent that their very existence has come to be criminalized. This is particularly pronounced in the case of Muslims. Recent 'anti-conversion' laws implemented across different states in India, to address what Hindu right-wing groups call 'love-jihad', have effectively criminalized consensual interfaith marriages. This has entailed indiscriminate arrests of young Muslim men while representing a concerted attack on women's agency (Srivastava 2021). There have also been many cases where stringent national security and terror laws have been invoked to arrest Muslim men for the alleged 'crime' of cow slaughter as, once charged under these clauses, securing bail becomes extremely difficult (Sahu 2020).

For the poor, the only accessible legal representation is through extremely slow-working and ineffective government-supported legal aid services, where lawyers are over-burdened, poorly compensated and rarely able to put adequate effort into cases. Consequently, it is not surprising that the population under trial is extremely high and increasing. Three out of every four people, 76.1 per cent of all prisoners in India, are under trial rather than convicted. Between 2015–2020, there was a 31.8 per cent increase of prisoners under trial (Gurmat 2022). In states like Jammu, Kashmir and Delhi, over 90 per cent of the prison population are under trials (Suresh 2022). Very high rates of case pendency, low convictions and the minuscule number of judges (14 judges per million people) means that until radical changes are introduced into the criminal justice system, these figures will continue growing.

Who can leave an Indian prison? Challenges to release post bail

A barrack-mate during my prison time, an 18-year-old pregnant Muslim woman accused of stealing a mobile phone, was granted bail a month after being arrested. Yet she could not leave prison as there was no one in the outside world with a house and an address willing to provide her bail security. Five months pregnant, she had to endure the deadly second wave of the COVID-19 pandemic inside Tihar Jail, where she contracted the virus and had a difficult recovery. Extremely depressed and not allowed to contact her family by the jail authorities while being kept in the COVID-19 aftercare ward, where there was no access to phones, she attempted suicide.

It is very common that, even after securing bail, getting out of prison becomes a difficult process for those from marginalized communities, as the so-called equal protection by law is mediated by property relations (Karnam and Nanda 2016). With the intention to ensure presence at trial, bail conditions require a specified bail amount in cash or other forms of security, along with sureties by individuals with verifiable local addresses. The Supreme Court in 2016 had strongly condemned this property-based bail system, categorically stating that 'it is against the spirit of law to incarcerate people only because of their poverty'. It ordered the legal services authority to take up cases of prisoners who are unable to furnish bail and are still in custody. Yet such cases continue to persist in significant numbers, despite judicial interventions.

Who labours in Indian prisons? Prison conditions, hierarchies and discrimination

Besides facing painfully long periods of incarceration with minimal legal support, prisoners from marginalized or minority communities are also subject to harsher forms of exploitation and discrimination in jail. Indian prisons are infamous for inhumane living conditions, very high rates of overcrowding and terrible access to health, education, employment and recreational facilities. The prison system itself runs on the highly underpaid labour of inmates from socially and economically disadvantaged backgrounds.[1] All tasks required for the running of the prison, such as

---

[1] There exists no uniform legal safeguard that guarantees a minimum wage for the work that prisoners perform in prisons across India. Wages for prison labour differ across states. Delhi Prison Rules 2018 stipulate that prisoners be paid minimum wage. However, maintenance costs are deducted from prisoners' due wages, and these can be as high as 65 per cent of

cooking, cleaning, office work and so on are performed by prisoners. Indian prisons replicate the caste-based division of labour in the assignment of tasks to inmates. Many states, even in their official manuals, dictate that labour within prison be allocated on the basis of caste. Lower-caste prisoners are usually allotted work that involves sweeping, cleaning of sewers and septic tanks, while upper-caste prisoners are employed in kitchens, medical rooms and offices (Shantha 2020).

Towards de-carceration and restorative justice

An old Muslim woman whom I befriended during my prison time told me once: "*hame andha kanoon nahi chahiye, hum chahte hai ki kanoon dekhe, kaun gareeb hai, kaun peereet hai* [we don't want a law that is blind, we want law to see, to see who is poor, who is oppressed]".

She was saying this about the figure of the blind-folded Justice Lady, bearing balance scales, that adorns Indian cinema's representation of a courtroom. She had been languishing in jail for more than two years without access to a lawyer, with no clarity on even the exact charges and accusations against her. Because of the gendered social stigma associated with a woman going to prison, her family had abandoned her. The old woman's piercing observation stayed with me. So much unimaginable pain, devastation and injustice has been caused by the lack of consideration in the criminal justice system to deeply entrenched caste, class and communal biases; the state-police machinery compounds, along caste and religious lines, the vicious cycles of inequitable access to education, health services and employment that produce and accentuate what comes to constitute 'crime'.

Angela Davis (2003: 16), in arguing for prison abolition, poignantly observed that the existence of prisons creates an ideological apparatus that prevents meaningful engagement with and responsibility towards addressing the real issues affecting those communities from which prisoners are drawn in disproportionate numbers. In countries like India, the criminal justice and prison systems continue to reproduce colonial legal apparatuses that criminalized and disadvantaged Dalits, Adivasis, Muslims and other religious minorities. It is imperative to pursue strategies of de-carceration and restorative justice.

---

the wages for 'unskilled' work. This basically means that the expenses of middle- and upper-caste prisoners, who largely come from upper-caste or religious minorities, who do not need to work inside prison to survive, are borne by the state, while poor prisoners partly pay for their own incarceration and subsidize state prison expenditure.

References

Davis, A. (2003) *Are Prisons Obsolete?*, New York: Seven Stories Press.

Economic and Political Weekly (2020) Action on prison data, *Economic and Political Weekly* 55.37, 12 September.

Express News Service (2022) Conviction rate 7% in SC/ST atrocity cases: Kota Shrinivas Poojari, *The New Indian Express*, 26 March.

Gurmat, S. (2022) Prison Statistics India 2020: 76 per cent of prisoners are undertrials; the number of Muslims, Sikhs, SCs, and STs among them disproportionate to their population, *The Leaflet*, 5 January.

Karnam, M. and Nanda, T. (2016) Conditions of undertrials in India: Problems and solutions, *Economic and Political Weekly* 51.13, 26 March.

Mint (2021) 65.90% prison inmates are from SC, ST and OBC categories, NCRB data says, *Live Mint*, 10 February, www.livemint.com/news/india/6590-prison-inmates-are-from-sc-st-and-obc-categories-ncrb-data-says-11612951470742.html (accessed 8 December 2022).

National Crime Records Bureau Ministry of Home Affairs (2020) *Prison Statistics India 2020*, New Delhi: NCRB.

NH Web Desk (2022) Zeeshan Malik's death in police custody: Fact finding team points at irregularities, torture, *National Herald*, 23 February, www.nationalheraldindia.com/india/zeeshan-maliks-death-in-police-custody-fact-finding-team-points-at-irregularities-torture (accessed 8 December 2022).

Sahu, M. (2020) In Uttar Pradesh, more than half of NSA arrests this year were for cow slaughter, *The Indian Express*, 11 September, https://indianexpress.com/article/india/in-uttar-pradesh-more-than-half-of-nsa-arrests-this-year-were-for-cow-slaughter-6591315/ (accessed 8 December 2022).

Sen, J. (2016) Three-quarters of death row prisoners are from lower castes or religious minorities, *The Wire*, 6 May, https://thewire.in/law/three-quarters-of-death-row-prisoners-are-from-lower-castes-or-religious-minorities (accessed 8 December 2022).

Shantha, S. (2020) From segregation to labour, Manu's caste law governs the Indian prison system, *The Wire*, 10 December, https://thewire.in/caste/india-prisons-caste-labour-segregation (accessed 8 December 2022).

Srivastava, R. (2021) 'Love jihad' law seen trampling women's hard-earned freedoms in India, *Reuters*, 15 January, www.reuters.com/article/us-india-women-law-religion-idUSKBN29K260 (accessed 8 December 2022).

Suresh, N. (2022) 3 in 4 prisoners are under trial, highest in 25 years, *IndiaSpend*, 18 February.

The Hindu (2020a) Demand for enquiry into Ugandan woman's death in Tihar jail, 10 August, www.thehindu.com/news/national/demand-for-enquiry-into-ugandan-womans-death-in-tihar-jail/article32318305.ece (accessed 8 December 2022).

The Hindu (2020b) Poor account for 71% of custodial deaths in India, 10 December, www.thehindu.com/news/national/poor-account-for-71-of-custodial-deaths-in-india/article61940135.ece (accessed 8 December 2022).

The Times of India (2021) Nearly 5 deaths daily in judicial custody in the last three years: MHA, 30 July, https://timesofindia.indiatimes.com/india/nearly-5-deaths-daily-in-judicial-custody-in-the-last-three-years-mha/articleshow/84902683.cms (accessed 8 December 2022).

37

Key Blindspots in Thinking around Peacebuilding that Policy Makers and Practitioners Need to Address

Katharine Thane

This chapter synthesizes key peacebuilding theory and practice to understand dominant approaches and their blindspots in intersection with freedom of religion or belief (FoRB). Peacebuilding approaches, literature and especially practice have not historically integrated considerations of FoRB, and integrating FoRB and peacebuilding remains in its infancy. Blindspots therefore persist. FoRB is an important puzzle piece for better informing processes that build and sustain peace. A 'FoRB-lens' considers people's different identities, experiences of inequality and subsequent needs arising from where they have been 'othered'. It enables us to uncover often hidden dimensions of inequality, while supporting practitioners to find more holistic solutions to conflict in partnership with those with different religious identities. Experiences and perpetrators will differ between contexts. Without the application of a FoRB-lens, peacebuilding will be undermined.

Despite its usefulness and increased emergence in international policy spheres, FoRB remains largely unintegrated in much peacebuilding work (and vice versa). There are several reasons why blindspots exist, including:

- FoRB and peacebuilding work has largely developed in silos, with different frameworks of reference and languages, and differing funding sources and donor expectations.
- Many peacebuilders have not moved beyond 'binary discursives' around religion in conflict, and by association, FoRB.

- FoRB has been misperceived as protecting religious institutions and (patriarchally inspired) malpractice. FoRB's misuse to protect certain groups at the expense of others in some political spaces has strengthened this misperception.

Using a FoRB-lens and shifting the power and ownership of conflict response to people affected by FoRB inequalities, including through deep listening across sectors, enables diverse support to be most effectively brought to overcome religious inequalities that exacerbate and entrench conflict.

Peacebuilding approaches and freedom of religion or belief

An analysis of peacebuilding approaches and FoRB illustrates where these blindspots emerge.

Engaging with religion

Appleby argues that there is an overarching 'ambivalence' or feeling of 'irrelevance' towards religion's role in peacebuilding (Appleby 2000). At best, religion is a prism through which peace can be inspired. At worst, it is 'inherently violent and destructive' (Philpott 2013). Hence, religion is often portrayed in 'binary terms'– both as a 'source of violence and reconciliation' (Silvestri and Mayer 2015). By association, FoRB has not historically been integrated in peacebuilding theory and practice.

The UN Special Rapporteur on FoRB (2022) calls to move beyond 'discursive binaries' around religion, to 'enable inclusive peacebuilding'. There are different ways in which scholars have sought to consider religion in more nuanced ways in relation to peacebuilding. For example, Omer (2015) encourages us to hold the 'multiplicity of religion in peacebuilding', and Wilson (2022) suggests an exploration of religious 'fluidity'. There is growing consensus that simplifying religion's role risks conflict escalation (USIP 2006).

Applying a FoRB-lens to conflict involves identifying the role of different experiences of inequality and needs in exacerbating and entrenching conflict. The World Bank (2018) recognizes religious and intersecting inequalities as 'fertile ground for grievances' and a 'mobiliser for conflict'. Some conflict analysis, including within faith-based organizations, engages with religious identities but mostly not through a FoRB-lens (Bouta et al 2005). With a few exceptions (for example, Bouta et al 2005; Hertog 2010; Stewart 2011; Palihapitiya 2018), academic peacebuilding literature has not considered the role of religious inequalities in conflict. One key challenge in the peacebuilding literature is the tendency to engage with religion as 'the proxy for other antagonisms' (UNSG 2018). Religious identities can also be unhelpfully subsumed within ethnic identities (for example, Lederach's (2017) Justpeace approach).

Many peacebuilding organizations work with faith actors, using their platforms, reach and influence for promoting messages of peace and early-warning reporting (Payne 2020). Although some suspicion remains of working with religious institutions, perceived as 'perpetuating structural and cultural' conditions for violence', there is a growing consensus that faith actors' absence in peace processes can be harmful (Nicholas 2014, 2015; PaRD and JLI 2019; Religions for Peace 2020; NRTP 2021; USIP 2021). Blindspots regarding FoRB, however, remain; working with faith actors or institutions alone does not guarantee a FoRB-lens application. Interfaith work remains the primary paradigm of peacebuilding work with faith actors.

Yet interfaith work, which often pluralizes an otherwise secular space, does not inherently mean that nuanced FoRB dynamics are considered. Self-nominated religious leaders familiar with access to power (Griffith-Dickson et al 2019) 'representing' entire belief traditions (Shoemaker and Edmonds 2016) may be more symbolic rather than supporting the community members' ownership needed for conflict transformation (Karam 2016). A FoRB-lens supports utilizing opportunities by engaging with the heterogeneousness of collectives.

Addressing blindspots in peacebuilding

Some peacebuilding initiatives have sought to incorporate FoRB, such as the Dutch government-funded JISRA (Joint Initiative for Strategic Religious Action) programme, headed by Mensen Met Een Missie (MM), Tearfund, Search for Common Ground (SfCG), Faith 2 Action and the Network for Religious and Traditional Peacemakers (NRTP), which brings together 50 religiously diverse national peacebuilding and development organizations pursuing FoRB in several conflict contexts globally. MM (2019) has worked on FoRB in conflict settings in Kenya, Indonesia and elsewhere. SfCG pursues FoRB through a 'localization' approach, supporting national colleagues to own FoRB work using culturally relevant language, for example, through national FoRB Roundtables (SfCG 2022a), catalysing the Universal Code of Conduct for Holy Sites (SfCG 2022b), and supporting peacebuilding work with a FoRB-lens in Nigeria through the Para-Mallam Peace Foundation and others (SfCG 2020). These initiatives demonstrate that (internationally linked) work and recognition at the intersection of FoRB and peacebuilding is increasing. However, the true extent of national work effectively pursuing FoRB, using non-FoRB terminology, is likely hidden. This gap is for those working on FoRB and peacebuilding internationally, to address learning through national partners.

Conclusion

Religious identities, and related inequalities and needs, are only now increasingly explored and programmed into peacebuilding work linked to international organizations. To overcome remaining blindspots for realizing SDG 16+, cross-sector learning, including in partnership with national colleagues, pursuing FoRB through locally owned language is needed. This would empower policy makers and practitioners to better realize peacebuilding and FoRB objectives alike. Although integration of FoRB within peacebuilding is increasing, the lack of consensus over religion's role, and by association, FoRB, means it is still in its infancy. Misuse of FoRB and subsequent (mis)perceptions of FoRB, as well as silos between sectors, also undermine integration, yet working with religion and faith actors is not a proxy for a FoRB-lens, as is sometimes intimated.

References

Appleby, R. (2000) *The Ambivalence of the Sacred: Religion, Violence, and Reconciliation*, Lanham, MD: Rowman and Littlefield Publishers.

Bouta, T., Kadayifci-Orellana, S.A. and Abu-Nimer, M. (2005) *Faith-Based Peace-Building: Mapping and Analysis of Christian, Muslim and Multi-Faith Actors*, The Hague: Clingendael Netherlands Institute of International Relations and Washington, DC: Salam Institute for Peace and Justice.

Griffith-Dickson, G., Hussain, D., Mandaville, P., Dickson, A., Farrag, S., Mian, M. et al (2019) *Building an EU International Exchange Platform on Religion and Social Inclusion*, London: The Lokahi Foundation.

Hertog, K. (2010) *The Complex Reality of Religious Peacebuilding: Conceptual Contributions and Critical Analysis*, Plymouth: Lexington Books.

International Partnership on Religion and Sustainable Development (PaRD) and Joint Learning Initiative on Faith and Local Communities (JLIFLC) (2019), Knowledge partnership between JLI and PaRD.

Karam, A. (2016) Realizing the faith dividend: Religion, gender, peace and security in Agenda 2030, United Nations Population Fund (UNFPA) Technical Report.

Lederach, J.P. (2017) *Justpeace*, University of Vienna.

MM (2019) Freedom of religion and belief, Mensen met een Missie, www.mensenmeteenmissie.nl/en/projecten/freedom-of-religion-and-belief/

Nicholas, S. (2014) Peacebuilding for faith-based development organisations: Informing theory and practice, *Development in Practice* 24.2: 245–57.

Nicholas, S. (2015) Peacebuilding for faith-based development organisations: Informing theory and practice, *CURVE*, Coventry: Coventry University.

NRTP (2021) SEA-AIR grant stories, Network for Religious and Traditional Peacemakers, www.peacemakersnetwork.org/sea-air-grant-stories/

Omer, A. (2015) Religious peacebuilding: The exotic, the good, and the theatrical, in R.S. Appleby A. Omer and D. Little (eds) *The Oxford Handbook of Religion, Conflict, and Peacebuilding*, Oxford: Oxford University Press.

Palihapitiya, M. (2018) Faith-based conflict early warning: Experiences from two conflict zones, *Journal of Interreligious Studies* 24: 61–77.

Payne, L. (2020) What can faith-based forms of violent conflict prevention teach us about liberal peace?, *Religions* 11.4: 167.

Philpott, D. (2013) Religious freedom and peacebuilding: May I introduce you two?, *Review of Faith & International Affairs* 11.1: 31–37.

Religions for Peace (2020) Faith leaders strongly echo the UN Secretary-General's call for a ceasefire, 14 April.

Search for Common Ground (2020) Draft report for context analysis, Advancing Religious Tolerance (ART.38) Project, Abuja: Search for Common Ground.

Search for Common Ground (2022a) Lebanon religious freedom roundtables, Abuja: Search for Common Ground.

Search for Common Ground (2022b) Universal code of conduct on holy sites, Abuja: Search for Common Ground.

Shoemaker, T. and Edmonds, J. (2016) The limits of interfaith? Interfaith identities, emerging potentialities, and exclusivity, *An Interdisciplinary Journal* 17.2: 200–212.

Silvestri, S. and Mayall, J. (2015) The role of religion in conflict and peacebuilding, The British Academy.

Stewart, F. (2011) Horizontal inequalities as a source of conflict: A review of CRISE findings, Washington, DC: World Bank.

UN Special Rapporteur on Freedom of Religion or Belief (2022) Rights of persons belonging to religious or belief minorities in situations of conflict or insecurity, Report of the Special Rapporteur on Freedom of Religion or Belief, A/HRC/49/44.

UNSG (2018) Religious conflicts normally product of political or geostrategic manipulation, proxies for other antagonisms, secretary-general tells security council, United Nations Meetings Coverage and Press Releases SG/SM/19104-SC/13393.

USIP (2006) Religious contributions to peacemaking: When religion brings peace, not war, *Peaceworks* 55.

USIP (2021) Religious actors in official peace processes, www.usip.org/programs/religious-actors-official-peace-processes

Wilson, E.K. (2022) *Religion and World Politics: Connecting Theory with Practice*, London: Routledge.

World Bank (2018) *Pathways to Peace: Inclusive Approaches to Preventing Violent Conflict*, Washington, DC: World Bank.

Young, E. (2018) Lifting the lid on the unconscious, *New Scientist*, 25 July.

PART X

Partnership

38

Partnerships and Religious Inequality

Amro Hussain

In 2019, as Director of the UK All-Party Parliamentary Group (APPG) for International Freedom of Religion or Belief (FoRB), I worked with the UK government to challenge laws in Pakistan which violate the right to FoRB and which unfairly target marginalized minorities. At the same time, Bill 21 was introduced in Quebec. This bill, which is now law, was designed to prevent Canadians who work for the state, including teachers and police officers, from wearing religious symbols at work. I mentioned this to British officials and said that this bill should be challenged because it was also a violation of the right to FoRB that would disproportionately affect marginalized religious minorities. I remember very clearly the blank, sideways looks that met my suggestion, the hesitation and the confused incredulity that filled the response – 'but Canada is a sovereign country? It's not for us to challenge what happens there'.

This reluctance was not a case of officials making a political decision to not criticize an ally but a genuine failure to see any inconsistency between their attitude towards Western countries and their willingness to point out FoRB violations in Pakistan and other countries in the Global South. Such bias limits the potential to build partnerships by turning religious and belief equality into something imposed on certain 'bad' groups and countries, rather than a goal which we pursue collectively. This discriminatory attitude is just one example of the barriers that we must overcome to build the necessary partnerships to create religious and belief equality.

Why are partnerships needed to create religious and belief equality?

Partnerships are necessary to amplify the voice of advocates for religious and belief equality and to build awareness about violations of FoRB. However, many advocates in this area tend to only speak out on behalf of their own religious or belief group, which can weaken the power of the movement by reducing the potential for coordinated action. Governments are more likely to respond to specific calls for change shared and delivered by a broad coalition of diverse communities than they are to many distinct, individual calls for change delivered by isolated groups.

Similarly, coordinated, multilateral international action can be more effective than bilateral pressure when pushing FoRB violators to change. When these coalitions are suitably diverse, it can also help challenge the limiting perception that religious and belief equality is a Western issue that is not applicable globally. For example, if several countries from the Global North and South apply sanctions against Chinese officials responsible for the persecution of Uyghur Muslims, this will likely be much more effective than if they were to be applied by one or two European nations. Moreover, religious and belief inequality often intersects with other vulnerabilities including poverty, gender and disability. For example, over 1,000 Hindu, Sikh and Christian girls are kidnapped, forcibly converted and married to men every year in Pakistan (Thompson 2021). These girls are vulnerable not only because of their religious identity but also their gender identity, and their lack of economic power. Thus, an approach to tackling religious and belief inequality issues which does not examine intersecting issues, and which does not incorporate partnerships with those dedicated to challenging those intersecting issues, will be limited in what they can achieve.

What barriers inhibit effective partnerships?

Equality for some

One of the principal barriers to effective partnerships in this area is group self-interest and a lack of commitment to religious and belief equality for all groups. An example of this is how often non-religious people are not given equal consideration by other groups advocating for FoRB despite also being protected by Article 18 of the Universal Declaration of Human Rights. They are often treated as an afterthought and regularly excluded from even the language surrounding religious and belief equality. This was the case with the International Religious Freedom Alliance, whose name was eventually changed to the International Religious Freedom or Belief

Alliance (IRFBA) but only after pressure from non-religious groups who pointed out how the original name was exclusionary.

There is nothing inherently wrong with advocating on behalf of one specific group. However, doing so at the expense of other groups, or at the expense of collaboration, is problematic. For example, I worked on a parliamentary inquiry into conflict between predominantly Christian farmers and predominantly Muslim pastoralists in Nigeria where Christian contributions were given priority, where only Christian groups or representatives were visited in country, where evidence provided by a diverse range of impartial academics and observers from globally respected institutions were dismissed if it contradicted the narrative presented by the Christian community, and where representatives from the Nigerian Christian community were exclusively allowed to comment on the final draft of the report. This risked creating a one-sided view of the conflict that could incite tensions further and alienate other religious groups, thereby potentially making life more challenging for the communities the report sought to help. Thus, failure to value groups equally is a barrier to partnerships that can also worsen religious and belief inequality.

Monopoly of space

Often, certain groups dominate spaces dedicated to religious and belief equality work. This can limit the capacity for partnership building, as other groups may feel excluded and less able or willing to be involved. For example, FoRB meetings and events held almost exclusively in Muslim spaces, chaired by Muslims, and dominated by issues primarily affecting Muslims would likely not be very welcoming for other groups and therefore not conducive to good partnerships.

Discriminatory attitudes

Discrimination can inhibit partnership, as demonstrated at the beginning of this chapter. I personally saw many cases of advocates from Western powers calling for changes in developing countries while ignoring similar religious and belief equality issues in their own nations. For example, very few British advocates raise the issue, or seem to notice, that the Church of England is elevated above other religious and belief groups in the UK in numerous ways, including being automatically granted seats in the House of Lords. However, if, for example, Hindu leaders were automatically granted seats in the Indian Parliament, it is likely they would see this as an unwelcome sign of religious and belief inequality. This sense of unfair treatment acts as a barrier to building genuine, global partnerships.

The usual suspects

Another major inhibiting issue is how partnership is enacted by those working on issues of religious and belief equality. Often, effective partnership is seen as merely getting a handful of older, male religious leaders in a room and usually it is the same handful over and over again. This is limiting for partnership development and religious and belief equality in several ways. First, partnerships conceived as talk-shops between the usual suspects with little interest in internal diversity, equity and inclusion, despite seeking to promote external diversity, equity and inclusion, will be limited in their ability to engage a wide range of partners and to build stronger and more diverse coalitions.

Second, this view of partnerships results in preaching to the converted. These meetings rarely engage those who are not already committed to the agenda. Therefore new and potentially productive relationships with other groups are not developed.

Finally, speaking in echo chambers can limit partnership development by facilitating an environment in which ideas aren't challenged and therefore may not be as persuasive, or as strongly supported, as they need to be to engage people who don't already share the same views. For example, many claims about the instrumental advantages of achieving religious and belief equality, such as improving economic growth or reducing conflict, are unquestioningly accepted by advocates. This means they are rarely challenged and that there is less incentive to develop or invest in the robust research needed to engage those who are not convinced.

Oppression of other rights

It is not uncommon for the rhetoric of religious freedom to be used to attempt to deny the rights of other marginalized groups such as women and members of the LGBTQ+ community. The resulting perception that issues such as religious equality and gender equality are in conflict reduces the likelihood of partnership between groups who, as mentioned previously, share many intersecting issues.

What are some examples of existing productive partnerships?

There are examples of productive partnerships working to advance religious and belief equality at various levels. These partnerships still face these challenges to different extents but, despite them, have been able to come together to achieve tangible successes. For example:

- At the governmental level, IRFBA brings together senior government representatives from 33 nations to advance freedom of religion or belief issues internationally.
- At the parliamentary level, the International Panel of Parliamentarians for FoRB supports politicians from the Global North and South to advocate for religious and belief equality by providing training, a network to share resources and connection to other parliamentary advocates.
- At the grassroots level, roundtables and forums have been developed in countries across the world to bring domestic advocates from different religious and belief groups together to discuss FoRB challenges and to coordinate action.

At all three levels, these initiatives have been successful in coordinating diplomatic action against FoRB violators, thereby applying cumulative political pressure that would not have been possible without these partnerships. There are also examples of partnerships extending across multiple levels. For example, at the UK FoRB Forum, the Prime Minister's Special Envoy for FoRB is often invited to attend meetings of civil society advocates, thereby combining grassroots and governmental work. Similarly, the 150 members of the UK APPG for FoRB are supported to raise religious and belief equality issues by a network of religious and civil society organizations from various faiths and beliefs. This partnership between legislators and civil society has proven very effective and resulted in driving FoRB up the UK government's agenda, as well as resulting in several policy changes including the appointment of the PM's Special Envoy for FoRB.

Where is there room to develop partnerships?

There are many sectors which have thus far not been sufficiently engaged in the struggle for religious and belief equality. Advocates should consider building connections with:

- *The private sector*. International companies have significant power to promote religious and belief equality by ensuring that their policies do not discriminate between religious and belief groups, by using their economic power to influence FoRB-violating governments, and by educating and training their staff on FoRB issues and on how to respect religious and belief differences.
- *Academia*. A better understanding of a range of issues which is grounded in robust academic research, such as the economic and social impacts of religious and belief inequality, would greatly enhance the capacity of policy makers and advocates to challenge these problems.

- *Non-FoRB civil society*. The non-governmental organizations working to challenge religious and belief inequality are often a small number of specific religious charities, whereas the bulk of the human rights and development sector, including major organizations like Amnesty International and Oxfam, currently do limited work in this area, if any, despite the fact that they are dedicated to promoting human rights and supporting marginalized communities.
- *Art and media*. Religious and belief discrimination is an enormous, global issue affecting countless people in countries around the world. However, the issue has a relatively small cultural footprint. It is not a topic that is widely discussed or represented in the news media, art or pop culture. This is in stark contrast to racial discrimination, which occupies a much greater space in culture and in the minds of the global public.
- *Diverse political actors*. Although there are politicians from across the political spectrum who advocate for religious and belief equality, this issue does tend to skew towards more right-wing parties. For example, the majority of officers on the APPG for FoRB have been from the political right (APPG FoRB 2022). Although this balance has improved over recent years, in my experience with the group, political representatives from the left were typically less active in this area than their counterparts from the right.
- *Development and security agencies*. There is ample evidence of how religious and belief inequality can lead to extraordinary violence and humanitarian crises. For example, long-term discrimination against Rohingya Muslims eventually led to their violent persecution by the Burmese military. Religious and belief inequality is strongly correlated with instability and conflict (Evans et al 2017: 31) and the UN framework of analysis for atrocity crimes highlights intergroup tensions and patterns of discrimination as a key risk factor for atrocity crimes (UN 2014: 9). However, religious and belief inequality is not typically mainstreamed into governmental thinking relating to security and international development. There is still much work to be done to get development and security professionals to take this issue seriously.

Conclusion

Partnerships are crucial to achieving religious and belief equality because they amplify the voice of advocates and facilitate powerful, coordinated action. However, the development of effective partnerships has been inhibited by issues such as group self-interest, discrimination, domination of FoRB spaces and agendas by specific groups, and a tendency to only engage those who are already interested or to use religious and belief equality as a way to undermine the rights of other groups.

There are examples of productive partnerships at multiple levels that have achieved success despite these problems, but they could be functioning more effectively and they could build even wider coalitions with groups in the private sector, academics, non-FoRB NGOs, artists, media professionals, more diverse political actors, and development and security agencies.

Unfortunately, there are no easy solutions for the problems which inhibit religious and belief equality partnerships. They require a fundamental change in outlook and a willingness to honestly and openly ask ourselves tough questions and to interrogate our actions and our ordinary ways of doing things. We all have blind spots, we all have biases and we could all improve the extent to which we are willing to engage and support the other. This is natural. But challenging ourselves to address these issues and to move out of our comfort zone is crucial because to build a world that embraces religious diversity, equity and inclusion requires that we embrace diversity, equity and inclusion, at both the individual and organizational level.

References

APPG FoRB (2022) List of members, the All-Party Parliamentary Group for International Freedom of Religion or Belief, https://appgfreedomofr eligionorbelief.org/appg/ (accessed 24 August 2022).

Evans, M., Rehmann, J., Petito, F. and Thane, K. (2017) Article 18: From rhetoric to reality, London: APPG FoRB.

Thompson, M. (2021) Abducted, shackled and forced to marry at 12, *BBC News*, 10 March.

United Nations (UN) (2014) *Framework of Analysis for Atrocity Crimes: A Tool for Prevention*, New York: United Nations.

39

The Need for
Secular-Religious Engagement

Kishan Manocha

In view of the significance of collaboration and participation for equitable engagement (and policy) as defined by the overall framing of SDG17, how best can we elaborate sound frameworks for partnership between the religious and policy-making sectors? What areas should policy makers increase their awareness of to foster and sustain a culture of dynamic, purposeful, trustful and impactful collaboration with religious actors?[1] What would ensure that each party serves as a reliable and responsible partner for the other?

Addressing these key questions would speak to some of the primary concerns raised by more sceptical policy makers, particularly those keen to keep religion out of the public sphere, in addition to speaking to the reservations of some religious actors, who may be concerned about the instrumentalization of partnerships by secular policy makers for narrow political purposes.

Key issues to consider

1. The importance of *mutual literacy* between the religious and policy-making sectors.

---

[1] For the purposes of this policy synthesis, 'religious actor' refers to individuals and entities who are motivated by faith, whether a religious or non-religious belief system or conscientiously held worldview, to participate in the life of society. The category of religious actor includes, but is not limited to, religious leaders, individuals, communities, institutions, and faith-based and faith-inspired organizations.

There are persistent and worrying levels of mutual ignorance when it comes to religious literacy. When domestic public officials and policy makers working in international organizations are reluctant to partner with faith groups, it is often a result of ignorance about religion and the important societal role of religious individuals, communities and organizations. This can also be termed 'faith illiteracy', arising in many instances from 'faith phobia' – an active objection to the principle of religious actors working in partnership with public authorities and institutions of governance.

A persisting misapprehension on the part of policy makers concerns conversion: that religious actors perform 'religion' or engage in the public sphere simply to win converts. Though this mistaken view arises more through ignorance than intent, it can nevertheless have serious consequences for the engagement of religious actors in public policy discussions, leading to their potential exclusion. There is a lack of appreciation on the part of many policy makers of the role that religious leaders and actors play, and the consequent power and influence they convey in all dimensions of life, not just a small portion of the activities termed 'religious'. This represents a major area of necessary learning for policy makers.

When thinking about effective engagement with religious actors in any setting, it is important that public officials also understand the concept of 'lived religion'; how religions operate in context, and not just the content of religious doctrines. A religiously literate public official should be able to discern and explore the religious dimensions of political, social and cultural expressions across time and space, while appreciating the diversity and complexity of communities, particularly the variety of interpretations and practice which shift according to context.

On the other hand, religious actors also appear to be in need of increased literacy on the mechanisms of secular discourse and governance, to better understand its principles, language and machinery.

2. Effective engagement of religious actors in the domestic public and international spheres requires *literacy on the concept of freedom of religion or belief* to ensure that policy works in parallel with the international obligations of states.

It is important that the renewed attention attributed to religious actors, who have assumed a critical role in development discourse, does not focus mainly on those actors who are seen to be able to make a difference – for example, due to their position, as politically influential, statistically significant or economically strong. A privileging of these actors can lead to a dichotomy between those deemed politically and socially 'relevant', and those seen to be 'irrelevant', who are excluded (either directly or indirectly); there is a danger that those belonging to the less 'relevant' groups will remain largely ignored.

While some religious minority communities might strongly benefit from increased attention, public awareness and recognition, it is likely others will lose out. This can lead to new forms of ignorance, stigmatization and discrimination. In line with the universalistic spirit of freedom of religion or belief (FoRB), it is important for any engagements to also be welcoming and inclusive of the prevalent religious and belief diversity in society so as not to reproduce any tensions or inequities.

3. *Seek common ground*; build and shape common vision and understanding while respecting difference.

In a plural world, meaningful and effective engagement between religious actors and policy makers demands dialogue and collaboration, including the responsibility to seek common ground. A framework for policy maker-religious engagement should also strive to safeguard the uniqueness of individual standpoints, the separate spheres of influence and the different responsibilities and missions of both religious and secular actors.

Often unconsciously, policy makers try to shape the attitudes of religious actors, to assimilate them into a more secular policy discourse. Vice versa, religious actors sometimes expect that policy makers will change their attitudes towards religion, accepting the discourse of morality and/or religious values. Nevertheless, it is important to keep religious concepts, values and ethics alive as an integral part of inclusive and effective partnerships; these elements cannot be assimilated or 'translated', and thereby softened, for secular discourse.[2]

The peaceful search for solutions to the issues facing society today is best facilitated by a process of public deliberation. Decisions should be made by reference not to sectional interests at stake but to universal principles, such as FoRB. Deliberation and democratic contestation of arguments does not require that each actor abandon their values, only that they are prepared to subject them to scrutiny, both for their conclusions and assumptions.

4. *Engaging religious actors in the public sphere and in policy making necessitates respect of their autonomy*, and in ways that does not instrumentalize them for narrow political purposes.

For policy makers to work effectively with religious actors, particularly religious leaders, they must appreciate their unique, sometimes complex roles within their communities.

---

[2] See Talal Asad's excellent book *Secular Translations* (2018) for more information on how religious ideas are translated into the secular domain.

If public officials seek to operationalize religious engagement to further a political agenda or legitimize differential treatment between religious communities, religious engagement is unlikely to achieve its aims. In fact, it runs the serious risk of becoming counterproductive. Equally, if religious actors assume an increasing role in the exercise of institutional power, this may have a detrimental effect on their credibility and legitimacy, especially for those in positions of leadership in religious communities if they are viewed to be permitting state interference in religious matters.

Strict respect for the principle of inclusive secularism is required on the part of public officials to avoid undermining the very authority which gives religious leaders their influence and credibility. The beliefs and priorities which religious actors hold need to be heard and recognized. When this happens, they are more likely to be empowered as conscious agents of change.

5. Efforts by policy makers, at the domestic or international level, to engage religious actors requires *sensitive understandings of religious roles.*

The religious sector is broad and complex. Policy makers often assume that publicly visible figures holding formal titles, or specific organized institutions, are the most relevant religious interlocutors for a given community, but this is not always the case.

In many settings, the direct influence of formal religious leaders – even on matters of religion – is questionable. Careful assessment of leadership patterns is needed: religious actors (and particularly leaders) who actively put themselves forward for engagement or are chosen by policy makers do not necessarily have the greatest following within their communities. Religious actors at the local and provincial level, particularly women and youth, are likely to be trusted and to have a more granular understanding of the specific issues and challenges facing their communities.

Recalibrating our understanding of the religious sector, going beyond official religious authorities and formal institutions, makes it possible to discern a far more complex religious landscape populated by a far wider array of actors and voices. We should not underestimate the extraordinary impact of local leaders and individuals of capacity in religious communities.

Although many religious traditions limit formal religious authority to older males, in practice, women play a major role in shaping understandings and interpretations of religion – both within families and as public religious leaders. Focusing only on men can serve to reproduce male domination of the religious space while missing opportunities for more effective and impactful engagement.

For similar reasons, younger or more junior leaders are often omitted from efforts to engage religious actors, even when they are often more credible and effective communicators, especially among their peers in local communities. Creative efforts need to be made to engage more young people of faith in policy engagement work. The challenge of religious engagement demands wise interventions that start with strategic knowledge of religious communities, institutions and issues pertaining to religious leadership.

40

Co-creation for Freedom of Religion or Belief

Mike Battcock

Strengthening the means of implementation and revitalizing the Global Partnership for Sustainable Development, the seventeenth Sustainable Development Goal (SDG17), is arguably the glue for the other 16 goals, for without effective partnerships, it will not be possible to enable the global, regional and local efforts necessary to facilitate investment and implementation of sectoral work to meet the SDGs. The Foreign, Commonwealth and Development Office (FCDO), formerly the Department for International Development (DFID), has recognized for many years the need for more representative, diverse partnerships and increased localization, which is particularly significant when working on issues of freedom of religion or belief (FoRB). The UK Aid Connect programme, which was launched in 2018, was convened around the pillars of innovation and partnership, with the whole impetus of the funding intending to bring together a wide range of different organizations to work together effectively as consortia, understanding that no one organization has all the answers to address complex challenges such as FoRB. UK Aid Connect was also clear from the outset of the need to involve organizations from the countries where the proposed programmes of work were taking place, a crucial measure for legitimate, sustainable interventions.

However, it was one thing inviting organizations to form consortia for UK Aid Connect funding, but quite another to get them to work together effectively. Co-creation phases were written into UK Aid Connect programmes, a first for UK Aid funding, to provide time for organizations to establish their governance structures, ways of working and programmatic areas of priority. At the programme reviews, all convening consortia partners were unanimous in highlighting the importance of the co-creation phase.

The FCDO started off outlining six to nine months for this process, but most organizations ended up spending at least nine months in this phase prior to project implementation. Bringing together divergent organizations from all over the world, from research institutions to development and rights organizations, think tanks and local religious organizations, was always going to be a challenge. The consortia leads all recognized that it was extremely difficult to build up the relationships between the organizations, and that if the process were to take place again, they would spend more time building up the governance structures and consortia relationships from the very beginning. It isn't surprising that organizations that hadn't worked together before struggled, particularly where lots of the organizations didn't really have a history of working collaboratively. It requires compromise and changes in ways of working, and it can be very difficult. But this is what makes consortia for development, and for FoRB, so important – enabling the combination of different expertise, experience and local, regional, national and international networks to convey cross-cutting legitimacy for effective programming.

Forging partnerships around redress for the religiously marginalized is a particular and complex challenge; the issues being dealt with are both contentious and contested. The communities are marginalized. Due to the very nature of the work, it's going to be difficult to set up partnerships where people are under attack and operating in fragile and conflict-affected settings. This presents a multitude of risks and practical challenges for programming, including very basic barriers, such as making payments to in-country partners and organizing travel. There will also be difficulties identifying the right people on the ground where the organizations embedded within marginalized communities are, more than likely, small and under resourced with limited capacity.

Making the Sustainable Development Goals on partnerships FoRB-sensitive

The omission of religion in the progress indicators of SDG17 is intriguing and highlights the need for programmes such as the Coalition for Religious Equality and Inclusive Development (CREID), which was funded through UK Aid Connect. Abuses on the grounds of religion or belief are one of the most prevalent human rights violations globally. Even if religion is not included as an SDG indicator by omission, rather than deliberate exclusion, it's still problematic that it is not included as a measurable indicator for change. However, there are clear difficulties in collecting this data. People will likely be suspicious of those gathering information on their religious affiliation in contexts where they are targeted on the basis of belief. This necessitates working with very good, strong, effective local organizations that have the trust and legitimacy within communities to be able to gather valid, disaggregated data.

Building partnerships for FoRB requires identifying organizations that have *real* relationships with religiously marginalized communities – not working with those that appear, particularly to outsiders (especially funders), embedded in communities when they are not. Identifying the right organizations to work with requires deep understanding of the context, the situation, the local language, the people and the history. This can make finding the organizations with legitimacy and genuinely strong relationships of mutual trust with communities very difficult, and there have been cases which have slipped through the cracks of the due diligence process.

With marginalized religious communities, there are also issues to consider with respect to representation, where groups may espouse to represent a particular marginalized community, where in reality they may only represent the wider religious group and not the marginalized groups within the minority community itself, particularly the women. This highlights the need for contextual situational analysis, identification of the right organizations and really working hard to understand how organizations are embedded within society. What not to do is to go with the showy organizations that present well, that look like they're doing alright, and not spending the requisite time to work out whether they do have the right connections and experience. The FCDO has a due diligence process that covers finance and the operational skills of the lead and convening partners of a programme but also seeks to understand whether the organization has the skills, experience, knowledge and connections to be able to deliver the programme of work that money is being provided for. However, for second and tertiary stages of this process, this is where the really interesting questions are, with the responsibility on leading partners to follow their own rigorous process to ensure they can deliver what they have proposed. The FCDO due diligence has become more rigorous over the last ten years. Yet there are gaps still in the ability to be able to identify organizations that are truly embedded in local communities.

Enabling communities to understand and advocate for their rights

There's a need to work with communities and understand what their problems are. If they feel their primary problems are development issues, one needs to work with those communities on development issues. It might be that one has to work with the development issues and at the same time build up an understanding of rights issues. CREID did lots of service delivery-related work with various very marginalized communities that went down very well within the communities. In this way, development can be used as leverage to work on longer-term rights issues, particularly where it can be politically contentious in some contexts to be explicitly working on rights issues, such as FoRB.

The CREID programme was a brilliant example within UK Aid Connect, bringing together research and rights institutions with religious community and development organizations. CREID's emphasis on participatory research brought the lived experience of communities to life, giving voice, and a platform, to the actual communities themselves. It is consequently through a multi-tiered process of co-creation, that inclusive, FoRB-sensitive partnerships can be fostered.

41

Promoting Freedom of Religion or Belief in Fragile Contexts: Emerging Lessons from the Coalition for Religious Equality and Inclusive Development on Legitimacy

Mariz Tadros

In this chapter, I reflect on the experience of the Coalition for Religious Equality and Inclusive Development (CREID) in establishing and deepening partnerships for the promotion of inclusive processes of change for redressing inequalities along the lines of religious affiliation, ethnicity, class, gender, geography and other identifiers. The CREID consortium is convened by the Institute of Development Studies (IDS) at the University of Sussex but governed through a set of partners that include faith-based actors, such as Al-Khoei Foundation and Refcemi, as well as secular human rights organizations, such as Minority Rights Group (MRG). The partners that comprise the consortium include academic, faith-based, development and policy actors based across several countries globally. However, the core governing members of the steering committee are all affiliated to organizations based in the UK, even if they have affiliates in the Global South.

Having a foot in a Western country (UK) and overseas (in the Global South) was critical to negotiate sensitivities around the positionality of the consortium; namely, that it is funded by the UK government in a global context in which many countries consider Western intervention an unwelcome hangover from a colonialist past of divide and rule. The challenges to the promotion of freedom of religion or belief (FoRB) internationally, from the vantage point of being a Western-based initiative, are immense. Unlike issues such as food security or climate change, for example, the promotion of FoRB domestically is not a cause for which foreign intervention or support is particularly welcomed. Many governments consider religious pluralism a matter of domestic sovereignty, one in which international support is neither solicited nor welcomed. At worst, many governments and communities consider Western championing of FoRB as driven by their own geostrategic interests, or at best, something advanced in an incoherent and hypocritical manner.

FoRB violations are a global phenomenon, experienced in both stable Western contexts as well as conflict-affected non-Western ones. However, there are particular challenges associated with Western support for FoRB in settings characterized by unpredictability in policy, volatility in the status quo, and fragility in the ever-changing and/or opacity of policy redlines. Through the CREID programme, we have come to realize that legitimacy, accountability and duty of care are key for successful partnerships for the promotion of FoRB. Next, I set out how and why these three factors are critical for FoRB promotion, and how CREID came to develop its partnerships around them.

1. Who has the legitimacy to speak on behalf of the religiously marginalized: beyond a common religious affiliation?

The legitimacy of the FoRB agenda in-country is as much relational as substantive. In other words, the promotion of FoRB is as much about who is championing it as it is about the content of the agenda. In large external aid programming, a key partner or focal point is often selected in-country to organize, galvanize and act as the intermediary between external actors and local stakeholders. From our experience in CREID, such a model does not work when seeking to gain legitimacy among local actors for the promotion of FoRB. In religiously heterogenous societies, where there are inter and intra sensitivities in who speaks on behalf of different groups, it is critical that mediation and representation be multivocal from the outstart. In lieu of one focal point, there may be many, according to where and with whom programmes are working. Having members of the religious majority represent minorities may be considered illegitimate, while having members of different religious minorities speak on behalf of all the others may equally be considered illegitimate.

Where sharing the same faith may be necessary to convey legitimacy in many contexts, CREID has found that who is considered to be legitimate representation in the eyes of religiously marginalized people can be very different from what is externally perceived. For example, Sunni Muslims' loyalty to Sunni Muslim leadership does not operate along the same lines as how Catholics would consider and/or defer to the Vatican. Also, in Myanmar, the majority of Muslims follow the Hanafi school, which is distinct from the Fiqh schools followed by many other Sunni Muslims in the Arab world.[1] Moreover, sometimes Muslims in Myanmar feel a greater affinity to Islamic doctrine as propagated in India and Pakistan than in the Middle East. In the CREID programme, we have learnt that to understand who is considered to have the power to legitimately represent a religiously marginalized group goes beyond affiliation with the same religion. Sensitivity to the multivocality of different leaderships, even among numerically small groups, is critically important. For example, in preparation for the Bishop of Truro's report in 2019, the British government undertook a consultation with some of the larger Christian denominational leaders in Iraq (such as the Chaldean Catholic). However, when His Grace Archbishop Nicodemus Daoud Sharaf, the Archbishop of the Syriac Orthodox denomination in Mosul, was asked about his opinion on the Bishop of Truro's report when he was speaking at the House of Lords on 10 July 2020, he expressed his anguish and anger that, although the report covers the Christians in Iraq, he was never approached to comment on the situation of the Syriac Orthodox Christian community. He believed that if the report were to make recommendations about how to support the Christians of Iraq, then all denominations should be consulted.

2. Disentangling the representation of faith and representation of the redress of religious inequalities' demands.

Conventionally, external actors engaged with faith leaders on the basis that they had the greatest legitimacy to represent members of their own religious minority groups/communities. This was manifest in activities involving, for example, interfaith dialogues, which often featured religious leaders coming together to represent and share perspectives from their respective communities. Depending on the context and the group, religious leaders often are seen to be legitimate in the eyes of their followers to represent their faith. However, representation of religious faith and representation of grievances on the basis of religion are not the same thing. In many contexts, members of religiously marginalized groups see religious leaders as having the authority and legitimacy to provide their community with leadership on matters of faith, but recognize the limitations of faith leaders to champion their citizenship rights. In highly authoritarian contexts, the space afforded to faith leaders to speak out against religious discrimination, as experienced

---

[1]   In Sunni Islam, there are four schools established according to the thinking of four leading Imams (religious scholars of Islamic interpretation of texts): Abu Haneefah, Maalik, Ash-Shaafi'i and Ahmad. They are considered authoritative sources of knowledge, among other sources. Different parts of the Sunni Muslim world have generally tended to follow different schools of jurisprudence, albeit on occasion there has been a borrowing from one school to the next in contemporary Islamic scholars' engagement with jurisprudential matters in Islam. For more info, see al-Jazīrī (2009).

by their communities, is very circumscribed, and sometimes almost entirely absent. In other cases, faith leaders are very close to the centres of power, in such a way that there is much at stake if they were to endeavour to hold authorities to account. We have learnt in CREID that assuming that faith leaders are most optimally positioned in all contexts to speak out on behalf of religiously marginalized members of their communities on FoRB violations is counterproductive for all concerned. It can be undermining for some religious leaders as it forces them, in the name of showing their patriotism, to deny the presence of religious discrimination so as not to incur the wrath of powerholders. Undoubtedly, it also does a disservice for the promotion of FoRB as members of religiously marginalized communities are then forced to challenge the position of their religious leader in legitimately representing them. For example, in Egypt, when Pope Tawadrous, the Patriarch of the Coptic Orthodox Church, denied the presence of any religious discrimination in Egypt, Coptic activists in the Diaspora challenged the legitimacy of his claims (Tadros and Habib 2022).

3. Multiple sources of legitimacy among religiously marginalized groups.

One of the key lessons learnt in CREID is that, in view of the diversity within any religious minority group, it is important to go beyond the idea that leadership in promoting FoRB is only exercised at an elite level, among a small circle of those who enjoy the privileges of being better off, economically, educationally and professionally, and also happen to be men. In Pakistan, the experience of CREID was that women who have social capital locally can, with support from partners, lead initiatives that directly seek to redress the religious inequalities that their communities face, and do so effectively. Through the formation of women's committees, women leaders from among the Christian, Shia and Hindu minorities in Pakistan were able to identify and respond to critical community needs, gaining legitimacy to effectively exercise leadership roles in their communities. In CREID, we learnt that there are different 'faces' and sources of legitimacy in any given context, very much reflecting the internally diverse, dynamic and multi-layered nature of any given community (Kanwer et al 2020). Our approach of working through a multitude of smalls (Tadros 2020) enabled us to identify and support legitimate FoRB actors and agendas which are embedded in communities and, to a certain extent, accountable to them. There are always multiple hierarchies in any given community across class, gender, geography, race, ethnicity and sometimes profession and caste as well which sometimes undermines full downward accountability. However, we endeavour to ask ourselves constantly, whether working at a global, national or local level, 'Is this legitimate in the eyes of the individuals that we have a commitment to accompany?'

References

al-Jazīrī, A. (2009) *Islamic Jurisprudence according to the Four Sunni Schools*, vol. 1, trans Nancy Roberts, Louisville, KY: Fons Vitae.

Kanwer, M., Israr, N. and Vahidy, U. (2020) Basic water and waste services for marginalised Christian communities in Lahore, Pakistan, Coalition for Religious Equality and Inclusive Development, 29 April, https://creid.ac/blog/2020/04/29/basic-water-and-waste-services-for-marginalised-christian-communities-in-lahore-pakistan/ (accessed 16 November 2022).

Tadros, M. (2020) Promoting FoRB in fragile contexts: Emerging lessons from CREID, CREID Learning Briefing 1, Brighton: Coalition for Religious Equality and Inclusive Development, Institute of Development Studies.

Tadros, M. and Habib, A. (2022) Who speaks for Coptic rights in Egypt today? (2013–2021), *Religions* 13.2: 183.

42

Epilogue

Mariz Tadros, Philip Mader and Kathryn Cheeseman

While the breadth of experience represented in this book defies synthesis, we will conclude with reflections on the possibilities for recasting a post-2030 development framework to redress religious inequalities in their intersections with other dynamics. The multivocality of the chapters indicates there is no one size fits all approach when it comes to integrating religious equalities into the SDGs and whatever framework may succeed them. However, they cumulatively challenge us to consider three salient sets of issues for redressing religious inequalities and promoting FoRB in development.

Addressing the oversight of religious inequalities

We began this book with an acknowledgement that only one indicator from one SDG mentions discrimination on the basis of religion as an axis of inequality. The chapters in this book have presented ample evidence for how religious marginalization means that wellbeing is denied or severely undermined in important ways for many people in different parts of the world. They present a deeply contextual and nuanced analysis of how systemic discrimination is enabled by factors interfacing with religious inequalities, such as socio-economic exclusion, gender, location and so forth. Concurrently, they also point to the importance of not subsuming religious affiliation under other identity categories, but rather the need to recognize it as a driver of inequality in its own right.

The case for including religious inequalities in development frameworks is about acknowledging that a person's association with a particular religious or religio-cultural heritage, even if they are not practising, can be a driver for their ostracization and vilification, their exclusion from services or, in extreme cases, their exposure to violence, both individually and collectively.

A wide array of people experience religious otherization: people associated with a minority religion in a context where religious majoritarianism is advocated; people who belong to the majority religion but diverge in their interpretations, practices or denominational affiliation; noneists (those who do not profess an affiliation to a particular religion) and atheists living in contexts where religiosity is expected; and people who hold norms and beliefs that they consider sacred but do not necessarily speak of as religion (such as many indigenous people).

Marshall (2021: 17) cautions that 'discrimination or persecution against people with a particular religious identity is not necessarily religiously motivated and hostility that seems to have a clear religious motivation is rarely motivated solely on religious grounds. The role of religion in discrimination and persecution can thus be overestimated or underestimated.'

The need to distinguish clearly between cases where religious inequality is the main problem and cases where it is not is one reason why it requires more active consideration and explicit attention in development frameworks. At times, the exposure of religiously marginalized people to discrimination can be primarily informed by a dynamic other than religion (Tadros and Thomas 2021). Nonetheless, it is critical to concede ways in which individual and community exposure to discrimination is not only a manifestation of patriarchy or class. Ideology of state and non-state actors, intergenerational transfer of prejudicial attitudes, fear of the religious 'other', or those that hold beliefs on what is sacred that are not recognized by the majority as a belief system, all directly lead to the targeting of individuals or communities on religious grounds.

In most cases, religious marginalization is compounded by other drivers of inequality, such as socio-economic exclusion, gender inequality and geographic oversight. The intention here is neither to create a hierarchy of the dispossessed, with the religiously marginalized featuring at the top, nor a hierarchy of problem significance. For example, where climate change has been described as 'the greatest threat the world has ever faced', impacting on the 'right to life, health, food, development, self-determination, water and sanitation, work, adequate housing and freedom from violence, sexual exploitation, trafficking and slavery' of the poorest,[1] in the lives of many religiously otherized people, the undeniable urgency of climate change may well be eclipsed by the risk of pogrom-like assaults or genocide, alongside deprivations caused by immediate, day-to-day discrimination. Addressing one problem should not detract from solving others.

---

[1] As Ian Fry, UN Special Rapporteur on the promotion and protection of human rights in the context of climate change, said in October 2022 (OHCHR 2022).

Operationalizing measurements for FoRB-sensitive indicators

There is a glaring lack of solid data on religious inequalities. Many governments do not collect data that allows the development progress and outcomes for people of different religious affiliations to be clearly seen. In part, this is because collecting such data is seen as 'sensitive'. It is often disputed by minorities, who do not trust governments to capture their real numbers and who often suspect they are intentionally underrepresented in official censuses. Conversely, governments do not want to share data on minorities in case they are pressed for more rights. The challenge of course is not only the collection of demographic data, but data on the intersections of religious affiliation and socio-economic equality at a sub-national and local level. Moreover, data by itself, without analysis of the drivers and dynamics of religious inequality, has no power to shed light on the power dynamics that inform patterns of respect for or violation of FoRB (Petri 2022).

There are various indices and indicators for the measurement of FoRB as part of human rights analyses and religious studies (Shaheed 2020; Marshall 2021). However, for international development, there is a need to embed ways of measuring religious inequalities and levels of inclusion/exclusion within existing frameworks of wellbeing. We would need debates between local and national policy makers, development policy makers and practitioners and members of religiously marginalized groups on the composition and wording of such indexes, so that they would be sufficiently overarching as to allow cross-context comparison, while being sufficiently attuned to phenomena on the ground to be relevant to people's lived experiences.

The question of developing and operationalizing better approaches to data generation and evidence gathering on the scale and depth of religious inequality, in its intersection with other inequalities, extends far beyond the SDGs, which are already halfway through their lifespan. International development actors, such as bilateral donors and multilateral development funders, can begin by including the measurement of their programmes' effects in terms of religious inequality and FoRB as an integral component of their monitoring, evaluation and learning (Aqeel and Gill 2022).

Moreover, if and when a post-SDG set of global development goals is negotiated, the question is what role religious inequality and FoRB should play in them. Not only should religious inequalities be included as an important dimension and axis of inequality to be reduced, this will also require the inclusion of appropriate measurements. As with the promotion of gender-sensitive development, we need to agree on the methods of gathering evidence and use this evidence to show that the benefits of inclusion are not only for women or for a religiously marginalized group, but for all (Tadros and Shutt, unpublished).

Resources and partnerships to redress religious inequalities and ensure freedom of religion or belief

Ultimately, as with all matters pertaining to redress of inequalities, evidence is key, but never sufficient, to elicit change. It also requires coalitions of like-minded actors and finding ways to work with the emotional or ideological biases of policy makers (Cairney 2016). Arguably, SDG17, to 'Strengthen the means of implementation and revitalize the Global Partnership for Sustainable Development', is the heart that pumps life into all other SDGs, and underperformance on the partnership goal, particularly in the form of financial support from rich to poor countries, remains the biggest obstacle to the goals achievement (Sachs et al 2020). As with all partnerships, galvanizing support for FoRB-sensitive development requires consensus building around its urgency and benefits. This will need to happen at both the international and national level.

One of the key issues to explore is how mainstreaming FoRB in international development offers the opportunity of de-ghettoizing this right. FoRB is highly relevant to the achievement of key global challenges, such as climate justice, redressing globally inequalities and building back better post-COVID-19. In this book, evidence from diverse contexts has been presented showing how religious inequality and unequal or obstructed progress on development agendas are linked. However, in future, we would need to gather evidence systematically across countries to positively amplify the links between the pursuit of FoRB and tackling global development challenges.

At the national level, the legitimacy of FoRB lies in its engagement through the right combination of actors, framings, approaches and entry points to change. The localization element in the SDGs foresees sub-national governments playing a crucial role in terms of deciding the means of implementation, measuring and monitoring progress on the SDGs, and aligning their local development strategies with the global goals (UNDP 2014). This devolution of the development agenda indicates that cities and regions would be a crucial level for any action on religious inequality as an integrated part of development frameworks. It also highlights how, in some cases, more effective action may be possible at the sub-national level than the national level, particularly in contexts where national governments are not committed or are actively opposed to equal treatment of different religious groups. Policy makers at the level of cities and regions can be strong partners. In any case, as so many chapters in this book show, the level of local and regional government is already where much of the action for FoRB, driven by community organizations and regional networks, is happening in reality.

However, one must not be naïve about establishing partnerships on a terrain as contested as religious inequality and development. As this book's title suggests, and chapter upon chapter has shown, marginalized communities are struggling for greater equality, recognition and more meaningful participation in the project of sustainable development. The theoretically well-established and well-intentioned consensus on partnership and participation for development (Chambers 2007) has all too often manifested in tokenistic or structurally disempowering forms of engagement that shut down critical voices and close off alternative development pathways (Cooke and Kothari 2001). Mainstream development interventions have repeatedly created economic and political arrangements that, by ignoring the cleavages built into 'communities' (Titz et al 2018) and the structural inequities of economic exchange relationships (Mader 2017), end up denying people meaningful voice and agency. Truly inclusive, sustainable development cannot come as an elitist project just outlined, and must be driven by people's own efforts to shape their collective destiny, which by necessity leads to tensions with forces that defend the unjust status quo (Selwyn 2017; Tadros 2022).

Working with a relational understanding of religious inequality, which recognizes that FoRB challenges the religious otherization and oppression dominant actors use to elevate their own position, means that partnerships for FoRB-sensitive development must be built with great attention to the issue of who speaks for whom and the national and local political contexts where partners work. The inherent conflictual nature of FoRB in contexts of religious inequality necessitates a strategy of 'a multitude of smalls' (Tadros 2020: 2), which pragmatically combines working for localized 'wins' as much as possible amid a broader push for structural change. Integrating FoRB into development frameworks would not only make development much more attentive to religious inequalities, which it must become to 'leave no one behind'. Making FoRB part of an internationally agreed vision for sustainable development also, crucially, would give more legitimacy and protection to actors struggling at different scales, in some cases against seemingly overwhelming odds, against poverty and prejudice.

References

Aqeel, A. and Gill, M. (2022) International assistance and impoverished religious minorities in Pakistan, in M. Tadros (ed) *What about Us? Global Perspectives on Redressing Religious Inequalities*, Brighton: Institute of Development Studies.

Cairney, P. (2016) *The Politics of Evidence-based Policy Making*, London: Palgrave Macmillan.

Chambers, R. (2007) Participation and poverty, *Development* 50.2: 20–25.

Cooke, B. and Kothari, U. (eds) (2001) *Participation: The New Tyranny?*, London: Zed Books.

Mader, P. (2017) How much voice for borrowers? Restricted feedback and recursivity in microfinance, *Global Policy* 8.4: 540–552.

Marshall, K. (2021) Towards enriching understandings and assessments of freedom of religion or belief: Politics, debates, methodologies, and practices, CREID Working Paper 6, Coalition for Religious Equality and Inclusive Development, Brighton: Institute of Development Studies.

OHCHR (2022) Climate change the greatest threat the world has ever faced, UN expert warns, Press Release, 21 October, Geneva: Office of the High Commissioner for Human Rights, www.ohchr.org/en/press-relea ses/2022/10/climate-change-greatest-threat-world-has-ever-faced-un-exp ert-warns (accessed 21 December 2022).

Petri, D. P. (2022) The tyranny of religious freedom rankings, *The Review of Faith & International Affairs* 20.1: 82–88.

Sachs, J., Schmidt-Traub, G. and Lafortune, G. (2020) Speaking truth to power about the SDGs, New York: Sustainable Development Solutions Network.

Selwyn, B. (2017) *The Struggle for Development*, Cambridge: Polity.

Shaheed, A. (2020) Interim report of the Special Rapporteur on freedom of religion or belief, A/77/514, Delivered to 75th session of the UN General Assembly, Geneva: United Nations.

Tadros, M. (2020) Promoting FoRB in fragile contexts: Emerging lessons from CREID, CREID Learning Briefing 1, Brighton: Coalition for Religious Equality and Inclusive Development, Institute of Development Studies.

Tadros, M. (2022) Religious equality and FoRB international development's blindspot, *Review of Faith and International Affairs* 20.2: 96–108.

Tadros, M. and Shutt, C. (unpublished) Gender in development: What lessons for addressing inequality on the grounds of religion or (non)-belief?, Brighton: Institute of Development Studies.

Tadros, M. and Thomas, C. (2021) Evidence review: Religious marginality and COVID-19 vaccination – access and hesitancy, Brighton: Institute of Development Studies.

Titz, A., Cannon, T. and Krüger, F. (2018) Uncovering 'community': Challenging an elusive concept in development and disaster related work, *Societies* 8.3: 71.

UNDP (2014) *The Sustainable Development Goals: What Local Governments Need to Know*, Brussels: United Nations Development Programme/United Cities and Local Governments.

Index

References to figures appear in *italic* type;
those in **bold** type refer to tables. References to endnotes show
both the page number and the note number (231n3)